# Worthington

## Rugby An
19

THIRTI... ...ΠON

Editor: ARWYN OWEN
Production Editor: JOHN BILLOT

**Llanelli's 10th cup victory. Skipper Robin McBryde waves the SWALEC Cup aloft in triumph at Ashton Gate in 1998.**

*Picture: Huw Evans Picture Agency Cardiff*

# THIRTIETH EDITION
# EDITOR'S NOTES
## by Arwyn Owen

Welcome to this 30th edition of the Rugby Annual for Wales. Regular readers will observe that, after 29 years under the Welsh Brewers banner, this publication is now named the Worthington Rugby Annual for Wales to tie in with all the local and regional cup and league competitions which are sponsored under the name of this extremely popular beer (see page 100).

As we advance with trepidation further into the professional era, the most pressing need for Welsh Rugby is for the WRU and major clubs to go forward together in harmony. The WRU could easily launch a new bonding process by withdrawing their demanded 10-year loyalty contract. It is no secret that clubs resent this: they see it as a policy of coercion and an unhealthy element in the modern game.

Unless they have signed up, clubs receive no funding from the WRU. Without that they cannot pay their bills. Only Cardiff are holding out because their financial situation is not under immediate threat. But the undercurrent of dissatisfaction remains and the ball is in the WRU court to move to restore confidence and amity.

What cannot be cured must be endured; but cures must be sought and the way is not by browbeating clubs into servitude. That is the pathway to trouble for the future and Welsh Rugby faces enough problems on the international playing fields as well as trying to find a fixture structure that will excite the paying public, improve playing standards and bring back some comfort to harassed club treasurers.

Most people find it ludicrous that the smallest clubs of the WRU can vote on matters affecting the major clubs. Such small clubs have little conception of the vast organisation and finance required to run the big clubs. The major clubs must have their own control without such interference being sanctioned by the WRU. All clubs are equal within the WRU, but some are more equal than others. That is the way it always has been and always will be. The big clubs are our show window and have special needs.

The lack of success by the home unions in the southern hemisphere during the summer of 1998 obviously is of concern. It was expected, but not by the record scores that crushed England in Australia and New Zealand. England, and Wales, toured with greatly depleted teams and the value of such tours must be questionable. It seems as if some countries are prepared to sacrifice their players in the pursuit of the big pay-off. That, of course, is the way to fund clubs. A vicious circle, indeed! It seems the dash for cash will never end.

Off the field, Welsh Rugby is a complete shambles. At the time of going to print there is still no sponsorship of the WRU National League. Numerous top and lower level clubs are in serious financial difficulties because of amateur management in this professional era. Plus a legal brawl between the governing body and Cardiff remains to be contested.

On the field, our national game is fast resembling second rate Rugby League with lineouts. Our players own natural creativity and flair are almost being completely 'snuffed out' by the present-day coaching methods which, in turn, are resulting in greatly reduced spectator support through the turnstiles.

Our domestic season saw Llanelli win the SWALEC Cup for a remarkable 10th time in their 13th final. We congratulate the Scarlets, wearing their modern image jerseys with an old motif of the challenging celtic warrior emblazoned proudly. No rivals can compare with their cup record, or Nigel Davies's achievement of eight finals and six times on the winning side, always for the Stradey team.

Swansea regained the national league title and delighted us with their spirit of adventure. Allan Bateman, most reliable of centres, became Welsh Player of the Year, a distinction well deserved; as with Llanelli's Darril Williams as most Promising Player. Ebbw Vale scrum half David Llewellyn was voted the first winner of the new award for Most Underrated Player of the season. Whilst Bedlinog battled through to emerge winners of the Worthington Welsh Districts Cup.

Our sympathy goes out to Gwyn Jones, the former Wales captain, whose career came to an abrupt end with a serious spinal injury while playing for Cardiff against Swansea. It serves to remind us that there is often danger in a physical game played at great pace. We have so many complaints to make against Rugby as it has changed that we are inclined to forget some of the tragic issues that are unfortunately part of the game. Hopefully, there will be many comforting events to report within the covers of the next Rugby Annual for Wales.

---

**Former Cardiff, Cambridge University and Neath full back Dennis Gethin, aged 53, was appointed in March 1998 as the sixth WRU secretary in nine years. A former solicitor and local government chief executive, he was selected from 95 applicants. Kevin Bowring, the national coach, left 'by mutual consent' after the record defeat by France. Under his control, in two-an-a-half years, Wales won 15 out of 29 matches, but only four out of 12 Five Nations games. He urged the WRU to scrap domestic promotion and relegation for the season, set up a meaningful Anglo-Welsh club competition, enter four regional teams in European competition and contract 25 players for the whole**  **DENNIS GETHIN of the Five Nations season. Bowring had been the 10th national coach, following David Nash (1967-68), Clive Rowlands (1968-74), John Dawes (1974-80), John Lloyd (1980-82), John Bevan (1982-85), Tony Gray (1985-88), John Ryan (1988-90), Ron Waldron (1990-91) and Alan Davies (1991-95).**

The Welsh team that defeated Scotland at Wembley in 1998. Back row (left to right): S Quinnell (rep), L Mustoe (rep), A Bateman, A Lewis, D Young, A Moore, M Voyle, Gareth Thomas, C Charvis, W Proctor, K Morgan, Leigh Davies (rep), S Roy (rep). Front row: J Humphreys (rep), R Appleyard, Neil Jenkins, R Howley (capt), Kingsley Jones, S Gibbs, Garin Jenkins, Arwel Thomas (rep), P John (rep).

Picture: *Huw Evans Picture Agency, Cardiff*

4

# FRANTASTIC! FRANCE SEND WALES CRASHING TO RECORD DEFEAT

*By* JOHN BILLOT

Welsh rugby has never been in such a sorry state. National coach Kevin Bowring commented after the Wembley defeat by New Zealand, "We will get better as a result of this experience." He could fool some of us some of the time, but not all of us all of the time. Not for one moment did he send a tremor through the ranks of England and France, who were lining up eagerly to inflict horrible scores against Bowring's team. Wales were involved in so many desperate rearguard actions that the new national ground could well be named the Dunkirk Stadium.

The team were not irredeemably bad, as was proved in victories over Scotland and Ireland, and even the opening quarter at Twickenham; but there has been only fragmentary evidence of revival. There are those, of course, who deny there has been any improvement whatsoever. Bowring is bitterly disappointed. He insisted he wanted to see his contract through to the end of the World Cup; but he made the inevitable errors of selection that continue to plague Welsh rugby.

| FIVE NATIONS CHAMPIONSHIP 1997-98 | | | | | | | |
|---|---|---|---|---|---|---|---|
| | *P* | *W* | *D* | *L* | *F* | *A* | *Pts* |
| France (1) | 4 | 4 | 0 | 0 | 144 | 49 | 8 |
| England (2) | 4 | 3 | 0 | 1 | 146 | 87 | 6 |
| Wales (3) | 4 | 2 | 0 | 2 | 75 | 145 | 4 |
| Scotland (4) | 4 | 1 | 0 | 3 | 66 | 120 | 2 |
| Ireland (5) | 4 | 0 | 0 | 4 | 70 | 100 | 0 |

*Numbers in brackets indicate finishing positions in previous season.*

Everyone makes mistakes: it is the magnitude that matters. Messing Neil Jenkins about ("I'm not a full back") was nothing short of criminal. Kevin Morgan and Mike Rayer (whatever had Rayer done not to be included in the Welsh squad?) obviously were far better equipped to wear the No 15 jersey. It was just that Bowring, obsessed by the idea that Arwel Thomas could transform Wales from outside half, could not leave his ace goal-kicker out and had to accommodate him somewhere. The Lions got away with it in South Africa not because Jenkins was enamoured with the idea, but because there were so many talented players in the team. The same depth of talent was never available to Bowring.

It could be said that some of the coach's selections were so weird it was almost a case for Scully and Mulder to investigate! Forwards should at least have looked fit. In this respect Bowring was badly let down. The surrender against France, when his side suffered a record Five Nations reverse by 51-0, was a bruising psychological experience and if a head had to roll it was always going to be Bowring's. Certainly, anyone can make blunders. A gravestone on Boot Hill, Tombstone, Arizona is a reminder of fallibility: 'George Johnson – hanged by mistake.' Another announced, "He called Bill Smith a liar." Bowring was totally honest and worked with tireless zest at his unenviable task. It was his choice of players that undermined confidence.

The claim to possess the sharpest and most menacing back line in the Five Nations looked valid enough on paper; yet against Italy, despite displaying their old state-of-the-art scrummaging power, and lording it in the lineout, Wales only managed a penalty try and then another moment of inspired opportunism from Gareth Thomas.

Bowring explained his theory about Arwel Thomas. "He brings more variety and a little unpredictability to our game. Arwel is showing more consistency now." The coach was prepared to accept that the Swansea star would produce most of the right options, but not necessarily in the right order!

"We let Wales down," was the admission of sorrowful skipper Rob Howley after Twickenham. England's backlash following defeat in Paris was awesome. Though Wales began purposefully to lead 12-6 after 24 minutes, the home side's riposte blasted Howley's team apart with eight tries and a 60-26 verdict. "We have to accept we are in the Five Nations' second division," volunteered Howley, in case anyone had forgotten.

Wales dumped six of the Twickenham team when Scotland arrived for the first Five Nations game to be staged at Wembley. Neil Jenkins ("I'll never play at full back again") resumed his old fly half role, but lasted only 18 minutes before a clash of heads meant stitches and blurred vision; so Arwel was back in the key spot and, ironically, won the match with three penalty goals and a magnificent conversion of the only Welsh try. Training sessions had been behind closed doors as Bowring excluded the media and urged his players to shut out memories of what had gone before. "We did not command the game, but at least we won," he said.

So it was on to Dublin with Bowring admitting, "I'll be happy to win in any old way!" There was a touch of tongue-in-cheek about this melancholy meditation, and his spirits were raised by three sparkling tries and another victory. At least Wales were kings of the celtic countries, which was no big deal considering the standards of the second division. Bowring admitted he had forsaken his flair concept and turned to form players and reliability. This brought in Swansea No 8 Stuart Davies, and we wondered again why his performances had been ignored for so long. Howley had called for a spirit of adventure. Everyone responded. A nation no longer mourned.

But not for long. Black Sunday at Wembley on April 5, 1998 was described by some as the lowest point of their lives. It sounded somewhat extreme, but was illustrative of the depth of feeling about what happened.

Lurching from one disaster to another is fairly commonplace for Welsh rugby – at club as well as international level – but measured by any yardstick this was an event to overshadow all others.

France garnished their success with seven tries for the biggest winning margin of all time in the Five Nations and Wales's tally of 145 shamefully was the most points ever conceded by a Five Nations team. Assailed from all quarters, Wales failed to score against France for the first time in the 90 years of their meetings. Another statistic was that the all-Swansea back row were each shown yellow cards. Wales emphatically were shown the door to disaster by a brilliant French team.

Bowring was a victim of his players' inept performances, but it is nothing new that the man in charge, for all his endeavours, pays the price of failure. During the siege of Constantinople in 1453, Ottoman admiral Suleiman Baltoghlu suffered the chop because he failed to prevent a Genoese corn convoy breaking the blockade. The luckless admiral fought bravely against the bigger galleons, but was sentenced to be impaled. This was commuted to a ruthless flogging and, some reported, having one eye torn from its socket.

Dismissal is rather less drastic these days and the coach at least has both eyes with which to take perhaps a jaundiced view of his experience and the state of Welsh rugby after it was mutually agreed he stand down.

# FIVE NATIONS RESULTS AND TEAMS 1997-98

## FRANCE v ENGLAND
### (Paris)

**February 7, 1998. France won by 24 (1G, 2DG, 2PG, 1T) to 17 (4PG, 1T).**

**FRANCE:** J L Sadourny (Colomiers); P Bernart-Salles (Pau), C Lamaison (Brive), S Glas (Bourgoin), C Dominici (Stade Francais); T Castaignede (Castres), P Carbonneau (Brive); C Califano (Toulouse), R Ibanez (Dax, capt), F Tournaire (Toulouse), O Brouzet (Begles-Bordeaux), F Pelous (Toulouse), P Benetton (Agen), T Lievremont (Perpignon), O Magne (Brive). Reps: M Lievremont (Stade Francais) for Benetton, T Cleda (Pau) for T Lievremont.

**ENGLAND:** M J Catt (Bath); D L Rees (Sale), W J H Greenwood (Leicester), J C Guscott (Bath), A S Healey (Leicester); P J Grayson (Northampton), K P P Bracken (Saracens); J Leonard (Harlequins), M P Regan (Bath), D J Garforth (Leicester), M O Johnson (Leicester), G S Archer (Newcastle), L B N Dallaglio (Wasps, capt), R A Hill (Saracens), N A Black (Leicester). Rep: D E West (Leicester) for Regan.

*Referee:* D T M McHugh (Ireland).

*Scorers:* For France, Philippe Bernat-Salles, Christophe Dominici (tries), Thomas Castaignede, Jean-Luc Sadourny (drop-goals), Christophe Lamaison (2PG, 1con). For England, Neil Back (1T), Paul Grayson (4PG).

## IRELAND v SCOTLAND
### (Dublin)

**February 7, 1998. Scotland won by 17 (4PG, 1T) to 16 (1G, 1DG, 2PG).**

**IRELAND:** C M P O'Shea (London Irish); R M Wallace (Saracens), K M Maggs (Bristol), M C McCall (London Irish), D A Hickie (St Mary's Coll); D G Humphreys (London Irish), B T O'Meara (Cork Constitution); R Corrigan (Greystones), K G M Wood (Harlequins, capt), P S Wallace (Saracens), P S Johns (Saracens), M E O'Kelly (London Irish), D S Corkery (Bristol), E R P Miller (Leicester), K Dawson (London Irish). Reps: N J Popplewell (Newcastle) temp for P S Wallace, V C P Costello (St Mary's Coll) for Dawson.

**SCOTLAND:** R J S Shepherd (Melrose); C A Joiner (Leicester), A V Tait (Newcastle), G P J Townsend (Northampton), K M Logan (Wasps); C M Chalmers (Melrose), G Armstrong (Newcastle, capt); G Graham (Newcastle), G C Bulloch (West of Scotland), M J Stewart (Northampton), D F Cronin (Wasps), G W Weir (Newcastle), R I Wainwright (Dundee HSFP), P Walton (Newcastle), S D Holmes (London Scottish). Reps: D Lee (London Scottish) for Shepherd, A G Stanger (Hawick) for Joiner, D I W Hilton (Bath) for Graham, S B Grimes (Watsonians) for Cronin.

*Referee:* Andre Watson (South Africa).

*Scorers:* For Ireland, penalty try, David Humphreys (1DG, 2PG, 1con). For Scotland, Alan Tait (1T), Rowen Shepherd (2PG), Craig Chalmers (2PG).

## ENGLAND v WALES
### (Twickenham)

**February 21, 1998. England won by 60 (7G, 2PG, 1T) to 26 (3G, 1T).**

**ENGLAND:** M B Perry (Bath); D L Rees (Sale), W J H Greenwood (Leicester), J C Guscott (Bath), A S Healey (Leicester); P J Grayson (Northampton), K P P Bracken (Saracens); J Leonard (Harlequins), R Cockerill (Leicester), P J Vickery (Gloucester), M O Johnson (Leicester), G S Archer (Newcastle), L B N Dallaglio (Wasps, capt), R A Hill (Saracens), N A Back (Leicester). Reps: P R de Glanville (Bath) for Greenwood, M J Catt (Bath) for Grayson, M J S Dawson (Northampton) for Bracken, D J Garforth (Leicester) for Vickery, D J Grewcock (Saracens) for Johnson, A J Diprose (Saracens) for Hill.

**WALES:** N R Jenkins (Pontypridd); G Thomas (Cardiff), A G Bateman (Richmond), I S Gibbs (Swansea), N K Walker (Cardiff); A C Thomas (Swansea), R Howley (Cardiff, capt); A L P Lewis (Cardiff), B H Williams (Richmond), D Young (Cardiff), G O Llewellyn (Harlequins), M J Voyle (Llanelli), C L Charvis (Swansea), L S Quinnell (Richmond), M E Williams (Pontypridd). Reps: L B Davies (Cardiff) for Bateman, W T Proctor (Llanelli) for Walker, L Mustoe (Cardiff) for Lewis, J M Humphreys (Cardiff) for B H Williams, C Stephens (Bridgend) for Voyle, R C Appleyard (Swansea) for Quinnell.

*Referee:* Colin Hawke (New Zealand).

*Scorers:* For England, David Rees (2), Neil Back, Kyran Bracken, Lawrence Dallaglio, Austin Healey, Will Greenwood, Matt Dawson (tries). Paul Grayson (2PG, 7con). For Wales, Allan Bateman (2), Gareth Thomas, Scott Gibbs (tries), Neil Jenkins (3con).

## SCOTLAND v FRANCE
### (Murrayfield)

**February 21, 1998. France won by 51 (5G, 2PG, 2T) to 16 (1G, 3PG).**

**SCOTLAND:** D J Lee (London Scottish); A G Stanger (Hawick), A V Tait (Newcastle), G P J Townsend (Northampton), K M Logan (Wasps); C M Chalmers (Melrose), G Armstrong (Newcastle, capt); D I W Hilton (Bath), G C Bulloch (West of Scotland), M J Stewart (Northampton), D F Cronin (Wasps), G W Weir (Newcastle), R I Wainwright (Dundee HSFP), P Walton (Newcastle), S D Holmes (London Scottish). Reps: S L Longstaff (Dundee HSFP) for Chalmers, G Graham (Newcastle) for Hilton, S B Grimes (Watsonians) for Cronin, A J Roxburgh (Kelso) for Walton.

**FRANCE:** J L Sadourny (Colomiers); P Bernart-Salles (Pau), C Lamaison (Brive), S Glas (Bourgoin), C Dominici (Stade Francais); T Castaignede (Castres), P Carbonneau (Brive); C Califano (Toulouse), R Ibanez (Dax, capt), F Tournaire (Toulouse), O Brouzet (Begles-Bordeaux), F Pelous (Toulouse), M Lievremont (Stade Francais), T Lievremont (Perpignan), O Magne (Brive). Reps: D Aucagne (Pau) for Lamaison, C Soulette (Beziers) for Tournaire, T Cleda (Pau) for Pelous, P Benetton (Agen) for T Lievremont.

*Referee:* Paddy O'Brien (New Zealand).

*Scorers:* For Scotland, Tony Stanger (1T), Craig Chalmers (3PG, 1con). For France, Philippe Bernat-Salles (2), Marc Lievremont (2), Christian Califano, Philippe Carbonneau, Thomas Castaignede (tries), Christophe Lamaison (1PG, 2con), Castaignede (1PG, 3con).

## WALES v SCOTLAND
### (Wembley)

**March 7, 1998. Wales won by 19 (1G, 4PG) to 13 (1PG, 2T).**

**WALES:** K A Morgan (Pontypridd); W T Proctor (Llanelli), A G Bateman (Richmond), I S Gibbs (Swansea), G Thomas (Cardiff); N R Jenkins (Pontypridd), R Howley (Cardiff, capt); A L P Lewis (Cardiff), G R Jenkins (Swansea), D Young (Cardiff), M J Voyle (Llanelli), A P Moore (Swansea), R C Appleyard (Swansea), C L Charvis (Swansea), K P Jones (Ebbw Vale). Reps: A C Thomas (Swansea) for N R Jenkins, J M Humphreys (Cardiff) for G R Jenkins, L S Quinnell (Richmond) for Appleyard.

**SCOTLAND:** D J Lee (London Scottish); A G Stanger (Hawick), G P J Townsend (Northampton), A V Tait (Newcastle), S Longstaff (Dundee HSFP); C M Chalmers (Melrose), G Armstrong (Newcastle, capt); D I W Hilton (Bath), G C Bulloch (West of Scotland), M J Stewart (Northampton), D F Cronin (Wasps), G W Weir (Newcastle), R I Wainwright (Dundee HSFP), E W Peters (Bath), A J Roxburgh (Kelso). Reps: G Graham (Newcastle) for Stewart, S B Grimes (Watsonians) for Cronin, R J S Shepherd (Melrose) for Lee.

*Referee:* Joel Dume (France).

*Scorers:* For Wales, Wayne Proctor (1T), Neil Jenkins (1PG), Arwel Thomas (3PG, 1con). For Scotland, Gregor Townsend, Damian Cronin (tries), Craig Chalmers (1PG).

## FRANCE v IRELAND
### (Paris)

**March 7, 1998. France won by 18 (1G, 2PG, 1T) to 16 (1G, 3PG).**

**FRANCE:** J L Sadourny (Colomiers); P Bernart-Salles (Pau), C Lamaison (Brive), S Glas (Bourgoin), X Garbajosa (Toulouse); T Castaignede (Castres), P Carbonneau (Brive); C Califano (Toulouse), R Ibanez (Dax, capt), F Tournaire (Toulouse), O Brouzet (Begles-Bordeaux), F Pelous (Toulouse), M Lievremont (Stade Francais), T Lievremont (Perpignan), O Magne (Brive). Reps: C Soulette (Beziers) for Tournaire, T Cleda (Pau) for Pelous, P Benetton (Agen) for M Lievremont.

**IRELAND:** C M P O'Shea (London Irish); R M Wallace (Saracens), R A J Henderson (Wasps), K M Maggs (Bristol), D A Hickie (St Mary's Coll); E P Elwood (Galwegians), C D McGuinness (St. Mary's Coll); R Corrigan (Greystones), K G M Wood (Harlequins, capt), P S Wallace (Saracens), P S Johns (Saracens), M E O'Kelly (London Irish), D S Corkery (Bristol), V C P Costello (St Mary's Coll), A Ward (Ballynahinch). Reps: N J Popplewell (Newcastle) for Corrigan, R P Nesdale (Newcastle) for Wood, P M Clohessy (Young Munster) for Wallace, M J Galwey (Shannon) for Johns.

*Referee:* Jim Fleming (Scotland).

*Scorers:* For France, Philippe Bernat-Salles, Raphael Ibanez (tries), Christophe Lamaison (2PG, 1con). For Ireland, Denis Hickie (1T), Eric Elwood (3PG, 1con).

## IRELAND v WALES
### (Dublin)

**March 21, 1998. Wales won by 30 (3G, 3PG) to 21 (1G, 3PG, 1T).**

**IRELAND:** C P Clarke (Terenure Coll); R M Wallace (Saracens), K M Maggs (Bristol), R A J Henderson (Wasps), D A Hickie (St Mary's Coll); E P Elwood (Galwegians), C D McGuinness (St Mary's Coll); R Corrigan (Greystones), K G M Wood (Harlequins, capt), P S Wallace (Saracens), P S Johns (Saracens), M E O'Kelly (London Irish), D S Corkery (Bristol), V C P Costello (St Mary's Coll), A J Ward

(Ballynahinch). Reps: R P Nesdale (Newcastle) for Wood, P M Clohessy (Young Munster) for P S Wallace, E R P Miller (Leicester) for Ward.

**WALES:** K A Morgan (Pontypridd); W T Proctor (Llanelli), A G Bateman (Richmond), L B Davies (Cardiff), G Thomas (Cardiff); N R Jenkins (Pontypridd), R Howley (Cardiff, capt); A L P Lewis (Cardiff), G R Jenkins (Swansea), D Young (Cardiff), M J Voyle (Llanelli), A P Moore (Swansea), R. C. Appleyard (Swansea), C L Charvis (Swansea), K P Jones (Ebbw Vale). Reps: J M Humphreys (Cardiff) for G R Jenkins, L Mustoe (Cardiff) for Young, S Davies (Swansea) for Jones.

*Referee:* Ed Morrison (England).

*Scorers:* For Ireland, Andy Ward, Vic Costello (tries). Eric Elwood (3PG, 1con). For Wales, Allan Bateman, Kevin Morgan, Neil Jenkins (tries), Neil Jenkins (3PG, 3con).

## SCOTLAND v ENGLAND
## (Murrayfield)

**March 21, 1998. England won by 34 (4G, 1DG, 1PG) to 20 (2G, 2PG).**

**SCOTLAND:** D J Lee (London Scottish); A G Stanger (Hawick), A V Tait (Newcastle), G P J Townsend (Northampton), S L Longstaff (Dundee HSFP); C M Chalmers (Melrose), G Armstrong (Newcastle, capt); D I W Hilton (Bath), G C Bulloch (West of Scotland), A P Burnell (London Scottish), D F Cronin (Wasps), G W Weir (Newcastle), R I Wainwright (Dundee HSFP), E W Peters (Bath), A J Roxburgh (Kelso). Reps: C A Murray (Hawick) for Chalmers, S B Grimes (Watsonians) for Cronin.

**ENGLAND:** M B Perry (Bath); A S Healey (Leicester), J C Guscott (Bath), W J H Greenwood (Leicester), A A Adebayo (Bath); P J Grayson (Northampton), M J S Dawson (Northampton); J Leonard (Harlequins), R Cockerill (Leicester), D J Garforth (Leicester), M O Johnson (Leicester), G S Archer (Newcastle), L B N Dallaglio (Wasps, capt), D Ryan (Newcastle), N A Back (Leicester). Reps: P R de Glanville (Bath) for Healey, D E West (Leicester) for Cockerill, D J Grewcock (Saracens) for Johnson, A J Diprose (Saracens) for Ryan.

*Referee:* Clayton Thomas (Wales).

*Scorers:* For Scotland, Tony Stanger, Shaun Longstaff (tries), Craig Chalmers (2PG), Derrick Lee (2con). For England, Matt Dawson, Austin Healey, Paul Grayson (tries), penalty try, Grayson (1DG, 1PG, 4con).

## ENGLAND v IRELAND
## (Twickenham)

**April 4, 1998. England won by 35 (3G, 3PG, 1T) to 17 (2G, 1PG).**

**ENGLAND:** M B Perry (Bath); M J Catt (Bath), W J H Greenwood (Leicester), J C Guscott (Bath), A S Healey (Leicester); P J Grayson (Northampton), M J S Dawson (Northampton); J Leonard (Harlequins), R Cockerill (Leicester), D J Garforth (Leicester), M O Johnson (Leicester), G S Archer (Newcastle), L B N Dallaglio (Wasps, capt), A J Diprose (Saracens), N A Back (Leicester). Reps: J P Wilkinson (Newcastle) for Catt, P R de Glanville (Bath) for Greenwood, D J Grewcock (Saracens) for Archer.

**IRELAND:** C P Clarke (Terenure Coll); R M Wallace (Saracens), K M Maggs (Bristol), M C McCall (London Irish), D A Hickie (St Mary's Coll); E P Elwood (Galwegians), C D McGuinness (St Mary's Coll); R Corrigan (Greystones), K G M Wood (Harlequins, capt), P S Wallace (Saracens), P S Johns (Saracens), M E O'Kelly (London Irish), D S Corkery (Bristol), V C P Costello (St Mary's Coll), A J Ward (Ballynahinch). Reps: D G Humphreys (London Irish) for Clarke, K P Keane (Garryowen) for McCall.

*Referee:* Derek Bevan (Wales).

*Scorers:* For England, Matt Perry, Richard Cockerill, Mike Catt, Phil de Glanville (tries), Paul Grayson (3PG, 3con). For Ireland, Denis Hickie (2T), Eric Elwood (1PG, 2con).

## WALES v FRANCE
## (Wembley)

**April 5, 1998. France won by 51 (5G, 2PG, 2T) to nil.**

**WALES:** K A Morgan (Pontypridd); W T Proctor (Llanelli), N Boobyer (Llanelli), L B Davies (Cardiff), G Thomas (Cardiff); N R Jenkins (Pontypridd), R Howley (Cardiff, capt); A L P Lewis (Cardiff), G R Jenkins (Swansea), D Young (Cardiff), M J Voyle (Llanelli), A P Moore (Swansea), R. L. Appleyard (Swansea), S Davies (Swansea), C L Charvis (Swansea). Reps: B James (Pontypridd) for Boobyer, J M Humphreys (Cardiff) for G R Jenkins, K D Jones (Ebbw Vale) for Appleyard, L Mustoe (Cardiff) for Lewis.

**FRANCE:** J L Sadourny (Colomiers); P Bernart-Salles (Pau), C Lamaison (Brive), S Glas (Bourgoin), X Garbajosa (Toulouse); T Castaignede (Castres), P Carbonneau (Brive); C Califano (Toulouse), R Ibanez (Dax, capt), F Tournaire (Toulouse), O Brouzet (Begles-Bordeaux), F Pelous (Toulouse), M Lievremont (Stade Francais), T Lievremont (Perpignan), O Magne (Brive). Reps: J M Aue (Castres) for Lamaison, D Aucagne (Pau) for Castaignede, F Galthie (Colomiers) for Carbonneau, C Soulette (Beziers) for Califano, M Dalmaso (Agen) for Ibanez, T Cleda (Pau) for Brouzet, P Benetton (Agen) for T Lievremont.

*Referee:* Peter Marshall (Australia).

*Scorers:* Jean-Luc Sadourny (2), Xavier Garbajosa (2), Thomas Lievremont, Stephane Glas, Fabien Galthie (tries), Christophe Lamaison (2PG, 5con).

10

#  'GHOST' TEAM COULDN'T SPOOK THE SPRINGBOKS

A cheeky try by Arwel Thomas, darting through a half-gap, was the only moment to remember for Wales on a day of desolation in Pretoria. The Springbok whirlwind blew them to oblivion. Only mistakes by non-stop attackers prevented South Africa from topping 100 points. As it was, a 96-13 rout was the worst Welsh defeat of all time and the home side's record tally. It was a chilling climax to an ill-fated trip.

Coach Dennis John was savagely critical of some of the star players who, for various reasons, withdrew or were unavailable. Actually, it was not so much a tour as a suicide mission with 18 frontline players left behind. This was indeed a shadow team and they never had a ghost of a chance against such giants of the rugby scene as South Africa.

It was 15 to one on tries and it would have been appropriate for television's William G. Stewart to have been calling the shots with too many tough questions for Wales to answer. Wing Pieter Rossouw snapped up three tries and Percy Montgomery, running like the wind to score two tries from full back, fired over 21 goal points for a tally of 31. It was all quite horrifying.

Three players captained Wales during this blackest of black hours: Kingsley Jones began in command in the absence of hamstring victim Rob Howley; Paul John took over when Jones was replaced; and Garin Jenkins assumed the captaincy when John departed the scene of the massacre. We knew how the 7th Cavalry felt that day at the Little Big Horn.

The tour was dogged by injuries. Seven replacements were hurried out, the last of them David Llewellyn, as cover for Howley, and the day after arriving, Llewellyn found himself winning his first cap as replacement with the tourists already up to their necks in tries. Perhaps Howley was not so disappointed as

---

## TOUR PARTY

**Coach:** Dennis John.
**Assistant Coach:** Lyn Howells

**Backs:** David Weatherley, Richard Rees, Mark Taylor, Arwel Thomas (Swansea), Darril Williams, Wayne Proctor, Garan Evans (Llanelli), John Funnell, Lennie Woodard, Byron Hayward (Ebbw Vale), Dafydd James, Paul John (Pontypridd), Robert Howley (capt), Leigh Davies (Cardiff).

**Forwards:** Mike Griffiths, Martyn Williams (Pontypridd), Darren Morris, Ben Evans (Neath), John Davies, Barry Williams, Scott Quinnell (Richmond), Garin Jenkins, Andrew Moore, Paul Arnold, Rob Appleyard, Colin Charvis (Swansea), Ian Gough (Newport), Mark Jones (Ebbw Vale), Nathan Thomas (Bath), Chris Wyatt (Llanelli).

*Replacements:* Geraint Evans (Neath) for Weatherley, Geraint Lewis (Pontypridd) for Quinnell, Kingsley Jones (Ebbw Vale) for Appleyard, Chris Stephens (Bridgend) for Mark Jones, Stephen Jones (Llanelli) for Proctor, Dean Thomas (Swansea) for Martyn Williams, David Llewellyn (Ebbw Vale) cover for Howley.

was suggested: a year earlier he had been struck down by injury that ended his Lions' tour in South Africa. That was a cruel blow. This time, it was a merciful relief to be spared the scars of catastrophe.

Scorching heat was the main problem in the opening match at Harare and Wales struggled unimpressively for a 12-6 interval lead before picking up the pace to defeat a poor Zimbabwe side 49-11. Byron Hayward's three tries on debut as replacement full back was the highlight in front of some 6,000 watchers in a stadium that holds 65,000. He was only the third Welsh player to score a hat-trick on debut, following Willie Llewellyn (1899) and Gareth Thomas (1995).

Richard Rees collected two tries on his first appearance and there were 19 points by Arwel Thomas, including two tries. David Weatherley returned home with a knee injury and before the next match Scott Quinnell followed with calf trouble.

## REPRIEVE FOR KINGSLEY

The Emerging Springboks blitzed Wales with four tries in the first 20 minutes and whipped the tourists 35-13 under the floodlights in the coal-mining town of Secunda, east of Johannesburg. Rob Appleyard, leading the pack, became the next to fly home with knee damage and Wales sent for Kingsley Jones, on holiday in New Zealand. It was an unexpected reprieve for the Ebbw Vale captain, who had been pencilled in when the squad originally was outlined, only for caretaker coach Dennis John to decide he did not fit in with his plans.

Border were expected to be the weakest opposition of the tour, but tackling again left a great deal to be desired and resulted in 24-8 defeat in East London. Border captain Glenn Gelderbloom was blunt: "Wales need to work on the intensity of their play, their pace and ball retention."

Another early storm awaited Wales in Durban. Natal roared into a 22-0 lead. Even without seven of their Springboks (playing against Ireland the following day), the Sharks dominated to win 30-23. Leigh Davies (knee) and Mark Jones (abscess on lower back) were selected for this game, but had to return home and during the match Wayne Proctor suffered a badly broken nose that ended his tour.

Arwel Thomas was awarded a lucky try when the referee failed to notice he did not ground the ball, but Hayward's try was a gem as he weaved through. Swansea coach John Plumtree, who spent six seasons playing for Natal, was there on holiday and summed up, "No Welsh players put in big hits. Good sides base their game on big tackling. Defence is everything and Wales must catch up." Dennis John reflected, "It is hard to appreciate the power and pace at which the South African teams start the match. It is something we are just not used to at home and we need to work on it."

Yet again it was a dismal start to the match against Gauteng Falcons, although Wales fought back with spirit and defeat this time was by just two points at 39-37. The home side were in front with a try after only two minutes. Still, there were four Welsh tries eventually and Hayward supplied 17 goal points. Wales were determined to offer some serious tackling, but let themselves down once more. They gave hope of success as they stole into a 20-17 lead and held it for 10 minutes. Such crumbs of comfort!

Then came Dean Thomas's dismissal for a savage straight-arm tackle that felled Len van Riet as the wing swung inside. The Swansea forward had been pitched into his first game 36 hours after arriving as replacement for Martyn

Williams and a 15-day suspension was the punishment.

So it was on to face the Springboks, who had honed a sharp edge with two victories over Ireland as they prepared for the big effort to crush Wales. It could have been easily more than 15 tries under the Loftus Versfeld floodlights. Home supporters roared their team on to try to reach 100 points. Desperately, Wales held them out. Someone Up There must have take pity at our plight!

## MATCH DETAILS

**June 6, 1998. Wales defeated Zimbabwe by 49 (3G, 1PG, 5T) to 11 (2PG, 1T) at National Sports Stadium, Harare.**

**ZIMBABWE:** V Olonga; R Karimazondo, J Ewing, B French, C Graham; K Tsimba, R Bekker; G Snyder, W Barratt, G Stewart, B Catterall, S Landman, L Greef, B Dawson (capt), M Mwerenga. Reps: D Walters for Karimazondo, D Trivella for Tsimba, I Nelson for Barratt, C McNab for Mwerenga.

**WALES:** D Weatherley; R Rees, D James, M Taylor, W Proctor; A Thomas, R Howley (capt); D Morris, G Jenkins, J Davies, M Jones, A Moore, N Thomas, S Quinnell, M Williams. Reps: B Hayward for Weatherley, J Funnell for Taylor, P John for Howley, B Williams for Jenkins, C Wyatt for Jones, C Charvis for Quinnell.

*Referee:* Johnnie Meuwesen (South Africa).

*Scorers:* For Zimbabwe, Ryan Bekker (1T), Kenny Tsimba (2PG). For Wales, Byron Hayward (3), Richard Rees (2), Arwel Thomas (2), Wayne Proctor (tries), Arwel Thomas (1PG, 3con).

**June 12, 1998. Emerging Springboks defeated Wales by 35 (2G, 2PG, 3T) to 13 (1G, 2PG) at Secunda Stadium, Secunda.**

**EMERGING SPRINGBOKS:** M Goosen; J Davies, D Kayer, R Fleck, L Venter; L Koen, H Husselman; S Wagner, O Nkumane, E Fynne, S Boome, B Thorne, P Krause, A Vos (capt), A Venter. Reps: C Stolz for L Venter, C Alcock for Husselman, N Trytsman for Thorne.

**Ebbw Vale fly half Byron Hayward became a Welsh hero on his debut when he went on as replacement full back against Zimbabwe and scored three tries. His performance ensured his selection in the No 15 jersey against South Africa.**

*Picture: Huw Evans*
*Picture Agency Cardiff*

**WALES:** D. Williams; L Woodard, L Davies, J Funnell, G Evans; B Hayward, P John (capt); M Griffiths, B Williams, B Evans, P Arnold, I Gough, R Appleyard, C Wyatt, C Charvis. Reps: D James for Funnell, M Jones for Arnold, N Thomas for Appleyard.

*Referee:* Jonathan Kaplan (South Africa).

*Scorers:* For Wales, Dafydd James (1T), Hayward (2PG, 1con). For Emerging XV, John Daniels (3), Robbie Fleck, Lourens Venter (tries), Louis Koen (2PG, 2con).

**June 16, 1998. Border defeated Wales by 24 (1G, 4PG, 1T) to 8 (1PG, 1T) at Basil Kenyon Stadium, East London.**

**BORDER:** D Heidtmann; D Maidza, G Gelderbloom (capt), K van der Merwe, K Molotana; W Weyer, J Bradbrook; H Kok, D du Preez, R Swanepoel, B Holtzhausen, A Fox, B Jacobs, M van der Walt, A Botha.

**WALES:** D Williams; R Rees, M Taylor, Geraint Evans, Garan Evans; A Thomas, P John; M Griffiths, G Jenkins (capt), B Evans, P Arnold, C Wyatt, G Lewis, N Thomas, M Williams. Reps: M Jones for Arnold, A Moore for Lewis.

*Referee:* T Henning (South Africa).

*Scorers:* For Wales, Richard Rees (1T), Arwel Thomas (1PG). For Border, Dale Heidtmann, Marcel van der Walt (tries), John Bradbrook (4PG, 1con).

**June 19, 1998. Natal defeated Wales by 30 (2G, 2PG, 2T) to 23 (2G, 3PG) at King's Park, Durban.**

**NATAL:** A Joubert; S Payne, J Thomson, T van der Mescht, S Brink; J van der Westhuyzen, K Putt; D Morkel, M Visser, J Smit, J Slade, S Atherton (capt), D Kriese, W Brosnihan, B McLeod-Henderson. Reps: D Strydom for Thomson, R Bennett for Strydom, H Martens for Putt, N Wenger for Slade, C McIntosh for Brosnihan.

**WALES:** B Hayward; W Proctor, D James, M Taylor, G Evans; A Thomas, R Howley (capt); D Morris, B Williams, J Davies, I Gough, A Moore, M Williams, C Charvis, K Jones. Reps: D Williams for Proctor, C Wyatt for Moore.

*Referee:* Andre Watson (South Africa).

*Scorers:* For Wales, Arwel Thomas, Byron Hayward (tries), Thomas (3PG, 2con). For Natal, Stephen Brink (3), Andre Joubert (tries), Joubert (2PG, 2con).

**June 23, 1998. Gauteng Falcons defeated Wales by 39 (3G, 1PG, 3T) to 37 (4G, 3PG) at Vanderbiljpark, Brakpan.**

**GAUTENG FALCONS:** P Matthys; W Geyer, W Lourens, E Meyer (capt), L van Riet; B van Straaten, D de Kock; G Williamson, D van der Walt, J le Roux, R Schroeder, W Boardman, D Strydom, N Rossouw, B Volschenk. Reps: J Girnun for van Reit, R van As for van Straaten, B Moyle for le Roux, J Booysen for Strydom.

**WALES:** D Williams; L Woodard, G Evans, J Funnell, R Rees; B Hayward, P John; D Morris, G Jenkins (capt), B Evans, P Arnold, C Stephens, G Lewis, C Wyatt, D Thomas. Reps: M Taylor for G Evans, S Jones for Rees, M Griffiths for Morris.

*Referee:* Carl Spannenberg (South Africa).

*Scorers:* For Wales, John Funnell, Paul Arnold, Lennie Woodard, Mark Taylor (tries), Byron Hayward (3PG, 4con). For Falcons, Werner Geyer (2), Dewet Strydom, Wynand Lourens, Moyle, Jaco Booysen (tries), van Straaten (1PG, 2con), van As (1con).

**June 27, 1998. South Africa defeated Wales by 96 (9G, 1PG, 6T) to 13 (1G, 2PG) at Loftus Versfeld, Pretoria.**

**SOUTH AFRICA:** P Montgomery; S Terblanche, A Snyman, P Muller, P Rossouw; F Smith, J van der Westhuizen; R Kempson, J Dalton, A Garvey, K Otto, M Andrews, J Erasmus, G Teichmann (capt), A Venter. Reps: H Honiball for Muller, B Skinstad for Andrews, W Swanepoel for van der Westhuizen, M Hendricks for Terblanche, A Aitken for Teichmann, O le Roux for Garvey, N Drotske for Dalton.

**WALES:** B Hayward; D James, M Taylor, J Funnell, G Evans; A Thomas, P John; M Griffiths, B Williams, J Davies, I Gough, A Moore, N Thomas, C Charvis, K Jones (capt). Reps: C Wyatt for K Jones, D Williams for Hayward, S Jones for Funnell, D Morris for J Davies, G Jenkins for B Williams, G Lewis for Charvis, D Llewellyn for John.

Referee: Paddy O'Brien (NZ).

Scorers: For Wales, Arwel Thomas (1T, 2PG, 1con). For SA, Pieter Rossouw (3), Percy Montgomery (2), Stefan Terblanche (2), Andre Venter (2), Joost van der Westhuizen, Krynauw Otto, Franco Smith, Johan Erasmus, Bob Skinstad, McNeil Hendricks (tries), Montgomery (1PG, 9con).

14

# BATH HERO CALLARD WINS IT
# 19-18 WITH INJURY-TIME KICK

All the drama of an unexceptional match surfaced during injury time at Stade Lescure in Bordeaux on January 31, 1998. Brive, the holders and favourites, were leading 18-16 in the Euro Cup final through five first half penalty goals by Christophe Lamaison and an Alain Penaud drop-shot. Then, 6,000 Bath fans in a crowd of 36,500 whooped with delight as Jonathan Callard kicked his side in front for the first time after 82 minutes with his fourth penalty goal. They led 19-18, but found Lamaison lining up yet another penalty attempt from a handy spot when Bath were ruled to have collapsed a maul. It was heart stopping time for everybody. He couldn't miss. But he did! So did Lisandro Arbizu, from in front of the posts with a last desperate drop-shot. That was how Bath sneaked it right at the end, the first English team to win the cup and keep their record of never having lost any cup final in 11 attempts. It was the club's 17th major trophy since 1984.

## THREE WELSH STARS HELP OUT

They had scored the game's only try when Dan Lyle charged from close range. He unloaded to Andy Nichol; on to Jeremy Guscott and he sent Callard sweeping over unopposed. Callard converted and so provided all 19 points. It was the first occasion for the final to be played in France and the first time a French team had lost, following the victories of Toulouse (over Cardiff) and Brive (against Leicester), both matches in Cardiff. Three Welsh players helped Bath to victory: Ieuan Evans on the wing and Richard Webster and Nathan Thomas in the pack.

**BATH:** J Callard; I Evans, P de Glanville, J Guscott, A Adebayo; M Catt, A Nicol (capt); D Hilton, M Regan, V Ubogu, M Haag, N Redman, N Thomas, D Lyle, R Webster. Reps: F Mendez for Regan, R Earnshaw for Thomas.

**BRIVE:** A Penaud; J Carrat, C Lamaison, D Venditti, S Carrat; L Arbizu, P Carbonneau (capt); D Casadei, L Travers, R Crespy, E Alegret, Y Manhes, L van der Linden, F Duboisset, O Magne. Reps:S Viars for S Carrat, D Laperne for Crespy, R Sonnes for Duboisset.

*Referee:* Jim Fleming (Scotland).

There were those who considered it was a measure of justice that Brive's luck ran out in the final. Pontypridd, especially, had suffered from the 'Brive Experience'; and after the notorious pool match there, BBC Wales broadcaster Phil Steele, the poor man's Max Boyce, sang a sad little ditty of the banned players, *"Barnard, McIntosh, John their names, and by the French magistrates they have been 'framed'!"* This referred to the decision to refuse the Ponty three permission to return to Brive for the play-off match while the police investigation was ongoing. To have shown some consideration to Pontypridd, the ERC should have instructed this play-off to take place on neutral ground in France so that Ponty could have included the three players concerned in their team. Alas, the ERC seem overawed by the influence of the French connection. Ponty qualified for the play-off as the best third-placed team.

Although Neil Jenkins kicked two penalty goals and converted tries by Mark Spiller and Dafydd James for a 20-18 lead, he missed two penalty shots that normally he would have put over blindfolded. So his team went out 25-20 as Jerome Carrat clinched it with a try that Lamaison converted. Ponty, without injured Kevin Morgan and David Manley as well as the banned trio, certainly gave a praiseworthy performance again in defeat.

Bath, with Ieuan Evans, Richard Webster and Nathan Thomas in action, performed impressively to defeat Pau 20-14 in the semi-final, watched by a full house of 8,200. Jonathan Callard kicked five penalty goals and Victor Ubogu scored the Bath try. The other semi was a cliff hanger with Brive going through 2-1 on tries in a 22-all draw at Toulouse. At 16-all, the match went to 30 minutes extra time. One minute from the end, Lamaison put over a simple penalty kick to tie the scores again in front of 26,000 onlookers and try count decided the issue. Wales's Derek Bevan was the referee.

## CALLARD KILLS OFF CARDIFF

There were no Welsh teams in the semi-finals for the first time after Cardiff failed 32-21 at Bath in the quarter-final stage. Again Callard was the nails-in-the-coffin man: he fired in five penalty goals and converted one of the tries by Phil de Glanville, Ubogu and Lyle. Cardiff's goal points came from three penalty goals and a conversion by Lee Jarvis. Leigh Davies scored both tries. Coaching supremo Alex Evans was annoyed that there were 17 penalties against Cardiff. "The referee decided to blow us off the paddock," he asserted. "When that happens, you lose your rhythm." Bath coach Andy Robinson countered, "Cardiff were guilty of the most cynical example of professional fouling I have ever seen." The referee was jostled by a spectator as he left the field and Bath, who had never lost a home Euro Cup game, conducted an enquiry. Jarvis finished as top scorer in the tourney with 134 points, followed by Callard with 114.

Cardiff reached the quarter-final stage by defeating Llanelli 24-20 in the new system of play-offs. The Scarlets trailed 21-3 into the second half; but a rousing fight-back cut the home lead to 21-20 before Lee Jarvis planted over his fourth penalty shot. Gregori Kacala, who had joined from Brive, and Justin Thomas scored Cardiff tries and Jarvis converted one. Craig Warlow slotted in a Llanelli penalty goal and converted one of the tries by skipper Robin McBryde, Wayne Proctor and Garan Evans.

## FISTS FLY ON THE FIELD – AND AGAIN IN THE BAR TOULZAC

When several French forwards took the law into their hands in the Euro Cup pool game and attacked Dale McIntosh after 22 minutes at Brive on September 14, 1997 it launched the Battle of Brive – on and off the pitch! He had late tackled Philippe Carbonneau. So McIntosh and home forward Lionel Mallier were ordered off and banned for 30 days. McIntosh was the first player to be charged with bringing the game into disrepute because he gave the V-sign to spectators as he walked off with a broad smile. However, the charge was dropped.

After the match, which Brive won 32-31, there was an incident in the Bar Toulzac, where Brive players Christophe Lamaison, David Venditti and Carbonneau were reported to have needed hospital treatment. McIntosh, Phil John and Andre Barnard were questioned by the police and the team's return home was delayed by a day until investigations had been made.

"They thought they could push us around, but we would not let them." said Ponty captain Neil Jenkins. Brive coach Laurent Seigne called Pontypridd's players "semi-civilised animals". He declared that Brive would refuse to play the return game at Sardis Road and Ponty should be kicked out. But Brive were instructed to play the second leg at Pontypridd.

The clubs were fined £30,000 each, with £15,000 to be paid within 21 days and the remainder suspended, dependent on their conduct, to the end of the tournament. Pau and Llanelli were also fined after their violent match on the same day, which Pau won 44-12. The fine was less in this case at £20,000, with £10,000 payable within 21 days, although the level of violence was described as "worse than the Brive-Pontypridd match".

Cardiff's opening fixture saw Jarvis drill six penalty goals and convert a late try by Leigh Davies, but they lost 26-25 at Bourgoin. Next it was a first home defeat in the three years of the tourney as Harlequins won 28-21, scoring three tries whereas Cardiff's reply comprised seven Jarvis penalty hits. Quins cited Tony Rees for careless use of the boot (Gareth Llewellyn's head was badly gashed) and the Cardiff lock was banned for 90 days. Alex Evans called the ban "incredible". He said "Rugby is a man's game played by men. It is not a sport for cissies. All this business of citing players is making a mockery of the game."

The return pool match with Brive playing at Sardis Road produced an electric 29-all draw and Lamaison's eight penalty goals equalled the competition record. Brive left the Pontypridd ground 20 minutes after the game ended: there was no fraternising on Brive's part!

## European Conference

# DISMAL AGAIN FOR WELSH CLUBS

Colomiers registered the biggest victory in their history by defeating

Agen 43-5 with seven tries in the final of the Euro Conference at Les Sept-Deniers Stadium, Toulouse on Sunday, February 1, 1998. For the second successive year no Welsh clubs aspired to the quarter-final stage. Although Newcastle went to the semi-finals, they lost 12-9 in Agen, doomed by a 50-yard penalty goal seven minutes from the end.

Newport were the most successful Welsh competitors with three victories from six games. They recorded the double over Montpellier. In the home win, fly half Chris John scored a gem of a try in his 27 points. No 8 Jan Machacek crossed for two tries and scored again in the 28-14 success in Montpellier for Newport's first victory on French territory.

Bridgend won their first and final games in their pool, thereby achieving the double over Grenoble and becoming the first Welsh club to win a Euro game in France during the three seasons. A late try by

## FINAL HEINEKEN CUP POOL TABLES

### POOL A

| | W | D | L | F | A | Pts |
|---|---|---|---|---|---|---|
| Toulouse ...... | 5 | 0 | 1 | 200 | 121 | 10 |
| Leicester ...... | 4 | 0 | 2 | 163 | 117 | 8 |
| Leinster ...... | 2 | 0 | 4 | 137 | 167 | 4 |
| Milan ........ | 1 | 0 | 5 | 111 | 206 | 2 |

**Results:** *Leinster 25, Toulouse 34; Leicester 26, Milan 10; Leinster 16, Leicester 9; Milan 14, Toulouse 19; Milan 33, Leinster 32; Toulouse 17, Leicester 22; Toulouse 69, Milan 19; Leicester 47, Leinster 22; Leicester 22, Toulouse 23; Leinster 23, Milan 6; Toulouse 38, Leinster 19; Milan 29, Leicester 37.*

### POOL B

| | W | D | L | F | A | Pts |
|---|---|---|---|---|---|---|
| Wasps ........ | 6 | 0 | 0 | 243 | 104 | 12 |
| Glasgow ...... | 3 | 0 | 3 | 132 | 167 | 6 |
| Swansea ...... | 2 | 0 | 4 | 157 | 161 | 4 |
| Ulster ........ | 1 | 0 | 5 | 95 | 195 | 2 |

**Results:** *Swansea 25, Wasps 31; Ulster 12, Glasgow 18; Swansea 33, Ulster 16; Glasgow 22, Wasps 46; Glasgow 35, Swansea 21; Wasps 56, Ulster 3; Ulster 28, Swansea 20; Wasps 43, Glasgow 5; Ulster 21, Wasps 38; Swansea 30, Glasgow 22; Glasgow 30, Ulster 15; Wasps 29, Swansea 28.*

### POOL C

| | W | D | L | F | A | Pts |
|---|---|---|---|---|---|---|
| Bath ........ | 5 | 0 | 1 | 141 | 119 | 10 |
| Brive ........ | 4 | 1 | 1 | 210 | 146 | 9 |
| Pontypridd .... | 2 | 1 | 3 | 154 | 147 | 5 |
| Scot. Borders .. | 0 | 0 | 6 | 129 | 222 | 0 |

**Results:** *Brive 56, Scottish Borders 18; Pontypridd 15, Bath 21; Brive 32, Pontypridd 31; Scottish Borders 17, Bath 31; Bath 27, Brive 25; Scottish Borders 16, Pontypridd 23; Bath 27, Scottish Borders 23; Pontypridd 29, Brive 29; Pontypridd 46, Scottish Borders 26; Brive 29, Bath 12; Bath 23, Pontypridd 10; Scottish Borders 29, Brive 39.*

### POOL D

| | W | D | L | F | A | Pts |
|---|---|---|---|---|---|---|
| Harlequins .... | 4 | 0 | 2 | 198 | 141 | 8 |
| Cardiff ...... | 4 | 0 | 2 | 184 | 146 | 8 |
| Munster ...... | 2 | 0 | 4 | 141 | 180 | 4 |
| Bourgoin ..... | 2 | 0 | 4 | 93 | 149 | 4 |

**Results:** *Bourgoin 26, Cardiff 25; NEC Harlequins 48, Munster 40; NEC Harlequins 45, Bourgoin 7; Cardiff 43, Munster 23; Munster 17, Bourgoin 15; Cardiff 21, NEC Harlequins 28; Munster 32, Cardiff 37; Bourgoin 18, NEC Harlequins 30; Bourgoin 21, Munster 6; NEC Harlequins 31, Cardiff 32; Cardiff 26, Bourgoin 6; Munster 23, Harlequins 16.*

### POOL E

| | W | D | L | F | A | Pts |
|---|---|---|---|---|---|---|
| Pau .......... | 4 | 0 | 2 | 203 | 89 | 8 |
| Llanelli ....... | 4 | 0 | 2 | 144 | 142 | 8 |
| Treviso ....... | 2 | 0 | 4 | 146 | 162 | 4 |
| Caledonia ..... | 2 | 0 | 4 | 89 | 189 | 4 |

**Results:** *Benetton Treviso 18, Pau 19; Caledonia 18, Llanelli 23; Pau 44, Llanelli 12; Caledonia 17, Benetton Treviso 9; Llanelli 39, Benetton Treviso 18; Pau 50, Caledonia 8; Benetton Treviso 52, Caledonia 6; Llanelli 14, Pau 10; Benetton Treviso 42, Llanelli 25; Caledonia 30, Pau 24; Llanelli 31, Caledonia 10; Pau 56, Benetton Treviso 7.*

**Play-offs:** *Brive 25, Pontypridd 20;
Cardiff 24, Llanelli 20; Leicester 90, Glasgow 19.*

**Quarter-finals:** *Bath 32, Cardiff 21;
Pau 35, Leicester 18; Toulouse 51, Harlequins 10;
Wasps 18, Brive 25.*

**Semi-finals:** *Bath 20, Pau 14; Toulouse 22, *Brive 22
(*Brive though on more tries rule)*

**Final:**
*Bath 19, Brive 18.
(at Stade Lescure, Bordeaux*

# FINAL EUROPEAN CONFERENCE POOL TABLES

### POOL A

|            | W | D | L | F   | A   | Pts |
|------------|---|---|---|-----|-----|-----|
| Agen ....... | 6 | 0 | 0 | 219 | 105 | 12 |
| La Rochelle ... | 2 | 0 | 4 | 128 | 139 | 4 |
| Ebbw Vale .... | 2 | 0 | 4 | 117 | 155 | 4 |
| Bristol ........ | 2 | 0 | 4 | 115 | 180 | 4 |

**Results:** *Ebbw Vale 16, Agen 27; Ebbw Vale 28, Bristol 15; La Rochelle 25, Ebbw Vale 24; Bristol 18, Ebbw Vale 16; Ebbw Vale 21, La Rochelle 19; Agen 51, Ebbw Vale 12.*

### POOL B

|            | W | D | L | F   | A   | Pts |
|------------|---|---|---|-----|-----|-----|
| Montferrand ... | 5 | 0 | 1 | 203 | 120 | 10 |
| Sale .......... | 3 | 0 | 3 | 163 | 117 | 6 |
| Newport ...... | 3 | 0 | 3 | 172 | 192 | 6 |
| Montpellier .... | 1 | 0 | 5 | 90  | 199 | 2 |

**Results:** *Newport 42, Montpellier 17; Montferrand 58, Newport 32; Sale 61, Newport 27; Newport 26, Montferrand 31; Newport 17, Sale 11; Montpellier 14, Newport 28.*

### POOL C

|            | W | D | L | F   | A   | Pts |
|------------|---|---|---|-----|-----|-----|
| Stade Francais .. | 5 | 0 | 1 | 337 | 131 | 10 |
| Ldn Irish ...... | 4 | 0 | 2 | 169 | 133 | 8 |
| Dax .......... | 3 | 0 | 3 | 139 | 180 | 6 |
| Farul Constanta . | 0 | 0 | 6 | 94 | 295 | 0 |

### POOL D

|            | W | D | L | F   | A   | Pts |
|------------|---|---|---|-----|-----|-----|
| Connacht ...... | 5 | 0 | 1 | 144 | 97  | 10 |
| Northampton ... | 3 | 0 | 3 | 161 | 116 | 6 |
| Begles-Bordeaux | 3 | 0 | 3 | 112 | 110 | 6 |
| Nice ......... | 1 | 0 | 5 | 94 | 188 | 2 |

### POOL E

|            | W | D | L | F   | A   | Pts |
|------------|---|---|---|-----|-----|-----|
| Colomiers ..... | 6 | 0 | 0 | 290 | 121 | 12 |
| Richmond ..... | 4 | 0 | 2 | 196 | 133 | 8 |
| Bridgend ..... | 2 | 0 | 4 | 130 | 259 | 4 |
| Grenoble ...... | 0 | 0 | 6 | 112 | 215 | 0 |

**Results:** *Grenoble 33, Bridgend 35; Richmond 43, Bridgend 14; Bridgend 24, Colomiers 49; Bridgend 12, Richmond 44; Colomiers 69, Bridgend 20; Bridgend 25, Grenoble 21.*

### POOL F

|            | W | D | L | F   | A   | Pts |
|------------|---|---|---|-----|-----|-----|
| Gloucester ..... | 5 | 0 | 1 | 170 | 101 | 10 |
| Toulon ........ | 3 | 1 | 2 | 136 | 104 | 7 |
| Beziers ....... | 2 | 1 | 3 | 150 | 147 | 5 |
| Padova ........ | 0 | 2 | 4 | 108 | 212 | 2 |

### POOL G

|            | W | D | L | F   | A   | Pts |
|------------|---|---|---|-----|-----|-----|
| Newcastle ..... | 5 | 0 | 1 | 264 | 98  | 10 |
| Biarritz ....... | 3 | 0 | 3 | 123 | 153 | 6 |
| Perpignan ..... | 2 | 0 | 4 | 98  | 138 | 4 |
| Edinburgh ..... | 2 | 0 | 4 | 109 | 205 | 4 |

### POOL H

|            | W | D | L | F   | A   | Pts |
|------------|---|---|---|-----|-----|-----|
| Castres ....... | 5 | 0 | 1 | 206 | 97  | 10 |
| Saracens ...... | 5 | 0 | 1 | 197 | 128 | 10 |
| Narbonne ..... | 2 | 0 | 4 | 168 | 138 | 4 |
| Neath ......... | 0 | 0 | 6 | 93  | 301 | 0 |

**Results:** *Neath 12, Castres 36; Neath 10, Narbonne 50; Saracens 69, Neath 30; Narbonne 52, Neath 21; Neath 12, Saracens 26; Castres 68, Neath 8.*

**Quarter-finals:** *Agen 40, Connacht 27; Colomiers 23, Montferrand 13; Newcastle 44, Castres 0; Stade Francais 53, Gloucester 22.*

**Semi-finals:** *Agen 12, Newcastle 9; Colomiers 19, Stade Francais 13*

**Final:** *Colomiers 43, Agen 5 (at Toulouse)*

Dan Jones scraped a 35-33 decision after Owain Lloyd (2) and Gareth Cull had crossed. Cull added 15 goal points and then provided another 20 points in the return game with six penalty shots and a conversion of Sam Greenaway's try. Cull aggregated 80 points in the tourney.

Ebbw Vale gained their first success in two seasons against French opponents with a 21-19 verdict over La Rochelle after trailing 13-0. Byron Hayward won it with his third penalty shot. If he had converted Kingsley Jones's try in La Rochelle, Ebbw would not have lost the return 25-24. Ironically, Hayward had already kicked 14 points.

Neath failed to win any of their games. Andrew Kembery was suspended for 30 days after being sent off for punching in a 68-8 drubbing in Castres. Darren Case collected two tries in his 25 points at Saracens, but the home side were 69-30 winners.

# THEY CALLED IT A DAY

**Ieuan Evans (left),** Wales's most-capped player and top try-getter, decided his international career had come to a close by the 1997-98 season and announced his retirement after 72 full caps. He scored 33 tries for his country and his 28 times as Wales captain was another record.

Jonathan Davies (below) made a total break with the playing side to concentrate on his television and broadcasting career and immediately became a much-respected critic with his shrewd assessments. He played for Wales both sides of his distinguished RL career, 32 appearances in all.

*Pictures by*
*Clive Lewis*
*for Western Mail & Echo Ltd.*

**Men with problems. Cardiff coaching director Alex Evans (right) and coach Terry Holmes. Aussie Evans left at the end of the season.**

## WRU National League

# Swansea – oasis of enterprise in a tactical desert

*By* JOHN BILLOT

The league often is a tactical desert to many teams. A wilderness of maul-and-drive, so that anyone with a touch of flair and adventure becomes an oasis of hope – and success. That was why national coach Kevin Bowring hung his hat on the peg of Arwel Thomas and prayed the twinkling tormentor could lead Wales out of the Slough of Despond. Alas, it was not to be on the international stage; but the outside half's venomous dummy and darting acceleration tore holes in defences and was a dynamic influence in Swansea's third championship title in seven years.

Thomas's goal kicking also made a substantial contribution with 246 league points (more than any other premier division player) and regularly he persuaded opponents into considering him beyond their control. The only wing forward to put the indian sign on him was Ebbw Vale's Kingsley Jones – and Arwel, as he had done with Philippe Carbonneau in Paris, felled the Ebbw captain with a short-arm and doubtless viewed the 'dirty deed' as well worth a yellow card!

Garin Jenkins led with customary verve, a rottweiler among hookers, and his pack outscrummaged opponents with steamroller ruthlessness. Stuart Davies was often a one-man Light Brigade on the charge while Colin Charvis and Rob Appleyard helped him form an arrow of back row destruction that pierced the hearts of the most defiant of defences. Andy Booth proved the personification of reliability, frequently producing that moment of rare opportunism that confounded those who thought him trapped. Scott Gibbs and Mark Taylor were dangermen with their bolting bursts and there was sinister speed on the wings from Simon Davies, Ricky Rees and Alan Harris.

Special praise should go to the unshakeable David Weatherley, an attacking full back capable of causing innumerable problems to the unwary. When Swansea saw off Cardiff's lumbering challenge at St. Helen's in the penultimate game, the title was a formality and completed with a first win at Pontypridd for four years and, at 45-27 against the title-holders, produced the most points they had ever scored at Sardis Road.

Cardiff finished in second place, but seemed to lose their way tactically with their runners often neglected while forward power was the obsession. They preferred the sledgehammer to the rapier. However, Swansea were the only winners of a league match at the Arms Park. Pontypridd finished in third spot. Those who called Sardis Road the House of Pain might reflect that the pain was Ponty's as Cardiff won the first match there and Swansea the last. Bath also triumphed there in the Euro Cup. So Ponty rightly felt their season was unfulfilled.

## DAVEY SETS DOUBLE RECORD

Ebbw Vales's achievement in earning fourth position was the highest they had ever managed in the top division and they will be joined by Div 1 champs Caerphilly, who thoroughly deserved promotion as the most consistently exciting team in the league. They set records with highest team aggregate in a season of 1090 points and most team tries with 137. This, of course, because the division was increased in size from 12 to 16 teams. Caerphilly's Brett Davey passed Neil Jenkins's record with 393 points, including the most in a match with 42 against Rumney.

Pontypool were saved by a whisker from the drop. There was another inspiring display by 37-year-old player/coach David Bishop in front of some 3,000, the biggest crowd of the season at Pontypool Park, for a relegation shoot-out with UWIC, who lost 14-8 and went down. Scrum half Bishop, in tears at the end, drained emotionally as he hugged former Pooler giant Ray Prosser, explained, "I just broke down. It was a feeling of enormous relief." For seven months his team had been at the bottom of the table, faced with a horrifying fate of life in a lower division. "If we had gone down I really don't know if we could have come back," said Bishop. "If we are going to gain promotion we must strengthen our team. That takes an awfully big squad – and that's expensive." Pontypool owe Dai Bish a huge debt of gratitude. Could any other single player have done what he did? The oldest hero playing marked his twilight season with memories we will never forget.

## PREMIER DIVISION

**WEEK 1:** Former Pontypridd starlet Lee Jarvis doomed his old team to 19-16 defeat as he scored all Cardiff's points, including a sparkling solo try. With the scores tied at 16-all, Jarvis hoisted over his fourth and winning penalty goal some 10 minutes from the end. The contest between the previous season's league champions and the cup winners brought a near-capacity crowd to Sardis Road, where Ponty had not lost a league match for almost three years. The last winners there had been Cardiff 12-6 on September 3, 1994. Ponty were leading this time 13-6 when Neil Jenkins suffered injured ribs in a tackle after 32 minutes. Simon Enoch took over as deputy, but a Gareth Wyatt penalty goal was the only further home score after Jenkins's departure. He had kicked two penalty goals and converted a try he craftily set up for Wyatt as Cardiff retired, thinking Jenkins would kick at penalty goal. Cardiff had won just one of their previous five meetings with Pontypridd. Llanelli roasted Neath by their record score against the visitors 52-23 in the blazing heat on August 16 with eight sizzling Stradey tries. Swansea collected seven tries in a 47-11 success at Ebbw Vale, where the home side were without half backs David Llewellyn and Byron Hayward. Newport had to play on the Sunday because their clubhouse had been booked for a wedding and a 19-3 lead was to prove no cause for celebration for the home side. Bridgend rallied to snatch 27-19 victory.

**WEEK 2:** Outside half Arwel Thomas, master of the dummy, scored one of the six Swansea tries and set up three others as they dumped Newport 38-14. Newport have not won at St. Helen's for 21 years. Busy Rupert Moon slashed through to launch two tries for Andrew Gibbs, but Llanelli could not cling on to their 21-16 interval lead. Newcomer Gareth Cull, recruited from Kenfig Hill, popped over two second half penalty goals for a haul of four such kicks and a 22-21 success for Bridgend. The lead swung five times, but Llanelli have not won at the Brewery Field for four years and the bogy struck again! Full back Kevin Morgan sparkled to score two of Pontypridd's nine tries as, even without injured Neil Jenkins, they slammed Ebbw Vale 56-12. Cardiff's fifth successive win at the Gnoll featured 26 points by Lee Jarvis, including a lovely try as Neath went down 46-12.

**WEEK 3:** This was a day of thrilling fight-backs. Bridgend, Pontypridd and Swansea all faced disturbing situations, but battled through to victory. The exceptions were Newport. They went down 24-19 at Ebbw Vale after the home side had been reduced to 13 men with the dismissals of Tongan full back Siua Taumalolo and wing Lennie Woodard in separate incidents late in the first half. Newport coach Steve Jones dejectedly expressed his black mood: "Every Newport player should hang his head in shame. I felt like packing it all in." Cardiff, with 80 per cent possession and overwhelming territorial advantage, saw their 27-10 lead eroded at the Brewery Field until Bridgend saved the match 27-all with a Gareth Cull penalty shot in the second minute of injury time. Cull supplied 17 points, including a try. Cardiff's tight tactics were inexplicable as they tried to sit on their lead. Swansea trailed 15-7 before their revival brought 27-18 home victory over Neath. Glyn Llewellyn, after 15 months with Harlequins, figured impressively for Neath, but scrum half Andy Booth inspired Swansea with a vital try. Another tense recovery featured the contest at Pontypridd, where Llanelli forged in front 13-0 and then 20-6. A sparkling solo try by scrum half Paul John turned the match and Ponty stole ahead for the first time at 21-20 and went on to win 27-23. Craig Warlow supplied 18 points for the Scarlets.

**WEEK 4:** With Bridgend and Swansea losing for the first time, Cardiff

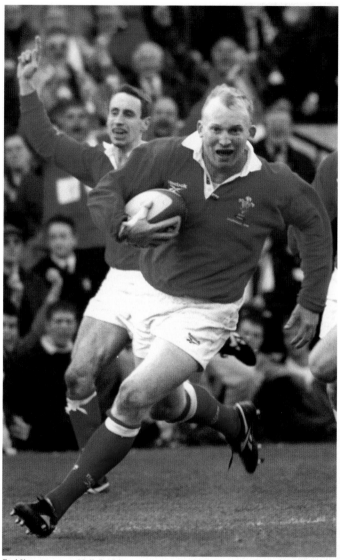

**Striding to score. Neil Jenkins powers away for a try in Dublin in 1998. Wales were 30-21 winners and Jenkins supplied 20 points.**

*Picture: Huw Evans Picture Agency, Cardiff*

**MERTHYR, WORTHINGTON MID-DISTRICT CUP WINNERS 1998 44-36 AGAINST CAERPHILLY**

*Picture: Wales News & Pictures*

were the only unbeaten premier division team. They were 30-24 winners against Ebbw Vale. Byron Hayward became the third player to pass 1,000 league points as he provided 19 for the Vale. Pontypridd joined Swansea in top spot, taking a 26-11 verdict at Newport with three sparkling solo tries from Paul John. The scrum half's 'disappearing act' to baffle defenders included one try from inside his half. This could be the most dynamic solo league try ever scored at Rodney Parade. The lead changed five times at Stradey. Then it was 22-all until Craig Warlow kicked his sixth penalty goal right at the end for the Scarlets to steal it 25-22. Warlow converted a Iwan Jones try to contribute 20 points. It is now 16 seasons since Bridgend won at the Gnoll. They slumped to the first defeat and heaviest reverse ever against Neath, 52-10. Australian wing Guy Barnard crossed for three tries on his debut to guide the Blacks to their first league victory. Justin Price added 22 points.

**WEEK 5:** Newport's fiery forwards had Cardiff on the rack, but a penalty goal by Lee Jarvis from two yards inside the home half gave Cardiff a lucky 26-25 decision in injury time. Gareth Thomas, transferred from Bridgend, marked his debut for Cardiff with two tries and Jarvis converted and kicked four penalty goals. The lead changed six times in the last 30 minutes and Shaun Connor, who put over six penalty goals and converted Jan Machacek's try, missed with a last chance penalty shot from 54 yards. It was so cruel for Newport as Cardiff escaped from the threat of a first league defeat. No 8 Stuart Davies drove over for three tries (two from push-overs) as Swansea rattled up their record score against Bridgend at the Brewery Field 63-15. Arwel Thomas kicked 18 points. Ebbw Vale's first victory over Llanelli for 12 years (also their first success at Stradey since 5-3 in 1970) came 15-12 with tries by Mark Jones and skipper Kingsley Jones and a conversion and penalty shot by Byron Hayward. Justin Price swung over the penalty goal in the fourth minute of injury time at the Gnoll to give Neath a share of events 22-all with Pontypridd. Tristan Davies scored on debut and Adam Palfrey and Lee Jones also crossed. Price converted two. Neil Jenkins landed four Ponty penalty shots and Martyn Williams and Kevin Morgan picked up their tries.

**WEEK 6:** Wales captain Gwyn Jones lay prone on the Arms Park after 13 minutes. He had been trapped at the bottom of a ruck and a neck brace was fitted on the field before he was taken off on a stretcher with a serious spinal injury. "It was a complete accident," explained Cardiff chief executive Gareth Davies. "Gwyn was caught at a very dangerous angle by the force of other players." A few days later Gwyn stated that he would never play again. Another moment of drama occurred when Swansea skipper Garin Jenkins rushed from the pitch into the crowd to try to help his father, who had suffered a heart attack. These incidents obviously affected the teams and the match became a very low key affair, though Swansea thoroughly deserved their 31-22 victory, their third at the Arms Park in eight league seasons. This was Cardiff's first defeat and again their pack lacked the zest of their opponents. Gareth Thomas scored two late tries after Lee Jarvis had fired in four penalty shots. Rob Appleyard, Scott Gibbs and Stuart Davies crossed for Swansea and Arwel Thomas followed his lovely left-footed drop-goal with a couple of conversions and three penalty kicks. Ebbw Vale's first bonus point came in an impressive 31-11 verdict over Neath. Pontypridd registered a slashing 46-10 win over Bridgend. Wayne

# HOW THEY FINISHED

## PREMIER DIVISION

|  | W | D | L | T | B | Pt |
|---|---|---|---|---|---|---|
| Swansea | 11 | 2 | 1 | 68 | 11 | 46 |
| Cardiff | 10 | 1 | 3 | 59 | 9 | 40 |
| Pontypridd | 8 | 2 | 4 | 55 | 9 | 35 |
| Ebbw Vale | 8 | 0 | 6 | 33 | 3 | 27 |
| Neath | 6 | 1 | 7 | 41 | 4 | 23 |
| Llanelli | 5 | 2 | 7 | 44 | 5 | 22 |
| Bridgend | 3 | 2 | 9 | 33 | 1 | 12 |
| Newport* | 0 | 0 | 14 | 23 | 0 | 0 |

*(\* 2 points deducted)*

## DIVISION ONE

|  | W | D | L | T | B | Pt |
|---|---|---|---|---|---|---|
| Caerphilly | 27 | 0 | 3 | 137 | 18 | 99 |
| Aberavon | 20 | 2 | 8 | 104 | 12 | 74 |
| Treorchy | 19 | 0 | 11 | 115 | 16 | 73 |
| Bonymaen | 17 | 0 | 13 | 86 | 9 | 60 |
| Dunvant | 17 | 1 | 12 | 87 | 6 | 58 |
| Merthyr | 14 | 4 | 12 | 91 | 8 | 54 |
| Llandovery | 14 | 0 | 16 | 88 | 12 | 54 |
| Rumney | 15 | 1 | 14 | 94 | 7 | 53 |
| Abertillery | 15 | 1 | 14 | 66 | 4 | 50 |
| Newbridge | 14 | 0 | 16 | 61 | 8 | 50 |
| Cross Keys | 14 | 1 | 15 | 79 | 6 | 49 |
| SW Police | 10 | 1 | 19 | 93 | 11 | 42 |
| Blackwood | 12 | 0 | 18 | 72 | 4 | 40 |
| Pontypool | 11 | 1 | 18 | 73 | 4 | 38 |
| UWIC | 8 | 0 | 22 | 87 | 11 | 35 |
| Maesteg | 7 | 0 | 23 | 59 | 2 | 23 |

## DIVISION TWO

|  | W | D | L | T | B | Pt |
|---|---|---|---|---|---|---|
| Tredegar | 18 | 0 | 4 | 80 | 14 | 68 |
| Tondu | 17 | 1 | 4 | 74 | 13 | 65 |
| Whitland | 16 | 2 | 4 | 76 | 14 | 64 |
| Tenby Utd | 13 | 0 | 9 | 69 | 7 | 46 |
| Pyle | 10 | 1 | 11 | 43 | 6 | 37 |
| Ystradgynlais | 10 | 0 | 12 | 46 | 5 | 35 |
| Narberth | 9 | 1 | 12 | 49 | 5 | 33 |
| Llanharan | 7 | 3 | 12 | 50 | 3 | 27 |
| Mountain Ash | 8 | 0 | 14 | 32 | 0 | 24 |
| Kenfig Hill | 7 | 1 | 14 | 40 | 2 | 24 |
| St Peter's | 6 | 0 | 16 | 52 | 5 | 23 |
| Abercynon | 6 | 1 | 15 | 37 | 1 | 20 |

## DIVISION THREE

|  | W | D | L | T | B | Pt |
|---|---|---|---|---|---|---|
| Llantrisant | 18 | 1 | 3 | 79 | 13 | 68 |
| Rhymney | 16 | 0 | 6 | 81 | 14 | 62 |
| Oakdale | 14 | 2 | 6 | 72 | 9 | 53 |
| Yst Rhondda | 14 | 0 | 8 | 65 | 6 | 48 |
| Blaina | 11 | 1 | 10 | 74 | 9 | 43 |
| Glam Wands | 11 | 0 | 11 | 61 | 9 | 42 |
| Felinfoel | 12 | 0 | 10 | 74 | 5 | 41 |
| Carmarthen Q | 10 | 1 | 11 | 67 | 8 | 39 |
| Builth Wells | 8 | 1 | 13 | 54 | 6 | 31 |
| Kidwelly | 6 | 0 | 16 | 51 | 4 | 22 |
| Glynneath | 6 | 0 | 16 | 41 | 2 | 20 |
| Penarth | 3 | 0 | 19 | 38 | 1 | 10 |

## DIVISION FOUR

|  | W | D | L | T | B | Pt |
|---|---|---|---|---|---|---|
| Vardre | 18 | 0 | 4 | 59 | 7 | 61 |
| Gilfach Goch | 17 | 0 | 5 | 78 | 10 | 61 |
| Carmarthen A | 15 | 2 | 5 | 64 | 11 | 58 |
| Pencoed | 13 | 1 | 8 | 56 | 5 | 45 |
| Seven Sisters | 11 | 2 | 9 | 54 | 7 | 42 |
| Garndiffaith | 11 | 0 | 11 | 52 | 5 | 38 |
| Abergavenny | 10 | 1 | 11 | 48 | 5 | 36 |
| Aberavon Q | 10 | 0 | 12 | 51 | 3 | 33 |
| Tonmawr | 8 | 2 | 12 | 50 | 5 | 31 |
| Bedwas* | 6 | 2 | 14 | 53 | 6 | 24 |
| Resolven | 7 | 1 | 14 | 35 | 0 | 22 |
| Tumble | 0 | 1 | 21 | 35 | 2 | 3 |

*(\* 2 points deducted)*

Proctor ran 100 yards from a loose ball to score one of his two tries as Llanelli won at Newport for only the second time in the league.

**WEEK 7:** Leaders Swansea and second-placed Pontypridd drew 24-all watched by 7,000 spectators at St Helen's, where Ponty have not won for 26 seasons. Both sides were critical of referee Nigel Williams, who awarded 35 penalties. Arwel Thomas kicked eight penalty goals and then missed for the only time with ninth attempt in injury time. Gareth Wyatt and Kevin Morgan crossed for Ponty. Neil Jenkins converted one, dropped a goal and landed three penalties. Frano Botica's 16 goal points doomed Cardiff to their second reverse. It was 26-24 and Cardiff can claim just two successes at Stradey in eight league visits. Newport had Ian Gough sent off

15 minutes from the end at Neath after unruly use of the boot and Chris John, who had joined from Newport two weeks' earlier, kicked the resultant penalty goal to give the home side a 23-22 verdict. Shaun Conner's 75-yard interception try launched Newport's bold bid. Three tries in eight minutes brought Ebbw Vale 33-26 victory at Bridgend. Gareth Cull kicked 16 home points.

**WEEK 8:** The only match to survive the storm saw Neath 31-6 winners over Llanelli with tries by Delme Williams, Mefin Davies, skipper Geraint Evans and Tristan Davies after three tonnes of sand had soaked up Gnoll surface water. Played later, Swansea blitzed Ebbw Vale 63-3 with nine tries and Arwel Thomas fired over 18 goal points. St. Helen's is very much Ebbw's bogy ground: they have not won there since March 1979, and then by a whisker 15-14. Bridgend doomed fellow strugglers Newport to relegation 24-13 with two tries by wing Gwilym Wilkins on his 100th appearance for the Brewery Field team. Cardiff produced some spectacular running to destroy Pontypridd 28-0. It was the first time for 16 seasons for Ponty to fail to score against the Blue and Blacks, who scored tries by Gareth Thomas (3) and Lee Jarvis.

**WEEK 9:** Ebbw Vale's dynamic performance to win 29-13 in one of the most entertaining matches of the season, saw them defeat title-holders Pontypridd for the first time in 10 years (since their double in 1987-88) with Byron Hayward scoring 19 goal points. Inspiringly led by skipper Kingsley Jones, and with Dai Llewellyn a questing scrum half, Ebbw obtained tries by Alun Harries and second row Kuli Falatai. Ponty, without injured Neil Jenkins, incurred their second league reverse. Swansea, now leading by five points from Cardiff, were 37-11 winners at Newport, where Arwel Thomas crossed for two tries in his 27 points. Cardiff overpowered Neath 50-11. Nigel Walker scored two of the seven tries; Lee Jarvis kicked 15 points. Bridgend drew a bad-tempered match 14-all at Llanelli.

**WEEK 10:** Llanelli's rally almost stole the game at Swansea: but Arwel Thomas kicked his seventh penalty goal some five minutes from the end to save matters at 26-all. There were 11 penalty goals in the match, four for the Scarlets by Craig Warlow, who converted two tries, including his own, for 21 points. The start was delayed until the Llanelli team had returned to the dressing room to discard their upper-body protective wear. Chris John scored 17 points for Neath to win 32-26 at Bridgend, who had never scored so many points against Neath without winning. Lee Jarvis supplied 18 points in Cardiff's 33-18 victory at Ebbw Vale. Pontypridd's well crafted 41-5 triumph over Newport featured 16 points by Neil Jenkins.

**WEEK 11:** Leaders Swansea wrested a worrying 36-28 victory at the Gnoll after Neath had threatened to steal it, by leading 21-17 with only some eight minutes left. But home errors let in Mark Taylor (from a rip-roaring 50-yard burst by Scott Gibbs), Natal forward Tyrone Maullin and Paul Moriarty for counter-attacking tries. Those three winning tries came in the space of some five minutes. Cardiff's highest score against Bridgend featured two tries by Rob Howley to make it 52-17 with eight tries. Pontypridd assembled a 36-25 score at Llanelli. It was three tries each, but Neil Jenkins provided 26 Ponty points with a try, drop-shot, four penalty goals and three conversions. Ebbw Vale were 18-10 winners at Newport with tries by Alun Harries and Jonathan Hawker.

High and low, it's just no go in trying to catch Arwel Thomas. The Swansea fly half flits away from Cardiff's jumping Lee Jarvis and diving Gareth Thomas.

*Picture: Gareth Everett for Huw Evans Picture Agency, Cardiff*

**WEEK 12:** Swansea ran in eight tries during the first 25 minutes and finished 71-19 winners against devastated Bridgend. Wing Ricky Rees collected four of the 11 tries in Swansea's record score against the visitors. Pontypridd also cut loose to swamp Neath 61-19. Llanelli led 12-6 at half time, but Byron Hayward supplied 21 points for Ebbw to win 26-15. Newport could not find a front row to go to Cardiff so the game was postponed. Then nine tries blasted Newport in Cardiff's record win over them 61-24. There were 21 Jarvis points and No 8 Steve Williams made it a maximum bonus with a try in the third minute of injury time. Phew!

**WEEK 13:** Cardiff's hopes of stealing the title crashed at Swansea. It was a 39-20 defeat as the Whites proved faster and more imaginative. Arwel Thomas produced 29 points with a try, three conversions and six penalty goals. In the process, he conned referee Derek Bevan into giving a penalty against an outraged Jonathan Humphreys! Scott Gibbs and Simon Davies were other home try-getters. Jamie Ringer and Lee Jarvis crossed for Cardiff. Jarvis converted both and fired over two penalty shots. Llanelli had no trouble disposing of Newport 66-10 with two tries by prop Martyn Madden on his debut on loan from Penzance. Pontypridd won 46-27 at Bridgend. Ebbw Vale trailed 28-3 at Neath, but rallied spiritedly before losing 28-24.

**WEEK 14:** There were 6,000 onlookers at Sardis Road to witness Swansea receiving the crystal glass championship trophy after 45-27 victory. Arwel Thomas kicked 20 points; the 33-year-old Paul Moriarty sped in for two sparkling tries (the first from 60 yards) and Andy Booth, Scott Gibbs and Colin Charvis also crossed. Neil Jenkins kicked five home penalty goals and converted one of the two tries by full back Simon Enoch. In their first home defeat by Swansea for four years, Ponty were lucky in one respect: Dale 'Big Mitts' McIntosh was fortunate not to be sent off for a vicious punch that put lock Andy Moore out of the match and in need of stitches in his mouth. Liam Botham's second try in the last minutes brought Cardiff 31-27 success over Llanelli. The Scarlets led 17-3 and Wayne Proctor's three tries saw him reach 100 tries for his club. Cardiff battled back spectacularly with 14 men for most of the match after Derwyn Jones was dismissed for the early bath by referee Robert Davies (Dunvant). Ebbw Vale defeated Bridgend 34-12 with 24 points from Byron Hayward, including two tries. Darren Case collected 21 points as Neath won 41-17 at Newport.

## DIVISION ONE

**WEEK 1:** Caerphilly full back Brett Davey set a league record with 42 points (3T, 3PG, 9con) in his team's 77-6 success against promoted Rumney, the previous season's Div 3 champions. Aberavon swamped Dunvant, who had lost the bulk of the previous season's successful team. Jason Ball kicked 17 points in the 47-3 victory. Darren Simpson's fourth penalty goal, fired over from half way in the 81st minute, saw Llandovery win 12-10 at Bonymaen. Scrum half Jonathan Hooper, a Tonyrefail product, made a dynamic three try debut for Merthyr as they defeated Pontypool 43-15. New full back Nick Fearns, from Newport, helped Maesteg to a 22-0 verdict over SW Police. Abertillery's Mark Fleet torpedoed Treorchy 29-11 with 18 goal points. Cross

### MOST POINTS

*Brett Davey (Caerphilly) Div 1 . . . . . . . . . 393
Mark Thomas (Dunvant) Div 1 . . . . . . . . . 295
Ioan Bebb (Cross Keys) Div 1 . . . . . . . . . . 262
* Record

Jonathan Mason (Rumney) Div 1 . . . . . . . . . 249
Arwel Thomas (Swansea) Prem Div . . . . . . . 246
Kevin Thomas (Felinfoel) Div 3 . . . . . . . . . 235

### MOST TRIES

Roger Bidgood (Caerphilly) Div 1 . . . . . . . . 17
Jason Riggs (Treorchy) Div 1 . . . . . . . . . . . 17
Paul Jones (Llandovery) Div 1 . . . . . . . . . . 16
* Including 13 for Ystrad Rhondda

*Robert Davies (Treorchy) Div 1 . . . . . . . . . . 15
Marc Evans (Whitland) Div 2 . . . . . . . . . . . . 15
Jamie Payne (Llantrisant) Div 3 . . . . . . . . . . 15

Keys, led by new skipper Ioan Bebb, accounted for Blackwood 17-5. Newbridge won 14-10 at UWIC.

**WEEK 2:** Ioan Bebb found the target with six penalty goals for Cross Keys to register an 18-10 win at Llandovery. Darren Simpson provided all the Drovers' points with a goal and penalty goal. Darren Starr scored two of Caerphilly's seven tries as they routed Blackwood 41-8. Wing Jason Riggs swooped for two tries as Treorchy shocked Aberavon to 43-20 defeat. SW Police had scrum half Neal Bundock and back row Ian Hemburrow ordered off by referee Mike Cox for illegal footwork and lost 29-20 at Rumney. Neither player was banned. Pontypool led 14-3 but visitors Bonymaen finished 15-14 winners despite having hooker Darren Polland sent off. Pooler prop Wayne Morgan also went for an early splash. UWIC were 31-18 ahead at half time at Dunvant, but the home side hit back and a hat-trick of tries by Mark Thomas in his 29 points helped bring 44-36 victory. A try by Colin Milkins saw Abertillery shade Maesteg 13-12. Played later, Newbridge lost to Merthyr 10-9 as Stuart Hancox converted a penalty try and kicked a penalty goal for the visitors.

**WEEK 3:** Abertillery have won only five times in 60 visits to Aberavon and the latest defeat came 27-5. Scrum half Andrew Jacobs crossed twice for the Wizards. Hooker Andrew Thomas nipped over for three tries from close-up lineouts as Treorchy triumphed 35-25 at UWIC. Blackwood had Julian Price and Gavin Thomas ordered off and lost 27-10 at SW Police. Played later, try-scorer Roger Bidgood set Caerphilly on the path to 18-10 success against Llandovery. Dunvant forced a 20-all draw at Merthyr with tries by Simon Daniel (2) and Adrian Killa. Player/coach David Bishop slanted over a 55th minute drop-shot to inspire Pontypool's 21-12 win at Cross Keys. Maesteg nudged out Rumney 16-14.

**WEEK 4:** Outside half Richard Thomas scored two tries and set up two for Aberavon to defeat Maesteg 46-25. Jason Thrupp also crossed twice for the Wizards. Caerphilly stunned Pontypool to 60-12 home humiliation with Owen Robbins a hat-trick scorer. Cross Keys collected the only try through Colin Ellis, but lost 12-5 at Newbridge, where Jason Williams kicked four penalty goals. Phil Sparrow's 15 points brought SW Police 25-16 success at Llandovery. Merthyr were denied 22-17 at Treorchy. David Lloyd's 12 points proved decisive. Chris Lay was Blackwood's star with 11 goal points as they stopped Rumney 26-10. Peter Roberts contributed all the UWIC points, but they failed 26-14 at Abertillery. Bonymaen lost 30-15 at Dunvant.

**WEEK 5:** When Rumney were awarded a penalty in the shadow of the posts, Llandovery players turned their backs, expecting a simple kick at goal. Instead, Simon Greedy tapped quickly and darted over for a cheeky try and 27-20 victory. Former Wales flanker Lyn Jones signed off for Treorchy with a try before returning to coach Neath. Lyn's try helped the Zebras to win 17-9 at Bonymaen. UWIC trailed only 27-28 until Nick Stork flew in for a long-distance try in Aberavon's 33-27 success. Abertillery forced a 15-all draw at Merthyr as scrum half Darren Wright pounced for the saving try. Brett Davey popped over 26 points as Caerphilly routed Newbridge 66-17 with eight tries. Cross Keys defeated Dunvant 26-11, but were unhappy about the incident that sent Craig Clements to hospital with a broken jaw. Ioan Bebb kicked 16 points. Phil Sparrow supplied 17 points for SW Police to beat Pontypool 52-19. Alex Davies fired over four penalty goals to make Maesteg 12-10 winners against Blackwood.

**WEEK 6:** Ian Hemburrow became the first forward in the league to reach 50 tries as he set SW Police on the path to 32-10 victory at Newbridge. Full back Chris Lewis stormed away on an 80-yard counter-attack to score a sensational try as Aberavon accounted for Merthyr 42-10. Prop Nigel Evans was ordered off, but Bonymaen twice came from behind to win at Abertillery 14-12. Wing Paul John crossed for the winners and the game's only try. Leaders Caerphilly took a 28-9 verdict at Dunvant, No 8 Adrian Wainwright scoring two of the four tries. A hat-trick of tries by skipper Glen George spearheaded Rumney to 27-18 success at Pontypool. Cross Keys gave a dismal display in losing 33-16 at Treorchy. Alex Davies kicked six penalty goals, but could not save Maesteg from 35-26 defeat at UWIC. Three tries by skipper Paul Jones helped Llandovery to their first home success 44-20 against Blackwood.

**WEEK 7:** Brett Davey became the first league player to pass 100 points as he helped Caerphilly stop Treorchy 21-13. In three successive weeks the Green Army had defeated the three teams who dropped with them from the top division: Newbridge, Dunvant and Treorchy. Three tries by Ian Hemburrow saw SW Police crush Dunvant 57-3 with nine tries. Scrum half Tom Walsh escaped numerous Abertillery tacklers to steal an audacious try for Cross Keys to win 25-12. Wing Andrew Wagstaffe whipped over for a hat-trick of tries as UWIC ended Merthyr's two year ground record 34-18. Jonathan Mason's conversion from the touchline brought Rumney 14-12 success against Newbridge. Captain Paul Jones crunched over for three tries as Llandovery triumphed 32-8 against Maesteg. Pontypool plunged to 46-19 defeat at Blackwood. Aberavon were 26-16 winners at Bonymaen.

**WEEK 8:** Aberavon's 18-month league ground record came under fire from Cross Keys skipper Ioan Bebb and he banged over four penalty goals, but the Wizards saved it in a 12-all draw. An Arwel Rowlands try and Darren Simpson penalty shot for Llandovery doomed Pontypool to 8-7 defeat. Blackwood were 19-10 winners at Newbridge with a hat-trick of penalty goals by Gareth Richards jolting the home side. Five yellow cards were displayed. Wayne Booth was the only try-scorer in Treorchy's 11-0 decision against SW Police. Scrum half Gareth Cooper was the star as UWIC edged Bonymaen 10-5.

**"It's been the worst week in my rugby life!"** Ebbw Vale captain **Kingsley Jones** had been left out of the Wales team to tour Zimbabwe and South Africa and Ebbw had been defeated in the SWALEC Cup final.

*Picture: Huw Evans Picture Agency, Cardiff*

Dunvant players agreed a no-win, no-pay deal against Rumney and the motivation brought Dunvant 20-8 reward. Leaders Caerphilly won 23-10 at Abertillery. Maesteg failed 26-18 against visitors Merthyr.

**WEEK 9:** Second-placed Aberavon's 23-17 victory at Caerphilly brought the Green Army's first defeat, though they stayed at the top. Wing Daran Griffiths scored two of the Wizards' tries. Ioan Bebb landed his sixth penalty goal in injury time for a 32-29 Cross Keys win against UWIC. Bottom team Pontypool enjoyed their first success 24-10 over Maesteg with 14 goal points by Gareth Curtis. Abertillery had centre Steve Barrett sent off and failed 46-19 at SW Police. Mark Cox provided 21 points, including two tries and wing Andrew Thomas swept over for three tries. Blackwood's desperate defence enabled them to register a tense 31-26 verdict against Dunvant. There was a hat-trick of tries for home fly half Chris Lay. Mark Thomas supplied 16 Dunvant points. A late rally saw Llandovery defeat Newbridge 19-13 with a 45-yard drop-shot by Dai Lloyd-Jones as a final flourish. Rumney had Gareth Phillips ordered off and visitors Treorchy were 29-13 winners. Merthyr won 22-10 at Bonymaen.

**WEEK 10:** Matthew Pearce converted a try and landed a 45-yard penalty shot, all in injury time, to present Maesteg with 22-20 success over Bonymaen. Captain Paul Kawulok, back after injury, collected a vital try and Jason Williams kicked 13 points for Newbridge to defeat Pontypool 28-13. Treorchy shattered Blackwood 54-13. Paul Jones scored three tries and David Lloyd put over 14 points. Prop Wayne Ford stormed over for two tries and Dean Evans added another two for Merthyr to stop Cross Keys 32-11. Paul Phillips's nine goal points and a try saw leaders Caerphilly win 24-19 at UWIC. A try by skipper Colin Laity inspired Aberavon to 15-5 victory against SW Police. Two late penalty goals from Mark Thomas steered Dunvant to a 26-23 verdict over Llandovery. Rumney were 24-19 winners at Abertillery.

**WEEK 11:** Scrum half Adrian Killa took centre stage with a hat-trick of tries as Dunvant powered to 47-19 success at Pontypool. Mark Thomas added 17 points. A try by outstanding forward Adrian Wainwright and four Paul Phillips penalty goals earned leaders Caerphilly a 17-13 verdict over Merthyr. Cross Keys preserved their 12-month home record 19-15 against Bonymaen with a sparkling 55-yard solo try by Tom Walsh. Keith Lee pounced for his 50th league try for Rumney; but his side lost 25-21 to visitors Aberavon as Ian Callaghan burst across for the clinching try. Full back Emyr Lewis weaved through for an audacious try and Llandovery shocked Treorchy to 28-15 defeat. Peter Roberts kicked five penalty goals for UWIC, but they lost 32-15 at SW Police. Abertillery slumped 13-0 at Blackwood. Newbridge registered 28-9 victory against Maesteg.

**WEEK 12:** Bonymaen, with only Pontypool below them in the table, notched up their first home success, a shock 18-17 over leaders Caerphilly after trailing 17-3. Stuart Davies scored all the winning points, including two tries. Caerphilly's second defeat enabled Aberavon to join them as joint leaders with a 30-22 verdict against Blackwood. After seven league games without a win, Abertillery jolted Llandovery 27-17. Andrew Price supplied 14 Abertillery points. Scott Eggar and Jason Riggs each scored three tries to spearhead

Treorchy to 79-29 victory over Pontypool with 13 tries. David Lloyd contributed 19 points to help raise a record tally against Pooler. Neil Morgan raced 45 yards for the clinching try as Merthyr stopped SW Police 13-9 at The Wern. Alex Davies's two tries in his 17 points brought Maesteg 32-21 reward against Cross Keys. Jason Williams's four penalty goals were invaluable as Newbridge won 22-13 at Dunvant. UWIC defeated Rumney 39-26.

**WEEK 13:** Bottom team Pontypool jolted second-placed Aberavon 10-all. The Wizards have not won at Pontypool since their 18-17 cup success in 1980 and were grateful that Jason Ball converted Andrew Jacobs's try and Nick Stork planted a penalty shot. Paul Thatcher converted his try and added a Pooler penalty goal. Julian Vernall's 21 points was the bedrock of Cross Keys's 36-23 success at SW Police, for whom Phil Sparrow scored three tries. Stuart Davies's drop-shot sealed a 21-15 win for Bonymaen at Rumney. Treorchy crashed 17-0 at Dunvant as Mark Thomas landed four penalty goals and Paul Matthews notched a try. Tim McManus motored away for two tries in a 31-11 triumph for Newbridge over Abertillery. Jason Williams kicked 16 points. Paul Phillips supplied 21 points in Caerphilly's 41-28 verdict over Maesteg. UWIC lost 47-19 at Llandovery. Merthyr were 12-7 winners at Blackwood.

**WEEK 14:** Former Wales full back Jonathan Mason was the fourth player to pass 1,000 league points (following Neil Jenkins, Aled Williams and Byron Hayward) as he helped Rumney draw 30-all at Merthyr. Wing Gafyn Stiff snatched a hat-trick of tries to give leaders Caerphilly a fortunate 30-22 verdict at Cross Keys. Alex Davies landed his fourth penalty goal in the sixth minute of injury time for Maesteg to sneak it 22-21 against Dunvant. Abertillery's pack dominated for a 36-13 success over Pontypool with two tries by Darren Miles. Treorchy, despite having Gavin Owen and Steve Evans sent off, stopped Newbridge 23-9. In the last minute, referee Gwyn Bowden added Newbridge's Damion Cooper to the ordered off list. Ian Laycock's injury-time try, converted by Chris Lay, saw Blackwood win at UWIC 23-22. Bonymaen registered their first bonus point in a 34-12 decision against SW Police. Aberavon were 25-14 winners over Llandovery.

**WEEK 15:** SW Police plundered five tries, two of them by Chris Howells, at Caerphilly, but 34 points amazingly was not enough to bring victory. Chris Brown swooped for three tries for the Green Army and Brett Davey's 21 goal points brought them 51-34 success. Dunvant were horrified that, after leading 21-3, they lost 22-21 at Abertillery, where Geraint Gladwyn pounced for the winning try a minute from the end. A Matthew Gibbs try sealed a notable 29-20 victory for bottom team Pontypool at UWIC. Llandovery led 8-9 at Merthyr, but the home side stole it 12-8 with a decisive try from Andrew Loring. Ioan Bebb fired over five penalty goals for Cross Keys, only for Simon Enoch to turn the game with a try and visitors Rumney took a 33-15 verdict. Aberavon cut Newbridge up 50-7. Blackwood lost 37-14 at Bonymaen. Treorchy were 29-16 winners at Maesteg.

**WEEK 16:** Aberavon outscored Dunvant 3-1 on tries at the Broadacre, but lost for the second time. It was 25-20 as Mark Thomas kicked 20 points. Leaders Caerphilly had Chris Brown sent off after 10 minutes, but still won 32-20 at Rumney with Brett Davey slotting 22 goal points. Brown was not banned.

Pontypool's courageous revival continued with a 19-12 revenge win over Merthyr despite losing wing Shane Aitken for an early bath. Aled Williams kicked a late penalty goal for Llandovery to edge Bonymaen 16-13. Treorchy suffered their first home defeat as Abertillery stormed back from 15 points down to complete a notable double over the Zebras 18-15. A late drop-shot by Andrew Green was decisive. Blackwood avenged earlier defeat with a 22-15 verdict against Cross Keys with Chris Way supplying three penalty goals and a drop shot. Maesteg had prop Simon Wilde dismissed and lost 46-19 at SW Police. Newbridge trounced UWIC 45-5.

**WEEK 17:** A conversion attempt struck the posts, so Newbridge failed 10-8 at Merthyr, where Nigel Berbillon and Neil Morgan scored home tries. After four successive defeats, Cross Keys bounced back 22-17 against Llandovery. Darren Miles collected the only try for Abertillery to make it 10-3 at Maesteg. Aberavon brushed aside Treorchy's challenge 26-6. Pontypool's run of three victories ended 36-7 at Bonymaen as wing Paul John raced in for four tries. Dunvant were 30-19 winners at UWIC. Rumney lost 21-7 at SW Police. Caerphilly racked up 10 tries in a 62-10 victory at Blackwood. Brett Davey supplied 17 points.

**WEEK 18:** All matches played later after storm. Mark Thomas's 23 points enabled Dunvant to jolt Merthyr 43-15. Bonymaen had prop Andy May ordered off at Newbridge and lost 22-3. Mark Ryce was a two-try scorer for Rumney as they hit Maesteg 43-28. Also a two-try getter was Richard Lewis in Blackwood's 28-9 verdict over SW Police. Brett Davey's late penalty goal nosed Caerphilly to tense 24-22 success in the Llandovery mud. David Bishop inspired Pontypool to 23-14 victory with a match-turning try against Cross Keys. Prop Kevin Matthews enjoyed two tries as Treorchy defeated UWIC 31-14. Aberavon won 19-5 at Abertillery.

**WEEK 19:** Merthyr's impressive performance brought a 35-7 revenge win over Treorchy with 20 points from Stuart Hancox, including a length-of-the-field interception try. Richard Diplock's weaving try helped Aberavon edge it 18-17 at Maesteg. Newbridge forward Damian Cooper broke his leg in two places and his side lost 16-12 at Cross Keys with 11 decisive points by Ioan Bebb. With Mark Glover, recruited from Neath, dominating the lineout, Dunvant were 21-6 winners at Bonymaen. Aled Williams supplied 13 points to bring Llandovery 23-3 success at SW Police. Darren Hawthorne scored two tries and Brett Davey kicked 17 points for leaders Caerphilly to stop Pontypool 47-20. Played later, Rumney blasted Blackwood 24-7. Abertillery won 33-16 at UWIC.

**WEEK 20:** Treorchy players, accepting a 10 per cent cut in wages to ease financial problems, had to accept another defeat as they lost at home 17-13 to Bonymaen. Llandovery added five tries in the last 15 minutes to shock Rumney 50-12. Mark Fleet supplied all Abertillery's points in a 16-13 success against Merthyr. A first minute try by Roger Bidgood set leaders Caerphilly up for a 20-5 decision at Newbridge. Ioan Bebb contributed 16 points but could not save Cross Keys from 29-21 defeat at Dunvant. Andrew Jacobs kicked 13 points as Aberavon stopped UWIC 27-12. Blackwood outscored Maesteg 6-1 on tries to win 37-11 and avenge their cup reverse. Played later, Pontypool defeated SW

**The Grangetown Galloper.** Martyn Madden scored two tries for Llanelli on this
debut against Newport. His try was to win the SWALEC Cup.

*Picture: Huw Evans Picture Agency, Cardiff*

Police 33-26 after Ian Hemburrow scored a try hat-trick for Police.

**WEEK 21:** Pontypool struggled off the bottom for the first time with a 22-12 success at Rumney. Tries by David Bishop and Ben Jefferies, plus four Matthew Silva penalty shots, saw Pooler triumph. Brett Davey's 14 points guided Caerphilly to 34-13 victory over Dunvant. After five defeats at the hands of Llandovery, Blackwood marked up a 32-27 verdict with Chris Lay providing 12 vital goal points. The previous week, Blackwood had lost 100-7 at London Welsh. A try by scrum half Colin Ellis set Cross Keys on the way to a 20-18 decision over Treorchy. Gethin Vobe's 18 goal points put the icing on a 53-15 UWIC win at Maesteg. After five consecutive league victories, Abertillery failed 30-20 at Bonymaen. Richard Morris snapped up two tries to make Aberavon 22-7 winners at Merthyr. Newbridge lost 34-3 at SW Police. Justin Price collected 14 points.

**WEEK 22:** Jeremy Cordle, son of former Glamorgan cricketer Tony, swooped for a try in his first league match as Abertillery defeated Cross Keys 22-15. Pontypool notched an impressive 46-22 success over Blackwood with 16 points by Matthew Silva. Brett Davey's 18 points inspired Caerphilly to 33-10 victory at Treorchy. Richard Diplock's two tries spearheaded Aberavon's 33-15 verdict against Bonymaen. Chris Wills was the only try scorer as Rumney won 10-3 at Newbridge. Maesteg's seven-try victory slammed Llandovery 42-20. Dunvant recorded 27-5 revenge over SW Police. Merthyr hit UWIC 41-22.

**WEEK 23:** Second-placed Aberavon plunged to their third defeat as Cross Keys snatched three tries in a 12-minute spell in the second half which brought 30-13 victory. Ioan Bebb kicked 15 points. Leaders Caerphilly fought back from 19-9 arrears to wear down Abertillery 35-26. Llandovery snatched the lead for the first time in the last minute to pip Pontypool 29-28 when Aled Williams twinkled across and added the conversion. Full back Richard Jones raced 90 yards for a memorable UWIC try, but the students went down 26-22 at Bonymaen. Wing Paul John grabbed three home tries. Rhys Williams supplied 15 Maesteg points only for Stuart Hancox to score the same number and help Merthyr win 30-20. Jonathan Mason's 18 points enabled Rumney to beat Dunvant 33-21. David Lloyd scored 23 points for Treorchy to end a sequence of six league defeats with a 28-10 verdict at SW Police. Jason Williams collected 15 points for Newbridge to win 33-13 at Blackwood.

**WEEK 24:** Caerphilly ensured they would finish as division champions by avenging their only home defeat and winning 22-0 in a mudbath at Aberavon. In the process, Brett Davey set a national league record of 289 points in a season. He kicked four penalty goals to pass the previous best tally of 285 by Neil Jenkins. Pontypool leapfrogged off the bottom and over Maesteg with 29-18 victory at the Old Parish. David Bishop schemed Pooler's success and set up two of their four tries. Stuart Davies kicked 14 points to inspire Bonymaen's 19-7 verdict at Merthyr. Chris Wall raced 60 yards for the winning try as UWIC nudged out Cross Keys 20-15. Newbridge trailed 17-5, but surged to 31-17 success over Llandovery. Treorchy defeated Rumney 32-24. Dunvant downed Blackwood 44-14. SW Police lost 36-17 at Abertillery.

**WEEK 25:** Relegation-haunted Maesteg lost 59-10 at Bonymaen, where Jonathan Young scored three of the nine tries. Stuart Davies added 14 goal points. After three successive defeats, Aberavon regained their poise 23-13 at SW Police. It was too close for comfort, but Caerphilly struggled through 24-18 against UWIC. Dunvant scraped a 28-25 verdict at Llandovery with Dunvant's Mark Thomas becoming the fifth player to top 1,000 league points. Played later, Treorchy were 23-10 winners at Blackwood. Pontypool were thankful for 22 points from Gareth Curtis to account for Newbridge 32-13. Rumney edged Abertillery 22-18. Merthyr lost 28-27 at Cross Keys with Ioan Bebb supplying 18 home points.

**WEEK 26:** Merthyr staggered Caerphilly 38-23 with Nigel Berbillion racing the length of the field for his second try while inflicting the leaders' third defeat. No 8 Chris Powell, son of former Neath star Steve Powell, snapped up two tries as Bonymaen cut up Cross Keys 36-12. Pontypool had Danny Hurford sent off at Dunvant and lost 20-14. Craig Blundson's two tries spearheaded Abertillery to 25-15 success over Blackwood. Treorchy lambasted Llandovery 51-12 with a try hat-trick from wing Andrew Lewis. Rumney's 24-12 win at Aberavon featured two tries by Mark Ryce. Newbridge won 40-10 at Maesteg. There were two sendings off and five yellow cards at Cyncoed as referee Hugh Banfield negotiated a difficult match, which saw UWIC pip the Police 29-27.

**WEEK 27:** Caerphilly ensured the division title with a 30-25 revenge victory against Bonymaen. Darren Starr's try in the last couple of minutes, from a midfield burst by Chris Murphy, decided it. Brett Davey set a club record as he reached 325 points. Cross Keys collected 11 tries, three of them by skipper Ioan Bebb as they routed Maesteg 71-16. Bebb added eight conversions for a tally of 31 points and his club's league record. Aberavon went down 23-8 at Blackwood. Rumney ripped UWIC apart 63-16. Keith Lee and Chris Wells each scored three tries. David Lloyd's 16 points inspired Treorchy to 36-14 success at Pontypool. Prop Chris Budgen crossed twice for Newbridge as they defeated Dunvant 46-15. Merthyr, trailing 24-5, stormed back to draw 24-all at SW Police. Abertillery lost 20-7 at Llandovery.

**WEEK 28:** Caerphilly's 60-17 victory over Cross Keys featured three tries by Pete Good and 20 points from Brett Davey. Aberavon faded badly at Llandovery to lose 41-16 as Aled Williams contributed 21 points. Chris Lay's two tries in his 19 points inspired Blackwood to 29-15 success over UWIC. Wing Lee Abdul raced in for the decisive try right at the end for Rumney to edge Merthyr 23-20. Relegation fears increased for Pontypool as visitors Abertillery won 25-19. A last-minute drop-goal by Stuart Davies saw Bonymaen 23-20 victors at SW Police. Maesteg lost 30-12 at Dunvant. Played earlier, Newbridge did for Treorchy 26-20 with 16 goal points from Jason Williams.

**WEEK 29:** Ioan Bebb's 19 points saw him reach a record 302 points in all matches for Cross Keys during the season as they overwhelmed SW Police 59-19. He scored a try and converted seven. Chad Bushell collected three Keys' tries. Brett Davey obtained 31 points, including a hat-trick of tries, to help Caerphilly beat his old club Maesteg 71-18 at the Old Parish ground. Merthyr's 40-12 success over Blackwood featured three tries each by Andrew Loring and Neil Morgan. There were 19 points for Phil Withers as Abertillery accounted for Newbridge 24-11. David Evans collected 28 points as Treorchy dusted up

Dunvant 63-21. Stuart Davies kicked 19 points for Bonymaen to blast Rumney 54-20. Chris Wall's three tries saw UWIC snatch 32-24 victory against Llandovery. Aberavon were 45-22 winners over Pontypool.

**WEEK 30:** It was relegation shoot-out: Pontypool v UWIC for the dreaded drop. Pooler escaped it with a 14-8 verdict – three Matthew Silva penalty goals and a try by prop Wayne Williams seven minutes from the end to a Rhys Shorney try and Jonathan Williams penalty shot. It was rugby on a knife edge for some 3,000 onlookers. Treorchy registered 73-24 success over Maesteg. David Evans scored one of the 11 tries and goal kicks brought him up to 23 points. Jonathan Mason contributed 21 points in Rumney's 66-32 destruction of Cross Keys. Champions Caerphilly were 42-17 winners at SW Police. Dunvant defeated Abertillery 45-18. Merthyr lost 39-27 at Llandovery. Bonymaen won 27-5 at Blackwood. Played earlier, Newbridge defeated Aberavon 31-25.

## DIVISION TWO

**WEEK 1:** All played later. Ceri Pritchard kicked 15 points for Mountain Ash to win 30-28 at Tenby. Matthew Chapman also supplied 15 points in Tredegar's 55-8 verdict at Pyle. Two Mark Addis tries helped Abercynon through 36-25 against Kenfig Hill. Whitland toppled Tondu 17-3. Ystradgynlais were 21-17 winners at Narberth. St. Peter's defeated Llanharan 24-14.

**WEEK 2:** Tredegar displayed style with seven tries at Mountain Ash, three of them by wing Ioan Lane to win 46-10. There were three tries also for scrum half Andrew Teale to help Tondu defeat Abercynon 48-5. Steve Pearce struck five penalty goals and a conversion in Whitland's 27-21 verdict at Pyle. Wayne Jervis supplied 16 points as Llanharan triumphed 21-10 against Ystradgynlais. Tenby were 13-11 winners at Narberth. St. Peter's lost 36-22 at Kenfig Hill.

**WEEK 3:** Two tries by scrum half Paul Young helped Tredegar defeat Narberth 32-3. There were 14 goal points for Austin Howells as Ystradgynlais dashed Kenfig hopes 24-16. Wing Mark Evans swooped for two of Whitland's seven tries in 43-6 victory over Mountain Ash. Llanharan snapped up a 26-19 verdict at Tenby. Pyle were 24-0 winners at Tondu. St. Peter's blasted Abercynon 35-13.

**WEEK 4:** A last-minute try by Colin Roberts denied Abercynon a first win as Pyle forced a 14-all away verdict. Former Llanelli outside half Steve Pearce supplied 10 goal points for Whitland to topple home side Narberth 20-13. Leaders Tredegar won 25-18 at Llanharan. Steve Matthews crossed for two St. Peter's tries, but visitors Ystradgynlais triumphed 20-6. Tondu were 24-0 winners at Mountain Ash. Played later, Kenfig Hill lost to Tenby 29-20.

**WEEK 5:** Mike Boys, former Ebbw Vale star runner, marked his debut for leaders Tredegar with a try in their 26-18 win against Kenfig Hill. Outside half Paul Williams scored two tries in his 21 points as Tondu defeated Narberth 36-24. Pyle were 41-17 winners against Mountain Ash with three tries by Gareth Owens. Gavin Scotcher's 15 goal points helped Tenby beat St. Peter's 35-20. Whitland drew 15-15 at Llanharan. Ystradgynlais stopped Abercynon 29-16.

**WEEK 6:** Mountain Ash collected their first points with a 20-16 verdict at Abercynon. The Old Firm had Andrew Lane sent off, but Paul Nicholas picked

**HOLLYBUSH, WORTHINGTON GWENT AND DISTRICT LEAGUE CHAMPIONS 1998  20-17 AGAINST HAFODYRYNYS**

*Picture: Wales News & Pictures*

up 12 points, including a try. Mike Boys and Andrew Thomas scored tries that gave leaders Tredegar 10-0 victory at St. Peter's. Three yellow cards were brandished at Llanharan, where Tondu drew 6-6. Mike Nottingham's two penalty goals earned Ystradgynlais 6-0 success against Tenby. Narberth's first victory came by a whisker 10-9 against Pyle. Kenfig Hill went down 25-16 to visitors Whitland.

**WEEK 7:** Second-placed Whitland, who had signed Swansea star Alan Reynolds, inflicted St. Peter's heaviest league defeat 49-6. Robert Phillips collected three of the seven tries. Neil Forrester embellished Pyle's 25-8 verdict over Llanharan with 10 goal points. Matthew Roderick's two tries earned Narberth 20-10 success at Mountain Ash. Tredegar were 21-13 winners over Ystradgynlais with 11 Matthew Chapman goal points. Abercynon lost 47-27 at Tenby. Tondu edged Kenfig Hill five tries to four in a 34-29 victory.

**WEEK 8:** Tenby's six tries in 41-21 success knocked Tredegar off top spot and allowed Whitland, 17-9 winners at Ystradgynlais, to take over. Abercynon's first victory was enjoyed 15-11 against Narberth with two tries by Gareth Davies. Kenfig Hill were pipped 15-14 by visitors Pyle through five Neil Forrester penalty goals. Llanharan stopped Mountain Ash 32-8, Neil Edwards scoring two of the tries. Tondu won 36-7 at St. Peter's with 12 points from Paul Williams.

**WEEK 9:** Tenby snuck in 20-19 at Whitland with two tries by Steve Hartland and this put Tredegar back on top after their 34-5 win against Abercynon. Tim Eddy dropped three goals in his 25 points and Chris McDonald swooped for three tries in Narberth's 50-26 victory over Llanharan. Bottom team Mountain Ash fought stubbornly before losing 18-16 to visitors Kenfig Hill. Darren Jones crossed twice for the Mules. St. Peter's were 24-15 winners at Pyle. Ystradgynlais lost 22-6 at Tondu.

**WEEK 10:** Second-placed Whitland succumbed to leaders Tredegar 17-9 without a try, whereas Paul Young and Matthew Chapman crossed for the visitors. David Griffiths was a three-try getter to colour Llanharan's 36-8 triumph at Abercynon. Kenfig Hill nudged in 11-9 against Narberth with Kenfig's Nicky Walsh scoring the game's only try. Mark Anderson's two tries was the springboard for Mountain Ash's second win, 17-10 at St. Peter's. Tenby took Tondu 34-13. Pyle lost 35-25 at Ystradgynlais.

**WEEK 11:** Tim Eddy's 28 points, including a try, helped Narberth sink St. Peter's 43-5. Leaders Tredegar won 18-16 at Tondu through Matthew Chapman's eight vital goal points. Whitland walloped Abercynon 67-7 with 11 tries. Marc Evans and Mike Buckingham each scored three. Paul Nicholas kicked 12 points for Mountain Ash to defeat Ystradgynlais 27-19. Pyle toppled Tenby 25-14. Kenfig Hill forced a 10-10 decision at Llanharan.

**WEEK 12:** Although losing at home for the first time, Tredegar stayed on top. Pyle's 13-7 verdict inflicted Tredegar's second defeat with a try by Andrew Twomey and conversion and two penalty goals from Neil Forrester. Second-placed Whitland also failed, Tondu stopping them 15-7 as Paul Williams kicked a penalty goal and converted Karl Hocking's try. There were two tries for Huw Woodland as Llanharan defeated St. Peter's 39-19. Kenfig Hill pipped Abercynon 14-13. Tenby registered 32-20 victory at Mountain Ash. Played later, Ystradgynlais won 33-16 against Narberth with two David Love tries in his 18 points.

**WEEK 13:** Leaders Tredegar owed their winning margin to eight goal points from Matthew Chapman in an 18-10 verdict against Mountain Ash. Stuart Monkley's two tries helped swell Ystradgynlais's tally to 34-7 over Llanharan. Paul Watkin provided two tries as Tondu won 22-0 at Abercynon. Stephen Pearce kicked 17 points for Whitland to defeat Pyle 22-11. Penalty goals earned Kenfig Hill 9-0 victory at St. Peter's. Narberth lost 15-0 at Tenby.

**WEEK 14:** Tredegar relinquished top spot by losing 17-0 at Narberth, where Colin Phillips pounced for two tries. Whitland, 27-9 winners at Mountain Ash took over the lead. Abercynon recorded their second victory, hitting St. Peter's 45-33 as Mark Addis went in for three home tries. Paul Williams's goal kicking helped Tondu win 16-9 at Pyle. Tenby failed 17-8 at Llanharan. Ystradgynlais triumphed 34-13 at Kenfig Hill.

**WEEK 15:** Tenby trounced Kenfig Hill 44-0 with former Swansea and Llanelli wing Warren Leach among the try-getters. Played later, Tondu defeated Mountain Ash 27-5 with two tries by scrum half Richard Morgan. Wing Barry Grabham scored the only try as Pyle stopped Abercynon 11-6. Chester Robinson, returned from Newport, crossed twice in St. Peter's 26-24 win at Ystradgynlais. Narberth drew 3-3 at Whitland. Tredegar clinched the division title with a 54-0 win in their final match against Llanharan.

**WEEK 16:** Whitland won 28-8 against Llanharan, but the leaders lost wing Marc Evans when he fell awkwardly and broke his leg in two places. Tredegar's 32-16 verdict at Kenfig Hill featured two tries each by Chris Lake and Paul Young. Tenby's Dean Bowen crossed for two tries and a 30-20 success at St. Peter's. Pyle played tenaciously before losing 20-13 at Mountain Ash. Ystradgynlais were 16-6 winners at Abercynon. Tondu made it 38-15 at Narberth.

**WEEK 17:** Skipper Dominic Setaro was a two-try scorer as leaders Whitland hammered Kenfig Hill 39-3. Robbie Savage put over four penalty goals for Abercynon to record their third victory 12-10 at Mountain Ash. Mike Barry's drop-shot saw Tondu defeat Llanharan 13-10. Pyle resisted Narberth's challenge 30-20. Ystradgynlais lost 16-8 at Tenby. Played later, Tredegar beat St. Peter's 50-3 with 20 points from Matthew Chapman.

**WEEK 18:** Former Wales star Mark Ring figured in the St. Peter's line-up as their new player/coach, but was on the losing side as visitors Whitland shaded them 18-15. Tredegar won 11-5 at Ystradgynlais with a Paul Young try. David Balkwill's two tries could not save Tenby from 23-17 defeat at Abercynon. Wayne Jervis's seven goal points proved decisive as Llanharan held off Pyle 22-19. Narberth toppled Mountain Ash 30-8. Tondu saw off Kenfig Hill 41-19.

**WEEK 19:** Barry Thomas's two tries in Whitland's 32-10 win over Ystradgynlais kept them level with Tredegar at the top as Tredegar defeated Tenby 23-14. Nathan Strong stormed in for three tries for Tondu to tame St. Peter's 43-18. Neil Forrester's four penalty goals for Pyle sealed Kenfig Hill's fate 17-11. Mountain Ash were 17-12 winners against Llanharan. Abercynon lost 26-17 at Narberth.

"The Bish" on the burst. As player/coach dynamic David Bishop inspired troubled Pontypool to cling to Div 1 status – but only just. Here in action in the vital last match victory against UWIC.

*Picture: Gareth Everett for Huw Evans Picture Agency, Cardiff*

**WEEK 20:** Dylan Meredith rustled up two tries to guide leaders Tredegar to 42-10 success at Abercynon. James Davies's try hat-trick was the highlight for St. Peter's as they overpowered Pyle 53-8. Tristan Edwards fired over four penalty goals to help Whitland win 17-10 at Tenby. Huw Watkins scored Kenfig's only try from 75 yards and landed two penalty goals for the Mules to beat Mountain Ash 17-9. Narberth were 24-11 winners at Llanharan. Tondu won 29-5 at Ystradgynlais.

**WEEK 21:** Tredegar full back Matthew Chapman crossed right at the end to snatch a tense 21-20 decision against Whitland. He contributed 16 points. Karl Hocking's three tries helped Tondu trounce Tenby 37-7. Narberth's Tim Eddy kicked 14 points to topple Kenfig Hill 34-18. Robbie Savage also fired in 14 goal points as Abercynon enjoyed their visit to Llanharan 34-12. Ystradgynlais lost 15-7 at Pyle. Mountain Ash were 24-13 winners over St. Peter's.

**WEEK 22:** Tondu ensured promotion when Karl Hocking's try from five yards out brought 5-0 victory at Tredegar, where only Pyle had won previously. Two tries by Carl Morgan fired Whitland to 39-20 success at Abercynon. Robbie Savage kicked five home penalty goals. Dean Bowen's two tries inspired Tenby to scrape in 24-22 against Pyle. Mountain Ash were 21-13 winners at Ystradgynlais. Kenfig Hill fought off the keen challenge of Llanharan 21-18. Narberth failed 21-8 at St. Peter's.

## DIVISION THREE

**WEEK 1:** All played later. Richard Langmead's 14 points included a try as Llantrisant were 32-13 victors against Rhymney. Paul Parry's 15 points also included a try as Builth Wells won 28-19 at Glynneath. Blaina's 30-10 success at Penarth featured two tries by Deri Mattravers. Kidwelly were 13-12 winners at Carmarthen Quins. Ystrad Rhondda took a 13-9 decision at Felinfoel. Oakdale beat Wanderers 27-0.

**WEEK 2:** A try by second row Glen Williams edged Rhymney through 14-13 at Carmarthen Quins. A hat-trick of tries by wing Gareth Martin featured Ystrad Rhondda's 38-18 victory over Oakdale. Felinfoel defeated Builth Wells 38-7 with 13 goal points from Kevin Thomas. Bruce Corlett included a try in his 12 points to help Blaina topple Wanderers 17-10. Wing Richard Davies snapped up a debut try for Glynneath as they won 21-8 at Llantrisant. Kidwelly were 33-3 winners at Penarth.

**WEEK 3:** Dean Pitt was a three-try hero for Blaina in their 36-7 success against Ystrad Rhondda. Rhymney roasted Penarth 52-9 with Anthony Forrester and Mike Roberts each scoring two of the seven tries. Llantrisant stole a 22-19 decision at Builth Wells with Richard Langmead on target with two drop shots. Kidwelly accounted for Wanderers 20-11 with two tries by Craig Thomas. Carmarthen Quins won 21-12 at Glynneath. Felinfoel were 28-15 losers at Oakdale.

**WEEK 4:** Rhymney, leaders and the only unbeaten side in this division, found it unexpectedly difficult before winning 18-16 at Wanderers through five penalty goals and a drop shot on debut by Matthew Pizey. Wing Kyle Fahiya scored the game's two tries. Kevin Thomas fired over 22 points for Felinfoel to fight off Llantrisant's challenge 47-37. David Meredith's three tries brought Penarth an amazing 43-34 verdict against Glynneath. Craig Miller kicked 23 points. Oakdale were 20-7 winners against Blaina. Kidwelly lost 24-14 at Ystrad Rhondda. Alistair Chambers put over five penalty shots for Carmarthen Quins to stop Builth Wells 15-5.

**WEEK 5:** Leaders Rhymney had Danny Rees and Keith Edwards ordered off, but were 32-22 winners against Ystrad Rhondda. Matthew Pizey scored 19 Rhymney points. Penarth's revitalised young side battled to 23-16 victory at Builth Wells with 18 points from Craig Miller. Jason Strange collected 20 Blaina points in a 50-20 success against Felinfoel. Wanderers registered their first win 36-16 over Glynneath with 16 goal points from Nick Bellamy. Jamie Payne scored the only try of the match and Llantrisant shaded Carmarthen Quins 16-12. Kidwelly defeated Oakdale 31-25.

**WEEK 6:** Oakdale inflicted Rhymney's first reverse as a second half penalty shot by Carl Thomas brought 11-8 success. A Phil Davies try ensured a 10-3 win for Wanderers against Builth Wells. Penarth came back to reality, losing 59-19 to visitors Llantrisant. Richard Langmead provided 19 points for the winners. Blaina took over as leaders with 28-7 victory against Kidwelly. Glynneath lost 15-7 at Ystrad Rhondda. Felinfoel were on top 27-19 against Carmarthen Quins.

**WEEK 7:** Kevin Thomas put over three penalty goals and converted two tries by Andrew Slimm for Felinfoel to steal a 21-19 verdict at Kidwelly. Andrew Thomas snapped up three of the nine Carmarthen Quins tries in a 61-20 crushing of Penarth. Leaders Blaina won 37-19 at Rhymney. Llantrisant swamped Wanderers 56-13 with 21 goal points from Richard Langmead. Oakdale pounded Glynneath 41-5. Ystrad Rhondda were 13-6 winners at Builth Wells.

**WEEK 8:** Felinfoel full back Devlin Leach was a four-try scorer and there were three by Wayne Lewis as they put Penarth to the sword 86-26. It was the Seasiders' most devastating league defeat. Leaders Blaina hammered Glynneath 55-10 with two tries by Andrew Dobbs. Steve Lewis swept in for three tries as Oakdale crushed Builth 57-5. Llantrisant won 16-12 at Ystrad Rhondda with two decisive penalty goals by Richard Langmead. Wanderers were 27-21 winners against Carmarthen Quins. Rhymney lost 20-7 at Kidwelly.

**WEEK 9:** Glamorgan Wanderers raised their record tally against Penarth 57-0. Skipper Garin Treharne scored two of the visitors' eight tries. Leaders Blaina were jolted in being held 18-all at Builth Wells. Bottom team Builth had won just one of their previous seven games. Another drawn tussle saw Oakdale struggle 12-12 at Llantrisant. Carl Thomas kicked four Oakdale penalty goals; Richard Langmead fired in three penalty shots and a drop-goal. Three penalty goals by Glen John proved crucial as Ystrad Rhondda edged out Carmarthen Quins 24-21. Glynneath scraped in 24-19 against Kidwelly. Felinfoel lost 22-5 at Rhymney.

**WEEK 10:** Second-placed Blaina suffered their second defeat, this time 16-3 to visitors Llantrisant, for whom Steve Cook scored the game's only try. Danny Rees's hat-trick of tries was a boost for Rhymney in their 46-10 decision against Glynneath. Leaders Oakdale fought off the challenge of Carmarthen

Quins 24-16. Nine tries saw Ystrad Rhondda wreck Penarth 60-3. Stuart Roberts's two tries enabled Felinfoel to defeat Wanderers 28-16. Builth went down 22-12 at Kidwelly.

**WEEK 11:** Kevin Jenkins fired over two crucial penalty goals to give Llantrisant 11-7 victory over Kidwelly. Felinfoel grabbed a 27-20 decision at Glynneath with 17 goal points from Kevin Thomas. Rhymney raised a 46-10 success at Builth Wells with David Nicholas a two-try getter. Richard Nancarrow's 10 goal points earned Blaina a 25-16 verdict at Carmarthen Quins. Oakdale won 25-5 at Penarth. Wanderers went down 16-5 to visitors Ystrad Rhondda.

**WEEK 12:** Leaders Oakdale won 22-12 at Wanderers with two tries by Steve Lewis. Ystrad Rhondda defeated Felinfoel 26-13. Richard Langmead's kicking was a key factor as he planted over two penalty goals and a conversion for Llantrisant to win 15-3 at Rhymney. Builth toppled Glynneath 24-0 for their first win. Played later, a hat-trick of tries by Jonathan Pleese helped Blaina to 41-15 victory over Penarth. Carmarthen Quins won 25-13 at Kidwelly with 15 points from Julian Howells.

**WEEK 13:** Ystrad Rhondda wrung a 9-3 decision at Oakdale with three penalty goals by Paul Morris to stay just one point behind leaders Llantrisant, who registered a slashing 34-0 victory at Glynneath. Richard Langmead supplied 14 points. Penarth enjoyed their third victory after six consecutive league defeats 28-12 and revenge at Kidwelly with 13 goal points from Craig Miller. Wayne Lewis's two tries spearheaded Felinfoel to 29-17 success over Builth Wells. Blaina recorded the double 15-3 against Wanderers. Carmarthen Quins lost 28-17 at Rhymney.

**WEEK 14:** Leaders Llantrisant defeated Builth 18-7 with two tries by Jamie Payne. Rhymney triumphed 50-12 at Penarth with Stuart Jarman a two-try scorer. Colin Owen collected three tries as Wanderers humbled Kidwelly 60-12. Jeff Relf kicked Oakdale to a tense 23-21 verdict at Felinfoel with 13 points. Ystrad Rhondda beat Blaina 27-20 with two decisive Gareth Martin tries. There were 10 tries for Carmarthen Quins to overpower Glynneath 64-7.

**WEEK 15:** South African fly half Clinton van Rensburgh scored the winning try for Builth Wells to climb off the bottom 13-5 against Carmarthen Quins. Llantrisant overwhelmed Felinfoel 52-5. Played later, Wanderers were 21-12 victors at Rhymney. New Zealander Moro Smith was a Wanderers' try-getter. Ystrad Rhondda won 15-12 at Kidwelly. Glynneath hammered Penarth 41-12. Oakdale triumphed 12-5 at Blaina.

**WEEK 16:** Rhymney scraped through 13-12 at Ystrad Rhondda with Wayne Booth's penalty shot the decisive score. Steve Lewis and Julian Long were try scorers to enable Oakdale to defeat Kidwelly 16-7. Wanderers enjoyed their second away win 25-13 at Glynneath. Played later, Builth Wells battered Penarth 48-0. Richard Langmead's eight goal points proved decisive for Llantrisant 21-16 at Carmarthen Quins. Eight Felinfoel tries hit Blaina 57-26.

**WEEK 17:** Smart scrum half Jason Alford pounced for a hat-trick of tries as leaders Llantrisant humbled Penarth 55-9. Julian Howells kicked 16 points for Carmarthen Quins to defeat Felinfoel 26-15. Tries by Danny Rees and Keith Edwards saw Rhymney 19-0 winners over Oakdale. Nick Bellamy's 11 goal points helped Wanderers to a third successive win 26-11 at Builth Wells. Ystrad Rhondda won 22-15 at Glynneath. Kidwelly lost 25-20 to visitors Blaina.

**WEEK 18:** Llantrisant faltered 16-15 at Wanderers, but stayed on top. Griff Rhys scored the vital home try. Ex-Wales prop Jeremy Pugh crossed to set Builth Wells on the way to 22-16 success at Ystrad Rhondda. Kevin Thomas produced 19 points for Felinfoel to dispose of Kidwelly 34-15. Greg Swaine's two tries failed to save Penarth from 27-20 defeat by visitors Carmarthen Quins. Glynneath went down 39-15 at Oakdale. Rhymney were 26-7 winners at Blaina.

**WEEK 19:** Felinfoel's eight tries had Penarth in turmoil and another defeat, this time 56-24 with Kevin Thomas contributing 24 points. Lowly Glynneath's third success of the season 19-18 surprised top order Blaina. Dave Harrett's three penalty goals proved decisive. Leaders Llantrisant overpowered Ystrad Rhondda 41-9. Similarly, Rhymney routed Kidwelly 42-6. Mike Price marked his debut with two tries in Builth's 32-13 victory over Oakdale. Wanderers went down 23-11 at Carmarthen Quins.

**WEEK 20:** Richard Langmead totted up 21 points, including a try, as leaders Llantrisant won 26-10 at Oakdale. Matthew Pizey's two tries set up Rhymney for 38-7 victory at Felinfoel. Penarth's passport to relegation moved a step nearer at Wanderers, beaten 24-3. Fellow strugglers Glynneath registered a 16-10 verdict at Kidwelly. Played earlier, Carmarthen Quins notched a 36-13 success over Ystrad Rhondda with a hat-trick of tries by wing Derek Wyke. Played later, Blaina lost to Builth Wells 22-7.

**WEEK 21:** Leaders Llantrisant and second-placed Rhymney ensured promotion. Llantrisant battered Blaina 41-13 with Jamie Payne fronting the way with two tries and Matthew Newlands running virtually the length of the field for his. Rhymney made it 42-15 at Glynneath with a hat-trick of tries by John Hodges. Kevin Thomas's nine goal points proved decisive as Felinfoel won 24-20 at the Wanderers. Builth Wells defeated Kidwelly 38-15. Oakdale forced a 21-all draw at Carmarthen Quins. Ystrad Rhondda took a 36-23 verdict at Penarth.

**WEEK 22:** Champions Llantrisant closed with a 12-5 success at Kidwelly. Relegated Glynneath won their final fixture 7-6 at Felinfoel as Simon Knoyle converted Craig Owen's try. Stuart Jarman pounced for two tries in Rhymney's stylish 24-8 verdict over Builth Wells. Sprightly Wanderers were successful 36-17 at Ystrad Rhondda. Oakdale punished Penarth 32-17. Carmarthen Quins triumphed 35-29 at Blaina.

## DIVISION FOUR

Vardre, captained by Martin Garland, were champions, winning 18 games, one more than closest challengers Gilfach Goch. Stefan Jones contributed 181 league points for the title-winners. Gilfach, led by Jonathan Jones, scored most points with 526, including 78 team tries. Craig Williams top-scored for them with 135 points. Vardre clinched the title with a 13-10 success at Tonmawr with a penalty try in the eighth minute of injury time, awarded for persistent scrum offences.

# NATIONAL LEAGUE RECORDS

## MOST POINTS IN SEASON

| | | |
|---|---|---|
| 393 | Brett Davey (Caerphilly) Div 1 | 1997/8 |
| 285 | Neil Jenkins (Pontypridd) Div 1 | 1993/94 & 95/96 |

## MOST TRIES IN SEASON

| | | |
|---|---|---|
| 24 | Wayne Lewis (Felinfoel) Div 5 | 1996/97 |
| 21 | Paul Jones (Llandovery) Div 2 | 1996/97 |
| 21 | Keith Lee (Rumney) Div 3 | 1996/97 |

## MOST POINTS IN MATCH

| | | |
|---|---|---|
| 42 | Brett Davey (Caerphilly) Div 1 v Rumney | 1997/98 |
| 39 | Colin Stephens (Llanelli) Div 1 at Newport | 1992/93 |
| 37 | Marc Evans (Kidwelly) Div 5 at Hendy | 1995/96 |
| 37 | Richard Langmead (Llantrisant) Div 4 v Tumble | 1996/97 |

## MOST TRIES IN MATCH

| | | |
|---|---|---|
| 7 | Marc Evans (Kidwelly) Div 5 at Hendy | 1995/96 |
| 6 | Ieuan Evans (Llanelli) Div 1 at Maesteg | 1992/93 |

## BIGGEST VICTORIES

| | |
|---|---|
| Felinfoel 106-14 at Cardiff Quins Div 5 | 1996/97 |
| Llanelli 97-10 v Newbridge Div 1 | 1996/97 |

## HIGHEST TEAM AGGREGATE IN SEASON

| | | |
|---|---|---|
| 1090 | Caerphilly (Div 1) | 1997/98 |
| 944 | Pontypridd (Div 1) | 1996/97 |

## MOST TEAM TRIES IN SEASON

| | | |
|---|---|---|
| 137 | Caerphilly (Div 1) | 1997/98 |
| 136 | Llanelli (Div 1) | 1992/93 |

## MOST TEAM TRIES IN MATCH

| | | |
|---|---|---|
| 18 | Ystrad Rhondda v Hendy Div 5 | 1995/96 |
| 18 | Felinfoel at Cardiff Quins Div 5 | 1996/97 |

## MOST PENALTY GOALS IN MATCH

| | | |
|---|---|---|
| 9 | Neil Jenkins (Pontypridd) at Pontypool Div 1 | 1993/94 |

## MOST CONSECUTIVE VICTORIES IN SEASON

| | | |
|---|---|---|
| 20 | Abercynon (Div 3) | 1993/94 |

## CHAMPIONS

| | Prem Div | Div 1 | Div 2 | Div 3 | Div 4 |
|---|---|---|---|---|---|
| 1991 | Neath | Newport | Dunvant | Llandovery | – |
| 1992 | – | Swansea | SW Police | Tenby Utd | Tumble |
| 1993 | – | Llanelli | Dunvant | Treorchy | Tondu |
| 1994 | – | Swansea | Treorchy | Abercynon | Builth Wells |
| 1995 | – | Cardiff | Aberavon | Ystradgynlais | Cardiff Inst. |
| 1996 | – | Neath | Dunvant | Blackwood | Merthyr |
| 1997 | – | Pontypridd | Aberavon | Rumney | St Peter's |
| 1998 | Swansea | Caerphilly | Tredegar | Llantrisant | Vardre |

*All records apply to top five divisions only*

# ON-LOAN PROP MARTYN GRABS
# HIS CHANCE FOR GLORY

*By* JOHN BILLOT

Desperate men take desperate measures. It worked for Llanelli. They had endured a gloomy season, financially and on the field. Just five league victories in 14 games told its own story. So they had to win the cup to rescue their reputation and bring some solace to the Stradey faithful: a faithful who had dwindled alarmingly through the turnstiles of a once-pulsating shrine of Welsh rugby.

When prop problems struck, in desperation they looked to far horizons and were forced to borrow Martyn Madden from Penzance/Newlyn. It proved a stroke of inspiration. Madden, 18st and with a surprising burst of pace when the need calls, is an ex-Cardiff Youth No 8 and Pontypool player who went to seek fortune, if not fame, down Cornwall way.

Madden is defined in the dictionary as meaning to irritate intensely. He certainly upset Newport with two tries on his Llanelli debut. But bigger events were in store. Ebbw Vale, in their first cup final, gallantly illustrated the three Rs of rugby – ruthless, relentless, remorseless – at

---

## TEAMS IN THE 1998 CUP FINAL

| LLANELLI | EBBW VALE |
|---|---|
| Darril Williams | Siua Taumalolo |
| Wayne Proctor | Alun Harries |
| Neil Boobyer | Jonathan Hawker |
| Nigel Davies | John Funnell |
| Garan Evans | Lennie Woodard |
| Craig Warlow | Byron Hayward |
| Rupert Moon | David Llewellyn |
| Aled Jones | Alun Phillips |
| Robin McBryde (capt) | Leighton Phillips |
| Martyn Madden | Mike Wilson |
| Vernon Cooper | Chay Billen |
| Mike Voyle | Kuli Faletau |
| Chris Wyatt | Richie Collins |
| Hywel Jenkins | Mark Jones |
| Iwan Jones | Kingsley Jones (capt) |
| Reps: Matthew Wintle for Boobyer, Andrew Gibbs for Wyatt. | Reps: Jason Strange for Hawker, Steve Jones for Leighton Phillips. |

*Referee:* Clayton Thomas *(Bryncoch)*

---

Ashton Gate (the new WRU stadium in Cardiff was still in course of construction) on May 23, 1998. They battled to stalemate at 12-all with time fast running out.

Then Rupert Moon took a hand. The Llanelli scrum half always has a nose for a half-chance, and he dodged through a lineout and, as Ebbw hauled him down, off-loaded to his nearest teammate. That was Madden, whose big moment had arrived. The 23-year-old from Grangetown, arrowed for the corner, a black bolt that blasted Ebbw hopes as he escaped a couple of flying tackles for the winning try seven minutes from the end. Craig Warlow converted magnificently from near the touchline and the Scarlets had won the cup 19-12 for the 10th time in their 13th final.

"It was our work without the ball that won us the game," smiled relieved captain Robin McBryde. "We had to make sure we tackled everything." Ebbw skipper Kingsley Jones, left out of the Welsh squad to tour South Africa when it was announced earlier, said desolately, "It's

## WRU CHALLENGE CUP WINNERS

| | | | |
|---|---|---|---|
| 1972 | Neath bt. Llanelli 15-9 | 1987† | Cardiff bt. Swansea 16-15 |
| 1973 | Llanelli bt. Cardiff 30-7 | 1988 | Llanelli bt. Neath 28-13 |
| 1974 | Llanelli bt. Aberavon 12-10 | 1989 | Neath bt. Llanelli 14-13 |
| 1975 | Llanelli bt. Aberavon 15-6 | 1990 | Neath bt. Bridgend 16-10 |
| 1976 | Llanelli bt. Swansea 16-4 | 1991 | Llanelli bt. Pontypool 24-9 |
| 1977 | Newport bt. Cardiff 16-15 | 1992 | Llanelli bt. Swansea 16-7 |

### SCHWEPPES CUP

### SWALEC CUP

| | | | |
|---|---|---|---|
| 1978 | Swansea bt. Newport 13-9 | 1993 | Llanelli bt. Neath 21-18 |
| 1979 | Bridgend bt. Pontypridd 18-12 | 1994 | Cardiff bt. Llanelli 15-8 |
| 1980 | Bridgend bt. Swansea 15-9 | 1995 | Swansea bt. Pontypridd 17-12 |
| 1981 | Cardiff bt. Bridgend 14-6 | 1996 | Pontypridd bt. Neath 29-22 |
| 1982* | Cardiff 12, Bridgend 12 | 1997 | Cardiff bt. Swansea 33-26 |
| 1983 | Pontypool bt. Swansea 18-6 | 1998 | Llanelli bt. Ebbw Vale 19-12 |
| 1984 | Cardiff bt. Neath 24-19 | | |
| 1985 | Llanelli bt. Cardiff 15-14 | | |
| 1986 | Cardiff bt. Newport 28-21 | | |

*Winners on more tries rule,  † Extra time*

been a bad week for me. We had 70 per cent of the ball, but Llanelli took their chances."

Some rated this as among the most disappointing of the 27 cup finals, but it was tense for the 16,000 watchers. Ebbw attacked mainly on a narrow front on a narrow pitch once play got under way after 15 minutes delay in order to allow spectators to take their seats following traffic hold-ups. Llanelli were primed as to what to expect having studied video recordings of Ebbw tactics and worked out counter moves.

Twice the Scarlets almost snatched tries: Chris Wyatt was nearly in at the corner and then Neil Boobyer dropped the ball in the act of diving over. So it was a goal-kicking exchange that produced the points: four penalty hits to Warlow; three penalty shots and a soaring drop by Byron

**Ebbw Vale full back Siua Taumalolo won the man-of-the-match Lloyd Lewis Memorial Award in the cup final. Here he is tackled by Llanelli's Wayne Proctor.**

*Picture: Huw Evans Picture Agency, Cardiff*

Llanelli, 1998 SWALEC Cup winners. Back row (left to right): A Buchanan, J Hyatt, M Madden, Iwan Jones, Aled Jones, A Gibbs, V Cooper, M Voyle, C Wyatt, H Jenkins, H Williams-Jones, G Jenkins (coach). Middle row: Nigel Davies, W Proctor, R Moon, Huw Evans (chairman), R McBryde (capt), S Gallacher (chief executive), C Warlow, Darril Williams, Garan Evans. In front: P Herbert, M Wintle, N Boobyer, Stephen Jones, Aled Thomas.

*Picture: Huw Evans Picture Agency Cardiff*

53

Hayward. Hayward might well have brought the cup back to Ebbw Vale, but he missed three penalty attempts. He suffered a touch of the Kingsley Joneses!

Mark Jones put himself about until referee Clayton Thomas, who had warned him once, reminded the Ebbw No 8, "I'm watching you like a hawk from now on!" This after Iwan Jones had been felled and Ebbw full back Siua Taumalolo raced through a gap and was steaming upfield like the proverbial runaway train. It was the most spectacular break of the day and earned the venturesome Tongan man-of-the-match selection for the coveted Lloyd Lewis Memorial Award.

Chay Billen dominated the lineout for Ebbw, who nudged into the lead at 12-9 for the first time 15 minutes from the end. Warlow equalised and the struggle intensified. Llanelli's back row proved more effective this time with Hywel Jenkins an influential No 8 and Wyatt and Iwan Jones performing with devastating impact. Old general Nigel Davies, in his eighth final, was always thinking of ways to worry the opposition, if only by sneaking off-side! But it was the maddening Moon-Madden menace that did for Ebbw as Llanelli yet again proved they are the team for the big event. Always put your shirt on the Scarlets in the cup final.

**SEMI-FINALS:** A delightful hat-trick of tries by dashing Tongan full back Siua Taumalolo was the highlight of Ebbw Vale's record 44-10 victory over Newport at Sardis Road. Lennie Woodard swooped for the other two tries in a sparkling team performance to blow away their rivals. Byron Hayward kicked 19 points with a drop shot, two penalty goals and five conversions. Second row Mark Workman crossed for Newport's try and Shaun Connor converted and dropped a goal. With so many props injured, Newport had to bring on permit player Mark Davis, capped in 1991 against Australia. He had been playing local police rugby all season.

Seven Sisters, the first village team to reach the semi-final stage, stole the lead three times at the Gnoll on the Sunday afternoon and it was 16-all just after the start of the second half. Llanelli brought on scrum half Rupert Moon during the interval and he proved the mainspring, as usual, when the Scarlets released their runners to finish with 10 tries, five of them during the closing 10 minutes. It was 61-16 as Seven found themselves very much at sixes as well as sevens. Chris Wyatt, the game's outstanding forward, and Neil Boobyer each crossed twice. Other tries came from Vernon Cooper, Wayne Proctor, Aled Jones, Moon, Garan Evans and Emyr Jones. Craig Warlow fired over three penalty goals and Stephen Jones converted one try. Ian Watts obtained the Div 4 club's try. Andrew James converted and landed two penalty goals and acting captain Hywel Evans dropped a goal. Regular captain Mark Chilcott missed the occasion because he broke a leg in the previous round.

**SEVENTH ROUND:** Two of the favourites crashed out. Pontypridd were on the threshold of a 27-26 victory at Rodney Parade when, in the last five minutes, Shaun Connor dropped a goal from around 30 yards to steal it for Newport 29-27. Newport, without a win in the premier division, relied on their forceful forwards for a supreme effort and thoroughly deserved a notable success. Connor said in the dressing room afterwards, "Everyone is smiling, which is a change. Usually it is like a morgue in here!" Coach Steve Jones summed up, "We planned to close them down. It was negative, but it worked." After Ian Gough ploughed over for a home try, centre Matthew Watkins intercepted and a bolting 70-yard run took him away for a try and a 17-10 lead. Ponty pulled ahead at 27-17 with two quick tries from deep inside their territory to start the second half. Gareth Wyatt went for the first; Dafydd James for the second. But Connor planted over three penalty goals and then completed 19 points with his winning drop-shot. Kevin Morgan scored Ponty's first try and Neil Jenkins converted all three tries and landed two penalty goals.

The other shock resulted in Swansea's exit 27-13 amid the Easter weekend snow flurries at Ebbw Vale. It was only Ebbw's fifth victory in 36 meetings with the Whites and avenged the semi-final defeat the previous season. Joking Swansea fly half Arwel Thomas had passed some disparaging remarks about the opposition, but Kingsley Jones blotted him out and Arwel was shown the yellow card after felling Kingsley with a wicked short-arm. It was no joking matter as Swansea conceded tries to Lennie Woodard, David Llewellyn and skipper Kingsley. Byron Hayward converted all three and fired over two penalty goals. Prop John Evans crossed for the only Swansea try; Arwel Thomas converted and put over two penalty goals.

Three tries by wing Garan Evans (though the first was a lucky score because he put a foot into touch at the corner) set Llanelli up for a 40-17 win over Neath. Rupert Moon's solo try was spectacular as he executed a sort of Chinese splits to touch down. Hooker Jason Hyatt and centre Nigel Davies also crossed for the Scarlets and Craig Warlow converted two and kicked two penalty goals. Richard Davies kicked Neath into the lead with a penalty shot, but the home side were 28-3 in front before Neath scored again, this time with tries by No 8 Lee Jones and wing Chris Higgs, both converted by Chris John. Hugh Williams-Jones came out of retirement to prop for Llanelli.

The duel between the two Div 4 teams saw Seven Sisters 39-0 winners over Garn, who had lock Richie Cox sent off for stamping after 16 minutes. Andrew James, 22-year-old Seven full back, supplied 19 points, including a try. Lloyd Paget (2) Adrian Hughes and prop Paul Elkins also crossed. Giant-killers Garndiffaith had come to the end of the trail, but their exploits had helped set the cup campaign alight.

**SIXTH ROUND:** The big surprise was the departure of holders Cardiff, firmly seen off at Ebbw Vale 24-9. Home tries were obtained by centre Jonathan Hawker and wing Alun Harries. Byron Hayward converted one and put over four penalty shots. There were no tries for Cardiff; just three Lee Jarvis penalty goals. Ebbw skipper Kingsley Jones, unimpressed that Cardiff had defeated them in both their league meetings,

Ebbw Vale, defeated SWALEC Cup finalists 1998. Standing (left to right): Alun Phillips, S Taumalolo, J Strange, P Pook, L Banks, K Falatau, Mark Jones, Steve Jones, C Billen, M Wilson, I Thomas, Leighton Phillips. Seated: R Collins, D Llewellyn, A Harries, J Funnell, Kingsley Jones (capt), B Hayward, L Woodard, J Hawker, G Bisp.

*Picture: Huw Evans Picture Agency Cardiff*

Scarlet Crusader. Chris Wyatt leads the Llanelli charge in the cup final at Bristol as his team won the cup for the 10th time. Llanelli figured in their 13th final.

*Picture: Huw Evans Picture Agency Cardiff*

and Vale had lost three previous cup encounters with the Blue-and-Blacks, fired his team with tireless zest. In doing so, he won back his place in the Wales side against Scotland.

Both Div 4 teams battled through to the quarter-finals. Garndiffaith, enjoying a fifth successive home tie for the season, put out Llanharan while Seven Sisters were 15-11 winners at Tredegar. It was 19-14 to Garn as they reached this stage for the first time. With captain Scott Crosby crooning the motivating melody for his rousing pack, they scored tries by Gareth Kirkup (2) and Ian Jenkins. Gareth Clark converted two. Huw Woodland picked up the Llanharan try and Wayne Jervis was on target with three penalty goals. Seven Sisters, quarter-finalists in 1985, shocked Div 2 leaders Tredegar with tries by scrum half Lloyd Paget and wing Dafydd Francis. Andrew James converted one and fired in a penalty shot. Dylan Meredith was Tredegar's try scorer and Matthew Chapman kicked two penalty goals.

Mark Taylor's four tries set Swansea up for a 66-12 success against Aberavon. Lee Davies converted eight tries. Newport were top scorers in this round, swamping UWIC 69-15 with 24 points from Shaun Connor. David Smith snapped up three tries. Fly half Phil Withers darted in for two tries to make Pontypridd struggle at Abertillery before Ponty won 33-24. "We nearly got turned over," admitted skipper Neil Jenkins. Ian Jones, on loan from Bristol, and Chris Higgs each scored two tries as Neath knocked out Builth Wells 41-0. Caerphilly led 18-13 after 20 minutes of the second half at Stradey, but Llanelli finished with a flourish for a 35-18 verdict.

**FIFTH ROUND:** Giant-killers Garn did it again. This time first division Rumney suffered a 17-11 fate after leading 11-0 at half time. Gareth Clarke kicked a home penalty goal and converted tries by Ian Jenkins and Steve Cross. Four penalty goals by Andrew James doomed Cross Keys 12-9 in extra time at Seven Sisters. "They were really scraping the barrel when they asked me to play," observed Paul Thorburn, called back after almost two years to play his 300th game for Neath. He fired over 21 points with five penalty goals and three conversions in a 36-17 decision at Llandovery. Cwmgors, Div 6A West leaders, had never come so far in the cup, but they could not curb Div 1 leaders Caerphilly and the visitors powered to 55-0 victory. There was only one try for Llanelli as they took an 8-0 verdict at Merthyr. Nigel Davies was the scorer and Craig Warlow landed a penalty goal. Arwel Thomas contributed 29 points, including two tries, as Swansea turned over Tondu 54-13. Richard Wintle scored three of the visitors' seven tries.

Lee Jarvis kicked 22 points for Cardiff to register a 62-6 success at Newbridge. Ebbw Vale also rattled up the tries: 10 in fact, with three each for Alun Harries and Lennie Woodard. Mike Boys (try) and Matthew Chapman (penalty goal) saw Tredegar through 8-3 at Penygraig. Full back Phil Sparrow raced 50 yards for a dazzling try, but it could not save SW

## RFU/Tetley Bitter Cup

## SELLA AND LYNAGH SPUR SARACENS

**Philippe Sella scored the first of seven winning tries and Michael Lynagh kicked 13 points to mark their last season with the Saracens in a 48-18 success over Wasps in the final of the Tetley Bitter Cup at Twickenham on May 9, 1998. Other tries in this first Saracens cup triumph came from Ryan Constable, Gavin Johnson, Danny Grewcock, Steve Ravenscroft, Kyran Bracken and Richard Wallace. Australian Lynagh converted five and dropped a goal. For Wasps, Paul Volley and Shane Roiser crossed and Gareth Rees converted one and kicked two penalty goals.**

Police from 26-8 defeat by visitors Newport. Aberavon put Maesteg out for the second successive season, this time 35-15. Wing Ian Hyde scored two tries for the Old Parish. Richard Tibbs supplied all Ynysybwl's points, including a try, but visitors Llanharan were 27-19 winners. Pontypridd compelled the exit of Treorchy 42-7, winning for the fourth time in four cup meetings.

**FOURTH ROUND:** For the first time, Bridgend lost to a small club. The visit to Garndiffaith was expected to provide the premier division club with a searching examination, but few anticipated the fourth division team would pull of such a shock. Garn snatched three second half tries on a day of drama at Lasgarn View, the last of which, during the final minute of extra time, brought Steve Cross the vital score, converted to make it 24-21. When Cross allowed Sam Greenaway to dodge inside him to put Bridgend ahead five minutes from the end, the Garn wing was devastated. Then, when Gary Morgan won yet another lineout and the Gwent minnows spread the ball, Cross took a short pass from full back Gareth Clarke and side-stepped Greenaway with a flourish to make historic amends. Clarke added his second conversion to end the match and leave Bridgend stunned.

Although Matthew James missed five penalty attempts, he put one over and converted one of the home tries by scrum half Ian Jenkins and back row man Danny Evans. There was a massed punch-up at one stage and referee Barrie Gregory took the unusual action of yellow-carding one of the replacements standing on the touch-line. "It would have been an injustice if we had won," said Bridgend director of rugby John Phillips. "We could not match their pride and passion. In Bridgend, and possibly a lot of other premier division clubs, there are some very much over paid, under-worked, big-headed people who have to face facts about what professional rugby is all about."

Cardiff accumulated 14 tries while defeating Div 6A East Abercarn 82-14. Tony Rees returned to Cardiff ranks after a 90-day ban for being sent off against Harlequins in the Euro Cup. Abercarn had No 8 David

**BRYNITHEL, WORTHINGTON GWENT AND DISTRICT CUP WINNERS 1998  17-10 AGAINST BLAINA UTD**

*Picture: Wales News & Pictures*

**RHIGOS, WORTHINGTON NEATH AND DISTRICT CHAMPIONS 1998 37-3 AGAINST CIMLA**

*Picture: Wales News & Pictures*

Maund ordered off for persistently killing the ball. Ebbw Vale's record cup tally 57-14 against Kidwelly featured three tries by Lennie Woodard. David Llewellyn raced 80 yards to score another of the nine tries. This in the opening minutes to set the scene. Full back Kevin Morgan was a three-try getter as Pontypridd disposed of Bonymaen 43-3 while Neil Jenkins provided 18 points. Cwmllynfell included 40-year-old golden oldie Mike Lewis, former Aberavon, Llanelli and Newport fly half, in their line-up, but the Div 6A Central team could not deny Neath and went out 32-13.

Pwllheli, defeated only twice as leaders of Div 6B West, coached by New Zealander Brian Going and with five Kiwi players in their squad, twice took the lead at Newport before losing 58-16. A week earlier Pwllheli had set a National League record win 135-0 over Milford Haven. Alex Lawson kicked 18 Newport points. Prop Hugh Williams-Jones, aged 34, played what he intended would be his final game for Llanelli in their hard-fought 21-16 verdict against Dunvant. Wing Julian Vernall collected a hat-trick of tries as Cross Keys put out Pontyclun 67-17. Newbridge raised their record cup score 50-0 against Abercwmboi. Abertillery, in their first cup meeting with Pontypool, were 28-18 winners after referee Hugh Watkins had issued a general yellow card warning. Pooler had Ryan Harvey sent off. Tredegar scraped through 17-16 at Morriston as Dai Davies scored their only try. Dai Lloyd contributed 22 points to help Treorchy win 62-8 at Kenfig Hill.

## DIDCOTT'S DEBUT WORTH 22 PTS

**EARLIER ROUNDS:** For the seventh time in eight seasons, Penarth failed in their first tie. This time, in the third round, they went out 34-12 at Tonyrefail. Glamorgan Wanderers also made their exit at this stage, defeated at their first attempt 25-18 by visitors Cwmllynfell. However, Tredegar out-gunned Ystrad Rhondda 41-10. Ynysybwl (Div 5) piled up the biggest third round tally 60-12 against Llandudno (Div 7) with four tries by Stuart Lloyd. Richard Tibbs supplied three tries and Jeff Lloyd 20 points. A hat-trick of tries by Alun Brown set Tondu to 33-25 success against fellow Div 2 team St. Peter's. Mark Addis and Craig Marshman each collected three tries as Abercynon (Div 2) overwhelmed Cowbridge (Div 5) 56-5.

Another three-try scorer was Leighton Winder for Mountain Ash (Div 2) to put out Crumlin (Div 6) 35-10. No 8 Anthony Thomas crossed for three tries as Aberavon Quins (Div 4) disposed of Dinas Powys (Div 5) 27-14. Dinas had reached the last 16 the previous season, but Cardiff at the Arms Park proved too much for them: it was 99-7. James Didcott's debut for Abergavenny brought him 22 points, including two tries, in 65-5 victory over Tumble in the second round. Simon Rogers was the star for Carmarthen Athletic with 20 points in their 30-17 success at Gwernyfed. David Rees kicked the winning penalty goal for Seven Sisters to defeat Risca 13-10. Penygraig were 96-0 winners at Llandaff North in the first round.

# SWALEC CUP 1997-98

## FOURTH ROUND

Aberavon 26, Bedwas 10
Aberavon Q 30, Felinfoel 17
Abercynon 7, Caerphilly 44
Beddau 14, UWIC 35
Blackwood 11, Maesteg 29
Cardiff 82, Abercarn 14
Carmarthen Q. 13, Llanharan 24
Cross Keys 67, Pontyclun 17
Cwmgors 22, Porthcawl 0
Cwmllynfell 13, Neath 32
Ebbw Vale 57, Kidwelly 14
Garndiffaith 24, Bridgend 21
Gilfach Goch 5, Seven Sisters 6
Glynneath 11, Merthyr 43
Kenfig Hill 8, Treorchy 62
Llanelli 21, Dunvant 16

Maesteg Q. 12, Llandovery 55
Morriston 16, Tredegar 17
Mountain Ash 22, Neath Ath. 12
Narberth 30, Wrexham 16
Newbridge 50, Abercwmboi 0
Newport 58, Pwllheli 16
Penygraig 29, Blaina 22
Pontypool 18, Abertillery 28
Pontypridd 43, Bonymaen 3
Swansea 25, Whitland 12
Tondu 26, Pyle 10
Tonyrefail 24, Croesyceiliog 21
Trimsaran 0, Builth Wells 18
Tylorstown 3, SW Police 32
Ynysybwl 15, Treherbert 13
Ystradgynlais 31, Rumney 32

## FIFTH ROUND

Aberavon 35, Maesteg 15
Abertillery 15, Aberavon Q 10
Builth Wells 23, Narberth 17
Cwmgors 0, Caerphilly 55
Garndiffaith 17, Rumney 11
Llandovery 17, Neath 36
Merthyr 0, Llanelli 8
Newbridge 6, Cardiff 62

Penygraig 3, Tredegar 8
Pontypridd 42, Treorchy 7
Seven Sisters 12, Cross Keys 9
SW Police 8, Newport 26
Tondu 13, Swansea 54
Tonyrefail 20, Ebbw Vale 60
UWIC 53, Mountain Ash 29
Ynysybwl 19, Llanharan 27

## SIXTH ROUND

Abertillery 24, Pontypridd 33
Ebbw Vale 24, Cardiff 9
Garndiffaith 19, Llanharan 14
Llanelli 35, Caerphilly 18

Neath 41, Builth Wells 0
Swansea 66, Aberavon 12
Tredegar 11, Seven Sisters 15
UWIC 15, Newport 69

## SEVENTH ROUND

Ebbw Vale 27, Swansea 13
Llanelli 40, Neath 17

Newport 29, Pontypridd 27
Seven Sisters 39, Garndiffaith 0

## SEMI-FINALS

Ebbw Vale 44, Newport 10
*(At Sardis Road)*

Llanelli 61, Seven Sisters 16
*(At The Gnoll)*

## FINAL

Llanelli 19, Ebbw Vale 12
*(At Ashton Gate, Bristol)*

**For the first time a player with an English club was voted Welsh Player of the Year. Allan Bateman, the schemer of the Welsh national team, plays for Richmond, who lured him back from RL ranks.**

*Picture: Huw Evans Picture Agency, Cardiff*

## *Player of the Year*

# ALLAN BATEMAN

The most organised and consistent centre in British rugby. That was the opinion of most critics during the 1997-98 season and Allan Bateman, the schemer of the Welsh team, was a worthy selection as Welsh Player of the Year. The Maesteg-born former Welsh Youth cap proved the complete midfield man. He first caught attention during his Neath days in combination with Colin Laity and helped the Gnoll team win the cup in 1989 (against Llanelli) and 1990 (against Bridgend).

Bateman secured his first cap against Scotland in 1990, but Warrington, well aware they were on to a good thing, quickly snapped him up in a deal worth around £100,000 to begin a notable RL career that brought him 13 appearances for Wales and he played twice for the Great Britain team. Richmond enticed him back to RU ranks and immediately Wales recalled him as a key figure. Indeed, no Wales team would be complete without Bateman.

Llanelli's exciting full back Darril Williams, aged 22, was chosen as Most Promising Player. Signed from Bonymaen for the start of the season at Stradey, he proved an invaluable recruit and helped the Scarlets win the SWALEC Cup. Talented Darril undoubtedly is a starlet to watch in the years to come.

A man who has entertained for a number of years with a number of clubs is Ebbw Vale scrum half David Llewellyn. The 27-year-old-man-of-many-tricks becomes the first winner of a new award as Most Overlooked Player. He was unlucky not to have gained some significant recognition for his irrepressible attacking qualities. His partnership with Byron Hayward ensured Ebbw a place among the top teams in the premier division and, of course, their first appearance in a cup final. Opponents regard him as an elusive runner and stealthy try-stealer.

### PREVIOUS PLAYERS OF THE YEAR

| | | | | | |
|---|---|---|---|---|---|
| 1969 | G.O. EDWARDS | 1979 | T.D. HOLMES | 1989 | PHIL DAVIES |
| 1970 | RAY HOPKINS | 1980 | D.S. RICHARDS | 1990 | ARTHUR EMYR |
| 1971 | BARRY JOHN | 1981 | CLIVE BURGESS | 1991 | SCOTT GIBBS |
| 1972 | J.P.R. WILLIAMS | 1982 | GWYN EVANS | 1992 | EMYR LEWIS |
| 1973 | T.P. DAVID | 1983 | T.D. HOLMES | 1993 | IEUAN EVANS |
| 1974 | T.J. COBNER | 1984 | M. TITLEY | 1994 | NEIL JENKINS |
| 1975 | T.M. DAVIES | 1985 | MARK RING | 1995 | NEIL JENKINS |
| 1976 | T.M. DAVIES | 1986 | J. DAVIES | 1996 | ROB HOWLEY |
| 1977 | P. BENNETT | 1987 | STUART EVANS | 1997 | ROB HOWLEY |
| 1978 | T.J. COBNER | 1988 | ROB NORSTER | | |

**LLANWERN, WORTHINGTON NEWPORT AND DISTRICT CUP WINNERS 1998  6-3 AGAINST PILL HARRIERS**

*Picture: Wales News & Pictures*

**RHYMNEY, WORTHINGTON BEN FRANCIS CUP WINNERS 1998  33-22 AGAINST NEWPORT**

*Picture: Wales News & Pictures*

**GILFACH GOCH, WORTHINGTON SILVER BALL WINNERS 1998 34-22 AGAINST BRITISH STEEL.**

*Picture: Wales News & Pictures*

# WALES LOSE AT WEMBLEY, BUT ENGLAND STUN THE BLACKS

Sensationally, England stopped New Zealand from enjoying another 100 per cent record in the UK and Ireland during the autumn of 1997. At Twickenham in December, was witnessed one of the epic rugby contests. The All Blacks were clear favourites after crushing Wales 42-7, mauling Ireland 63-15 and dashing English hopes 25-8 at Old Trafford in the first of their two meetings. England had fallen to South Africa by a record Twickenham score 29-11 the week before this second tussle with the Blacks, whereas New Zealand had triumphed in 11 successive matches at test level during the year, scoring 70 tries in the process.

Understandably, the Blacks were confident that a 70,000-plus Twickenham crowd would see another New Zealand success. Some critics, wildly unrealistic when making comparisons with NZ teams of the past who had come up against much stronger opposition in depth, were propounding the view that this was the most awesome All Blacks team of all time. They certainly did not give the impression of being awesome as England built an amazing 20-3 lead! Never had a New Zealand team looked so dismayed in England. Many contend that it was the greatest match to be staged at Twickers. Few could disagree.

England scored three tries in the space of 15 minutes. It was a stunning feat; but NZ teams never accept defeat is likely and their rally played its part in making this an incredible match. They hit back so forcefully that they forged ahead 26-23. The tourists crossed the gain-line on 42 occasions compared to England's paltry 19 and the second half onslaught had England reeling. They had played Australia (drawn 15-all), NZ, South Africa and now NZ again on successive weeks without a win and another defeat appeared to loom. It would have been a savagely cruel fate to lose after such a vibrant start and rescue was at hand. Paul Grayson stepped up to pop over a simple penalty goal to save the match for the Men in White at 26-all.

"We were lucky to get away with a draw," admitted acting NZ captain Justin Marshall. His team had been annoyed at the criticism of their tactics by England team manager Roger Uttley before the game. Uttley said, "It strikes me as odd that every time we get the ball in their 22, the whistle goes, giving us a penalty. They are happy to concede penalties rather than let us have the ball from a ruck or maul, because we could score a try from that position."

New Zealand 13 tries, Llanelli none. This was not so much a match as a visitation. In fact, this record defeat for the Scarlets at 81-3 was the biggest score by any touring team to Wales, surpassing the 78-7 by Australia against Swansea in 1994. Four of the tries came from expressive full back Christian Cullen, the Human Corkscrew, as the home defence leaked woefully. They just ran out of tacklers and it is doubtful if 20 Llanelli defenders could have checked the 15 flowing Blacks. We wondered if we were witnessing the last occasion when New Zealand would be pitted against a club? What club side can possibly hope to live with that?

Llanelli were just cannon-fodder with just a Craig Warlow penalty goal after 14 minutes to show for their endeavours. It was 25 years on from that famous day when Delme Thomas's heroes had defeated the All Blacks and that night the pubs in the town ran dry. Perhaps, unwisely, the Stradey scoreboard displayed that famous 1972 scoreline: Llanelli 9, Seland Newydd 3, before the 6pm kick-off under the floodlights on a wet and windy November night in front of some 13,000 spectators. The action was shown live on S4C and a nation watched in horror.

Coach Gareth Jenkins, a member of the 1972 side that toppled the giants, exclaimed, "Our players admitted they did not know what hit them. They just couldn't live with it. We've been beaten by the All Blacks before, but we've always felt able to compete." This time, it was not just that Llanelli were unequal – they viewed it as unreal!

The Wales A side produced more dogged tacklers than were seen at Stradey and it was not until the last quarter that the Blacks overwhelmed the defence with five further tries for 51-8 victory. Half time saw NZ only 13-5 in front: it had been try for try with Dafydd James giving Wales A the lead with a smart try following a quickly taken throw-in and strong run and dummy by Gareth Thomas to release the wing. Full back Todd Miller collected a gift try and Carlos Spencer converted and kicked two penalty goals.

Then Byron Hayward's penalty shot brought the home side back in contention on a night of steaming scrums under the Sardis Road floodlights. But this All Blacks second string piled on remorseless pressure to crack stubborn defenders. Hayward's battering-ram tackle to fell the monster 19-stone Jonah Lomu, in the New Zealand wing's first game back after 15 months out with a kidney disorder, was a feature of the Welsh spirit. A near-capacity crowd enjoyed the exciting manner in which the Welsh forwards took the game to their opponents during the opening half. Chris Wyatt and Martyn Williams, in particular, set an inspiring example as their team put in some serious tackling.

Ireland made a spirited start, out of the blocks with a furious offensive and there were two tries by skipper Keith Wood; but the black tidal wave gathered momentum and swept the Green Gladiators to their record defeat 63-15. Next, Emerging England were 59-22 victims at Huddersfield. Paul

Grayson inflated the home points tally with five penalty goals; but full back Miller snapped up three tries and Lomu powered in for two which won him back a Test place in the next match.

England managed a try at Old Trafford but, a week after drawing with the Wallabies at Twickenham, Lawrence Dallaglio's team were never going to stop the juggernaut. There was some merit, however, in the fact that England were not totally overwhelmed, as some suggested, and a score of 25-8, and only 3-1 on tries, implied a resolute effort.

The New Zealand midweek team endured a torrid time against England Rugby Partnership (a new term ostensibly for England A) at Ashton Gate. The Blacks scraped in 18-11 in front of more than 18,000 watchers. The Partnership nosed in front 11-10 with 15 minutes remaining, displaying commendable passion and fire, but Aaron Hopa bored in for a vital push-over try to swing matters for the tourists.

"We will probably have to play at a higher level than we have ever played before," warned coach Kevin Bowring before Wales faced the Blacks at Wembley, where 76,000 gathered to respond to the London Welsh Male Voice Choir on the pitch with rousing renditions of favourite Welsh tunes. The scene was set for an eventful occasion and it proved by no means a dismal display by the losers. Wales failed again against the Blacks, this time 42-7. Gareth Thomas kept dangerman Lomu subdued, Neil Jenkins saved a try with a tackle on Josh Kronfeld, and Gareth Llewellyn's stomping charge paved the way for Nigel Walker's try at the posts, which Jenkins converted. Neil Jenkins would have scored, but the ball was jolted from his grasp in a tackle as he crossed the line.

Everyone held their breath when Lomu flattened full back Kevin Morgan, but the Ponty man struggled back to his feet to battle on bravely. The superb all-round kicking of Andrew Mehrtens again was a dazzling feature for the tourists while Christian Cullen became the first full back to

Eyes front for this hypnotic sidestep. Leigh Davies goes into his dance routine to baffle the All Blacks in this first match Wales played at Wembley.

*Picture: Huw Evans Picture Agency, Cardiff*

72

score a hat-trick of tries against Wales. Wing Jeff Wilson twice thought he was away for tries, but each time Nigel Walker whipped back to catch the flier. Leigh Davies proved more dangerous than the other midfield attackers when he replaced Scott Gibbs (nine stitches in a gashed eyebrow). Arwel Thomas replaced injured Allan Bateman and took over the fly half spot with Neil Jenkins switching to centre.

Cullen's first try came when he ran a Rob Howley kick back at Wales. A long pass from Kevin Morgan was intercepted and led to Cullen's second try and then dazzling combined passing saw the full back complete his hat-trick. It was a match of four hookers: Jonathan Humphreys replaced Barry Williams and NZ brought on tour skipper Sean Fitzpatrick for Hewitt. Zinzan Brooke completed the scoring with the last kick of the match as the No 8 dropped a goal. It was the final flourish by the Blacks. But a shock awaited them from England at Twickenham.

## MATCH DETAILS

**November 8, 1997. NZ defeated Llanelli by 81 (5G, 2PG, 8T) to 3 (1PG) at Stradey Park.**

**LLANELLI:** Darril Williams; Wayne Proctor, Neil Boobyer, Stephen Jones, Warren Leach; Craig Warlow, Rupert Moon; Rhys Jones, Robin McBryde (capt), Sean Gale, Steve Ford, Mike Voyle, Chris Wyatt, Hywel Jenkins, Iwan Jones. Reps: Paul Morris for Jenkins, Aled Thomas for Moon, Andrew Gibbs for Iwan Jones, Hugh Williams-Jones for Rhys Jones.

**NZ:** C Cullen; J Wilson, F Bunce, A Ieremiah, G Osborne; A Mehrtens, J Marshall (capt); C Dowd, N Hewitt, O Brown, I Jones, R Brooke, A Blowers, T Randell, J Kronfeld.
Reps: J Stanley for Wilson, J Preston for Mehrtens, Z Brooke for Kronfeld.

*Referee:* Brian Campsall (England).

*Scorers:* For Llanelli, Craig Warlow (1PG). For NZ, Christian Cullen (4) Jeff Wilson (2), Norm Hewitt (2), Ian Jones, Josh Kronfeld, Justin Marshall, Alama Ieremiah, Zinzan Brooke (tries), Andrew Mehrtens (2PG, 2con), Wilson (2con), Jon Preston (1con).

**November 11, 1997. NZ defeated Wales A by 51 (5G, 2PG, 2T) to 8 (1PG, 1T) at Sardis Road, Pontypridd.**

**WALES A:** Matthew Back (Swansea); Gareth Thomas (Bridgend), Neil Boobyer (Llanelli), Jason Lewis (Pontypridd), Dafydd James (Pontypridd); Byron Hayward (Ebbw Vale), Andy Moore (Richmond); Ian Buckett (Swansea), Garin Jenkins (Swansea), Chris Anthony (Swansea), Gareth Llewellyn (Harlequins, capt), Chris Stephens (Bridgend), Mark Spiller (Pontypridd), Chris Wyatt (Llanelli), Martyn Williams (Pontypridd). Reps: Lee Jarvis (Cardiff) for Thomas, Huw Harries (Harlequins) for Hayward, Neil Eynon (Pontypridd) for Buckett, Stuart Roy (Pontypridd) for Stephens, Dean Thomas (Swansea) for Wyatt.

**NZ:** T Miller; T Umaga, S McLeod, W Little, J Lomu; C Spencer, M Robinson; M Allen, A Oliver, C Barrell, M Cooksley, C Riechelmann, T Blackadder (capt), S Surridge, M Carter. Reps: G Slater for Barrell, A Hopa for Reichelmann.

*Referee:* John Pearson (England).

*Scorers:* For Wales A, Dafydd James (1T), Byron Hayward (1PG). For NZ, Scott McLeod (2), Todd Miller, Anton Oliver, Mark Robinson, Jonah Lomu, Steve Surridge (tries), Carlos Spencer (2PG, 5con).

**November 15, 1997. NZ defeated Ireland by 63 (5G, 6PG, 2T) to 15 (1G, 1PG, 1T) at Lansdowne Road, Dublin.**

**IRELAND:** K W Nolan; D A Hickie, R A J Henderson, M C McCall, J P J McWeeney; E P Elwood, C D McGuinness; N J Popplewell, K G M Wood (capt), P S Wallace, P S Johns, M E O'Kelly, E O Halvey, E R P Miller, K Dawson. Reps: K M Maggs for McWeeney, B T

O'Meara for McGuinness, R P Nesdale for Wood, D J Erskine for Halvey.

**NZ:** C M Cullen; J W Wilson, F E Bunce, A Ieremiah, G M Osborne; A P Mehrtens, J W Marshall (capt); C M Dowd, N J Hewitt, O M Brown, I D Jones, R M Brooke, T C Randell, Z V Brooke, A F Blowers. Reps: S J McLeod for Bunce, J P Preston for Mehrtens, C Riechelmann for R M Brooke, J A Kronfeld for Blowers.

*Referee:* A J Spreadbury (England).

*Scorers:* For Ireland, Keith Wood (2T), Eric Elwood (1PG, 1con). For NZ, Wilson (2), Osborne (2), Marshall, Mehrtens, Ieremiah (tries), Mehrtens (6PG, 5con).

**November 18, 1997. NZ defeated Emerging England by 59 (5G, 3PG, 3T) to 22 (1G, 5PG) at McAlpine Stadium, Huddersfield.**

**EMERGING ENGLAND:** J Mallinder (Sale); J Bentley (Newcastle), N Greenstock (Wasps), M Allen (Northampton), T Beim (Sale); P Grayson (Northampton), A Healey (Leicester); G Rowntree (Leicester), M Regan (Bath), D Garforth (Leicester), S Shaw (Wasps), D Grewcock (Saracens), R Jenkins (Northampton), C Sheasby (Wasps), N Back (Leicester, capt). Rep: K Yates (Bath) for Garforth, M Corry (Leicester) for Jenkins, N McCarthy (Gloucester) for Regan, D Sims (Gloucester) for Shaw.

**NZ:** T Miller; T Umaga, S McLeod, W Little, J Lomu; C Spencer, M Robinson; M Allen, A Oliver, G Slater, M Cooksley, C Riechelmann, T Blackadder (capt), S Surridge, J Kronfeld. Reps: J Stanley for Umaga, A A Hope for Surridge.

*Referee:* P de Luca (Argentina).

*Scorers:* For Emerging England, Nick Greenstock (1T), Paul Grayson (5PG, 1con). For NZ, T Miller (3), J Lomu (2), J Kronfeld, S Surridge, C Riechelmann (tries), C Spencer (3PG, 5con).

**November 22, 1997. NZ defeated England by 25 (2G, 2PG, 1T) to 8 (1PG, 1T) at Old Trafford, Manchester.**

**ENGLAND:** M B Perry (Bath); D Rees (Sale), W J H Greenwood (Leicester), P R de Glanville (Bath), A A Adebayo (Bath); M J Catt (Bath), K P P Bracken (Saracens); J Leonard (Harlequins), R Cockerill (Leicester), D J Garforth (Leicester), M O Johnson (Leicester), G S Archer (Newcastle), L B N Dallaglio (Wasps, capt), A J Diprose (Saracens), R A Hill (Saracens). Reps: A S Healey (Leicester) for Adebayo, N A Back (Leicester) for Diprose.

**NZ:** C M Cullen; J W Wilson, F E Bunce, A Ieremiah, J T Lomu; A P Mehrtens, J W Marshall (capt); C W Dowd, N J Hewitt, O M Brown, I D Jones, R W Brooke, T C Randell, Z V Brooke, J A Kronfeld. Reps: J P Preston for Wilson, S J McLeod for Ieremiah, A F Blowers for Z Brooke.

*Referee:* Peter Marshall (Australia).

*Scorers:* For England, Phil de Glanville (1T), Mike Catt (1PG). For NZ, I Jones, J Wilson, T Randell (tries), A Mehrtens (2PG, 2con).

**November 25, 1997. NZ defeated England Rugby Partnership by 18 (1G, 2PG, 1T) to 11 (2PG, 1T) at Ashton Gate, Bristol.**

**ENGLAND RUGBY PARTNERSHIP:** T Stimpson (Newcastle); J Bentley (Newcastle), N Greenstock (Wasps), M Allen (Northampton), S Brown (Richmond); R Butland (Bath), M Wood (Wasps); K Yates (Bath), M Regan (Bath), P Vickery (Gloucester), D Sims (Gloucester), R Fidler (Gloucester), T Rodber (Northampton, capt), P Sanderson (Sale), C Sheasby (Wasps). Reps: A Long (Bath) for Regan, P Grayson (Northampton) for Butland, R Winters (Bedford) for Sims, S Benton (Gloucester) for Wood, J Worsley (Wasps) for Sanderson.

**NZ:** T Miller; T Umaga, J Stanley, S McLeod, G Osborne; C Spencer, J Preston; M Allen, A Oliver, C Barrell, C Riechelmann, M Cooksley, T Blackadder (capt), M Carter, A Hopa. Reps: W Little for Stanley, S Fitzpatrick for Oliver.

*Referee:* Robert Davies (Wales).

*Scorers:* For ERP, Wood (1T), Stimpson (2PG). For NZ, Spencer, Hopa (tries), Spencer (2PG, 1con).

**November 29, 1997. NZ defeated Wales by 42 (4G, 1DG, 2PG, 1T) to 7 (1G) at Wembley Stadium.**

**WALES:** K Morgan (Pontypridd); G Thomas (Bridgend), A G Bateman (Richmond), I S Gibbs (Swansea), N Walker (Cardiff); N R Jenkins (Pontypridd), R Howley (Cardiff); C D Loader (Swansea), B Williams (Richmond), D Young (Cardiff), M J Voyle (Llanelli), G O Llewellyn (Harlequins), R Appleyard (Swansea), N Thomas (Bath), R G Jones (Cardiff, capt). Reps: A C Thomas (Swansea) for Bateman, J M Humphreys (Cardiff) for Williams, S W Williams (Cardiff) for N Thomas, S C John (Cardiff) for Loader, L B Davies (Cardiff) for Gibbs.

**NZ:** C M Cullen; J W Wilson, F E Bunce, W K Little, J T Lomu; A P Mehrtens, J W Marshall (capt); C W Dowd, N J Hewitt, O M Brown, I D Jones, R W Brooke, T C Randell, Z V Brooke, J A Kronfeld. Reps: S B T Fitzpatrick for Hewitt, M Allen for Brown, A F Blowers for Randell.

*Referee:* Wayne Erickson (Australia).

*Scorers:* For Wales, Nigel Walker (1T), Neil Jenkins (1con). For NZ, Christian Cullen (3), Taine Randell, Justin Marshall (tries), Andrew Mehrtens (2PG, 4con), Zinzan Brooke (1DG).

**December 6, 1997. NZ defeated England A by 30 (2G, 2PG, 2T) to 19 (1G, 4PG) at Leicester.**

**ENGLAND A:** T Stimpson (Newcastle); S Brown (Richmond), S Potter (Leicester), M Allen (Northampton), A Adebayo (Bath); R Butland (Bath), S Benton (Gloucester); G Rowntree (Leicester), M Regan (Bath), P Vickery (Gloucester), D Sims (Gloucester), R Fidler (Gloucester), R Jenkins (Harlequins), P Sanderson (Sale), B Clarke (Richmond, capt). Reps: V Ubogu (Bath) for Vickery, R Winters (Bedford) for Jenkins, M Mapletoft (Gloucester) for Butland.

**NZ:** T Miller; T Umaga, S McLeod, A Ieremiah, G Osborne; C Spencer, M Robinson; M Allen, A Oliver, G Slater, C Riechelmann, M Cooksley, T Blackadder (capt), M Carter, S Surridge. Reps: J Preston for Robinson, A Blowers for Carter, A Hopa for Cooksley.

*Referee:* Alan Lewis (Ireland).

*Scorers:* For England A, Benton (1T), Stimpson (4PG, 1con). For NZ, McLeod, Oliver, Riechelmann, Umaga (tries), Spencer (2PG, 2con).

**December 6, 1997. England 26 (1G, 3PG, 2T) drew with NZ 26 (2G, 4PG) at Twickenham.**

**ENGLAND:** M B Perry (Bath); D L Rees (Sale), W J H Greenwood (Leicester), P R de Glanville (Bath), A S Healey (Leicester); P J Grayson (Northampton), K P P Bracken (Saracens); J Leonard (Harlequins), R Cockerill (Leicester), D J Garforth (Leicester), M O Johnson (Leicester), G S Archer (Newcastle), L B N Dallaglio (Wasps, capt), R A Hill (Saracens), N A Back (Leicester). Reps: T R G Stimpson (Newcastle) for Rees, M J S Dawson (Northampton) for Bracken, M P Regan (Bath) for Cockerill, C M A Sheasby (Wasps) for Back.

**NZ:** C M Cullen; J W Wilson, F E Bunce, W K Little, J T Lomu; A P Mehrtens, J W Marshall (capt); M R Allen, N J Hewitt, O M Brown, I D Jones, R M Brooke, T C Randell, Z V Brooke, J A Kronfeld. Reps: S J McLeod for Bunce, C J Spencer for Little, C C Riechelmann for Kronfeld.

*Referee:* Jim Fleming (Scotland).

*Scorers:* For England, David Rees, Richard Hill, Lawrence Dallaglio (tries), Paul Grayson (3PG, 1con). For NZ, Andrew Mehrtens, Walter Little (tries), Mehrtens (4PG, 2con).

---

## ACKFORD CLAIMS NZ CONNED THE REF

Former England second row Paul Ackford, in an article for the *Daily Telegraph*, stated after the NZ victory over England in Manchester, "Cheats prospered at Old Trafford. The All Blacks' willingness to concede penalty after penalty to prevent a try was as intentional as it was skilful. Australian Peter Marshall, one of five full time referees in that country, was as suckered as the rest of us."

# The day that star forward Barry wore a mask of horror!

## WALES 70, ROMANIA 21

"We believe we are a try-scoring team. We are progressing in attitude, but we need to be more ruthless," said coach Kevin Bowring after Wales collected 11 tries in overwhelming Romania. There would have been 12 tries, but Barry Williams, the outstanding forward in the match, lost the ball unhampered while wending his way in the in-goal area. He had already scored one try and the look of bafflement on his face when the ball dropped from his grasp was a mask for the artistic to copy and hang in a suitable gallery!

In this, the biggest score by Wales in a home match, Arwel Thomas contributed 23 points with two tries, five conversions and a penalty goal. It was just one point behind the record set by Neil Jenkins against Canada in 1993 and repeated against Italy in 1994. Had Arwel remained on the pitch he could have broken the record because Lee Jarvis, who replaced him to win his first cap, converted the final try.

Keeping the ball alive was the prime aim and there were just two lineouts in the first 30 minutes, and only eight in the entire match (six won by Romania). Rob Appleyard proved a dynamic blind-side breakaway and Leigh Davies, called up when Scott Gibbs withdrew with recurring ankle trouble, scored an explosive opening try as he thrust past three or four tacklers. Paul John again sparkled at scrum half while Arwel Thomas delighted in the spaces created and made a notable mark on proceedings.

Bowring commented, "We relaxed when we should have upped the tempo and let them back into the game. This was a performance upon which we must build in order to face the better teams." WRU Director of Rugby Terry Cobner observed, "The team will be disappointed that they did not score more than 100 points. We made 28 errors and you can't afford to do that at international level. We are not yet ready to beat the big boys."

For the first time since they opposed Scotland at Swansea in 1954, Wales staged a home match away from the Arms Park and a near-capacity crowd of just over 11,000 watched in dazzling sunshine at The Racecourse, home of Wrexham FC, on Saturday August 30, 1997.

**WALES:** K Morgan (Pontypridd); W T Proctor (Llanelli), A G Bateman (Richmond), L B Davies (Cardiff), G Thomas (Bridgend); A C Thomas (Swansea), P John (Pontypridd); C D Loader (Swansea), B Williams (Richmond), D Young (Cardiff), S Moore (Moseley), M Rowley (Pontypridd), R Appleyard (Swansea), N Thomas (Bath), R G Jones (Cardiff, capt). Reps: N Walker (Cardiff) for Proctor, L Jarvis (Cardiff) for Arwel Thomas, L Mustoe (Cardiff) for Young, S M Williams (Cardiff) for Rowley.

**ROMANIA:** V Maftei; L Colceriu, R Gontineac, G Solomie, I Rotaru; S Guranescu, M Iacob; G Vlad, M Radoi, A Salageanu, T Branza (capt), V Nedelcu, F Corodeanu, C Draguceanu, E Septar. Reps: P Mitu for Maftei, C Stan for Salageanu, I Ruxanda for Septar.

*Referee:* Ian Ramage (Scotland).

*Scorers:* For Wales, Leigh Davies (2), Allan Bateman (2), Arwel Thomas (2), Paul John, Kevin Morgan, Barry Williams, Steve Williams, Nigel Walker (tries). Arwel Thomas (1PG, 5cons), Lee Jarvis (1con). For Romania, Rotaru, Draguceanu (tries), Guranescu (3PG, 1con).

**Slipping a tackle. Gareth Thomas, the escapology expert of the Welsh team, launches another attack in the runaway victory over Romania at Wrexham.**

*Picture: Huw Evans Picture Agency, Cardiff*

# Transfer-listed Thomas points the winning way for Wales

## WALES 46, TONGA 12.

Gareth Thomas, the Bridgend centre transfer-listed by his club, scored two rousing tries and helped make two others in this expected victory on Sunday November 16, 1997. It was the first international match staged at Swansea for 43 years, though the attendance of 6,589 was the lowest in a Wales home game during the Twentieth Century. In the 1880s Wales games attracted crowds of only some 5,000 and the gate receipts at the Wales v NZ Native team, the Maoris, in 1888 amounted to just £120!

Undoubtedly, the wet and windy conditions and the fact that the match was televised live contributed to the sparse crowd; but it was an important workout for Wales just 13 days before they faced the awesome All Blacks.

Neil Jenkins was restored to his customary role of outside half after Wales had played 11 matches with Jonathan Davies (twice) and Arwel Thomas (9 times) in that position.

Pontypridd's Gareth Wyatt, normally a wing, scored a sparkling debut try playing at full back. "In the first half, we didn't quite find the rhythm we were looking for and played more like individuals than a team," admitted coach Bowring.

**WALES:** G Wyatt (Pontypridd); G Thomas (Bridgend), L Davies (Cardiff), S Gibbs (Swansea), N Walker (Cardiff); N Jenkins (Pontypridd); P John (Pontypridd); C Loader (Swansea), B Williams (Richmond), S John (Cardiff), S Moore (Moseley), M Voyle (Llanelli), R Appleyard (Swansea), N Thomas (Bath), G Jones (Cardiff, capt). Reps: D James (Bridgend) for Thomas, R Howley (Cardiff) for P John, J Humphreys (Cardiff) for Williams, C Anthony (Swansea) for S John, S Williams (Cardiff) for Moore.

**TONGA:** Gustavo Tonga; Teviti Tiueti, Fepi'kou Tatafu, Peter Tanginoa, Semisi Faka'osi'folau; Siua Taumalolo, Sione Mone Tu'ipilotu; David Briggs (capt), Viliami Ma'asi, Nualu Ta'u, Saia Latu, Kuli Faletau, Katelimoni Tu'ipilotu, Tomasi Matakaionogo, Holani Pohiva. Reps: Heamani Lavaka for Briggs, Simon Hafoka for Matakaionogo, Maama Molitika for Pohiva, Sione Tai for Tatafu.

*Referee:* Santiata Borsani (Argentina).

*Scorers:* For Wales, Gareth Thomas (2), Lee Davies, Gareth Wyatt, Chris Anthony, Nigel Walker (tries), Neil Jenkins (4PG, 2con). For Tonga, Tatafu, Tai (tries), Tonga (1con).

---

## DISILLUSIONED NEATH CHAIRMAN QUITS

**Neath chairman John Williams relinquished his post after 15 years' association with the club's committee. "The game I knew and loved is disappearing and so are the foundations that held it together – loyalty, friendship, warmth and camaradarie," he lamented. "Who wants to be involved in a game where television now dictates that you have to kick-off at 6pm on a Sunday?**

**"Who wants to be told you have to go and play English clubs in 30,000-seater stadia with fewer than 5,000 people rattling around? I don't. I have had enough of it all. We have torn apart a hundred years of rugby culture and tradition in Wales in the space of a couple of years. There isn't the money in Wales to sustain the current market for players."**

# THEY CAME, THEY SAW AND
# THEY NEARLY CONQUERED
## WALES 23, ITALY 20.

The spirit of Roman general Aulus Plautius and his disciplined legions, who drove Prince Caradog and his wild Welsh Silures into the mountains, burned fiercely in the Italian team that so nearly shocked modern Wales to defeat at Stradey Park on February 7, 1998. Many reckoned it should have been a draw, though the Italians were indignant that referee Steve Lander denied them a try when they surged over from a lineout. That try would have given the visitors their first win over Wales in five meetings and further underlined their growing power after victories over Ireland, Scotland and the destruction of Denmark 102-3.

Former Cardiff Coach Roy Bish, who coached Italy for four years in the 1970s, pointed out, "The collective play of Italy was superior to that of Wales, who were left without having solved any of their problems. Rugby in Italy is ninth in pecking order, so they are doing marvels with very limited resources. We don't seem to understand the concept of play, whereas the Italians understand it and their game is progressing."

Yet again Wales neglected the wide ball. Scott Quinnell and Scott Gibbs were criticised for seeking contact too freely when the occasion cried for ball release and search for space. Coach Kevin Bowring, understandably, was disappointed. "We would all have liked a better performance," he admitted. "We will need to improve going into the Five Nations. We made too many errors in contact and it wasn't the quality we are looking for."

The Welsh claim to possess the most menacing back line in the Five Nations seemed somewhat ambitious when their only scores came from a penalty try following seven successive scrums on the visitors' line and from another brilliant moment of opportunism by Gareth Thomas in the 77th minute. He relishes the long-distance challenge and raced more than half the length of the field for his 12th try in 24 appearances. A minute later, he brought down Corrado Pilat a yard from the goal-line to save his country from defeat.

This was the first international match at Llanelli since Arthur Gould's team beat Ireland by a try to nil in March 1893 to win the Triple Crown for the first time.

**WALES:** N Jenkins (Pontypridd); I Evans (Bath), A Bateman (Richmond), S Gibbs (Swansea), G Thomas (Cardiff); A Thomas (Swansea), R Howley (Cardiff, capt); A Lewis (Cardiff), B Williams (Richmond), D Young (Cardiff), G Llewellyn (Harlequins), M Voyle (Llanelli), R Appleyard (Swansea), S Quinnell (Richmond), M Williams (Pontypridd). Replacements: J Humphreys (Cardiff) for B Williams, C Charvis (Swansea) for M Williams.

**ITALY:** C Pilat; P Vaccari, C Stoica, L Martin, Marcello Cuttitta; D Dominguez, A Troncon; Massimo Cuttitta, C Orlandi, A Castellani, W Cristofoletto, G Croci, M Giovanelli (capt), J Gardner, A Sgorlon.

*Referee:* Steve Lander (England).

*Scorers:* For Wales, Gareth Thomas (1T), penalty try, Neil Jenkins (3PG, 2con). For Italy, Cristian Stoica, Andrea Sgorlon (tries), Diego Dominguez (2PG, 2con).

Sevens

# Record eighth victory for Fiji: Baa-Baas keep their title

Fiji were winners of the Hong Kong Sevens for a record eighth time as they triumphed in a bruising final 28-19 against Western Samoa. Bruce Rauqe, borrowed from Australia because of injuries, proved a valuable guest and scored the decisive try in the last minute. It was Fiji's first title since 1992 and a near capacity crowd of 37,000 watched.

Fiji had been surprised by Argentina, who held the world sevens champions to a 21-all draw in their pool round; but Fiji put out Australia 21-7 in the quarter-finals and then NZ 24-7 in the semi-final.

Barbarians retained their title with a hard-fought 38-28 decision against Leicester in the final of the Middlesex Charity Sevens at Twickenham. The Baa-Baas defeated London Welsh 24-19 in their opening game.

Wales defeated Hungary 69-5 in the Jerusalem Sevens when the event was staged for the first time; but Fiji overwhelmed the Welsh side 37-3 and another defeat was 26-17 by Western Samoa.

Bonymaen won the Cwmtawe Sevens for the first time in a thrilling 36-33 final against Ystalyfera. Bonymaen shocked six-times champions Swansea out 45-7 in the quarter-final with four tries by Peter Roberts. St. Cyres (Penarth) won the Old Penarthians' Sevens on their first appearance in the tourney, defeating Ysgol Glantaf 24-19 in extra-time with a try by Martin Liddiat, who raced some 40 yards with only one boot!

## Barbarians

### TAUMALOLO TAMES TIGERS WITH 33 pts

Ebbw Vale full back Siua Taumalolo scored three of the Barbarians' tries and added nine conversions for a tally of 33 points in the 73-19 victory over Leicester. It was a record win in fixtures between the teams and a record by the Tongan star for the Baa-Baas against the Tigers, who were without a dozen of their international players.

Pontypridd's Steele Lewis and Greg Prosser helped the Barbarians recover after trailing 28-7 to register a notable 40-33 success against Combined Services at Portsmouth in November. Then Ponty players figured prominently when the Baa-Baas defeated East Midlands 50-40 at Northampton in March. Paul John, Martyn Williams, Steele Lewis and Matthew McCarthy were the Ponty contingent. Other Welsh players in action were Newport's Sven Cronk and former Bridgend prop David Rees, now playing for Rugby. Remarkably, Rees was appearing 10 years after his original selection: he had withdrawn to attend his brother's wedding.

For the first time since the Barbarians began in 1890-91 they did not play in Wales.

# TOP TEAMS THREATEN STRIKE ACTION OVER WRU FUNDING

Wales's premier division clubs warned of strike action in a desperate move to obtain further funding from the WRU. Chairman of the top clubs, Eddie Jones, of Pontypridd, stressed that the clubs were prepared to refuse to play fixtures planned for Saturday, April 18, 1998.

The clubs presented the WRU with a business plan and emphasised that each of the eight leading clubs needed £750,000 per year from outside sources to meet the commitments of the professional game. Under the existing agreement, clubs received only £400,000 from the WRU in a season. Chairman Jones insisted, "There is more money in the pot which should be coming to us. The money we are receiving is only half the amount we would have if we shared all the proceeds raised by the tournaments we play in. We are not asking for anything that is not ours. The money we are getting is insufficient to run professional sides."

Mr Jones asserted, "Two or three of the clubs in the premier division are in dire trouble. They would not be if they were getting the money they should from the WRU. Unless they get it, they won't survive the summer. The genuine feeling is that unless they get the funding they are entitled to, they will pull the plug, cancel all the players' contracts and revert to amateur status. That would mean a lot of players going out of Wales and the union losing a lot of revenue. But it is a realistic option. We are in the same situation as the referees, when they could not make any headway until they resorted to strike action. We are not messing around."

Bridgend chairman Derrick King had an equally ominous view – "Drastic action is needed for all eight premier division clubs to survive until next season." First division clubs also expressed urgent concern regarding funding, protesting that they received only £75,000 each per season.

Mr Jones met WRU officials on April 14 to discuss the worrying financial position and the need for an acceptable fixture structure that would bring back the lost crowds. The strike threat was averted when the clubs secured significant pledges that the situation would be improved. WRU funding of £40,000 per club per month would continue through the summer.

Cardiff had not benefited from any union funding because of their dispute with the WRU over the imposition of a 10-year loyalty contract. The club refused to sign up, considering it a restraint on them and took the case to the High Court, with a hearing scheduled for November 1998. Other clubs had to agree to the condition or they could not pay their players.

Cardiff chairman Peter Thomas called for the WRU to be reshaped and controlled by a small board of directors. He urged a special general meeting of the WRU to replace committee members with a more professional system. "We no longer have faith in Glanmor Griffiths as chairman of the

WRU, or any of the executive body," he said. "They are clinging to power and destroying our national game."

At an extraordinary general meeting of the WRU on May 24, 1998, the union's proposal that participation in the premier division should be conditional on each club signing a 10-year loyalty clause was approved by the vast majority of the 370 delegates. Only five voted against with six abstentions. Glanmor Griffiths said, "Hopefully, now Cardiff will change direction and come on board by agreeing to sign a binding agreement to the union. I only hope that Cardiff realise the full membership is behind our request."

## WELSH RUGBY 'A SHAMBLES'

But Cardiff showed no inclination to submit, although it had cost the club and union around £200,000 in legal fees, with further substantial expense looming. Cardiff expressed a view that they would be better served by joining England's clubs in the Allied Dunbar premiership. They declared that they saw their future in England if the WRU clubs were ready to expel them.

The WRU intimated that they would be prepared to consider paying Cardiff retrospective funding if they complied with the loyalty condition. The club had not received the £400,000 paid to other premier clubs for the 1997-98 season and could lose another £250,000 up to the time of the High Court action.

Newport director of rugby Tommy David, who resigned in December for family and work reasons, considered Welsh rugby "a complete shambles." He stated, "There are so many Mickey Mouse games, which mean absolutely nothing." He urged that the premier division of eight teams be expanded to 10 or 12 to bring back supporters.

---

### JPR STILL MOST-CAPPED IN BIG GAMES

Full back JPR Williams won all his 55 caps for Wales against Five Nations countries, Australia, South Africa and New Zealand. Since then, caps have been awarded for appearances against less powerful rugby countries. Wing Ieuan Evans, who holds the Welsh record of 72 caps overall, played 54 times against the major countries and appeared in 18 matches against other opposition. Lineout forward Gareth Llewellyn won 42 of his 62 caps against top countries and is the most-capped forward.

Robert Jones is the most-capped scrum half overall with 54, but 44 were against the big guns, which puts Gareth Edwards top of the major league list because his 53 caps were all against heavyweight opposition. Neil Jenkins is third most-capped Welsh player with 57; 40 of those were at outside half, nine at full back and eight in the centre. But of his 40 appearances at fly half, only 28 were against major countries – which means Cliff Morgan is most-capped in that position against the top teams with 29.

# PONTY'S JENKS WINS DUEL
# WITH CARDIFF'S JARVIS

Pontypridd were the winners of the inaugural WRU Challenge Trophy when they defeated Cardiff 15-10 in the final at Sardis Road on March 28, 1998. The tournament was designed to fill the void created by the reduction of the premier division to just eight teams; but the competition, even with the injection of seven overseas teams, failed to fuel the imagination of the rugby public and attendances at the majority of matches were depressingly poor. Indeed, the tourney was viewed with derision by some and a number of respected officials and coaches were unimpressed. It was rated a Mickey Mouse event. There was confusion at the start when the WRU ruled no conversion kicks would be taken; but clubs raised objections and the decision was swiftly reversed.

Pontypridd and Cardiff also objected to playing the final at a neutral venue, so it was decided on the toss of a coin and Ponty enjoyed home advantage with a crowd of 5,000 to see a scoring duel between home skipper Neil Jenkins and ex-Ponty starlet Lee Jarvis. Jenkins won with five penalty goals to a Jarvis try, conversion and penalty goal. Though there were no Pontypridd tries, they were well pleased at finishing as the only team with a 100 per cent record in the tournament. "The boys put in a massive effort," said Jenkins. "We would have liked to have scored a few tries, but it wasn't one of those matches."

There was surprise, not to say amazement, that Cardiff left out Jarvis from their starting line-up; but he was brought on after 23 minutes to replace Bob Ross at outside half; and inside two minutes drove through tackles to get the ball down for the only try on the narrow side. His conversion was superbly judged for a 7-6 lead after Jenkins's two penalty shots. Jarvis extended the advantage to 10-6 with a straight penalty goal, but that was the end of Cardiff's points collection.

Jenkins found the target with two further penalty kicks and it was 12-10 to the home side at the interval and thoroughly justified. Andre Barnard's disallowed drop-goal right at the start no longer rankled: Ponty were on course for victory. Jarvis missed with two long-range penalty attempts in the second half, and the only other addition was Jenkins's fifth penalty goal when a loose lip gave him an extra 10 yards. It is said that referee Derek Bevan can hear a caterpillar crawl! Jenkins exchanged jerseys with Jarvis and went up to receive the trophy wearing Cardiff colours! Cardiff's woe was enhanced when Robert Howley twisted an ankle in diving at Paul John after 53 minutes, but he recovered in time to lead Wales against France at Wembley a week later.

**PONTYPRIDD:** Andre Barnard; Gareth Wyatt, Steele Lewis, Dafydd James, David Manley; Neil Jenkins (capt), Paul John; Aled Griffiths, Andrew Lamerton, Mike Griffiths,

Stuart Roy, Sean Bundy, Geraint Lewis, Dale McIntosh, Martyn Williams. Reps: Greg Prosser for Bundy, Matthew Lloyd for G Lewis.

**CARDIFF:** Craig Morgan; Gareth Thomas, Leigh Davies, Mike Hall, Simon Hill; Bob Ross, Robert Howley; Andrew Lewis, Jonathan Humphreys (capt), Lyndon Mustoe, John Tait, Tony Rees, Greg Kacala, Emyr Lewis, Jamie Ringer. Reps: Lee Jarvis for Ross, Steve Williams for Ringer, Justin Thomas for Morgan, Jason Hewlett for Howley, Derwyn Jones for Tait, Spencer John for A Lewis.

*Referee:* Derek Bevan (Clydach).

**SEMI-FINALS:** Pontypridd were without Neil Jenkins, recovering from an eye socket injury suffered against Scotland, but their backs proved too smart for Neath in a 30-15 success at Sardis Road. The visitors' points came from tries by No 8 Lee Jones and Tristan Davies, with a conversion and penalty goal from Chris John. Flanker Geraint John (2), Dafydd James, Gareth Wyatt and Kevin Morgan crossed for Ponty. Matthew McCarthy converted one and added a penalty goal.

Llanelli led 23-3 at half time at Cardiff, where the home side gave a drab display until they wore down the brighter Scarlets to score late tries and win 31-23. Owain Williams, Bob Ross, Jarvis and Steve Williams snapped up Cardiff tries; Jarvis converted four and put over a penalty shot. Frano Botica and Darril Williams were Llanelli try-getters. Botica converted both and was on target with three penalty kicks.

The overseas contingent, which were not scheduled to play in the closing stages, whatever their results, comprised Rugby Canada, Namibia, Spain, Northern Transvaal and three Argentine sides, Cordoba, Rosario and Tucuman. Only Tucuman won a game: they succeeded 22-10 at Ebbw Vale. Tucuman drew 40-all at Llanelli and N Transvaal drew 34-all at Swansea.

Gareth Wyatt scored three tries as Pontypridd defeated Namibia 34-3. The visitors had full back Attie Samuelson ordered off for a wild kick. Matthew de Maid's two tries helped Ponty topple Tucuman 40-15. Six penalty goals by Neil Jenkins doomed Northern Transvaal 18-0. The Bulls included nine of the team that had beaten the 1997 Lions. Lee Jarvis topped 100 points in the tourney. He contributed 25 points for Cardiff to hit Rugby Canada 45-22; then supplied 18 points in the 53-16 verdict against Rosario. He crossed for two tries during the 52-21 success against Cordoba.

---

### ONLY ONE WIN BY OVERSEAS TEAMS

**Wales coach Kevin Bowring praised the introduction of the Challenge Trophy. He commented, "The tournament certainly has helped us to develop players. There was a great cross-section of styles from the international teams that came to play in Wales and our players can only have benefited from that."**

**Pontypridd rugby director Cenydd Thomas pointed out, "The fact that the Welsh clubs lost only one match against the seven overseas teams shows the game in Wales is far more buoyant than some might say."**

---

Neil Jenkins, Pontypridd captain, receives the WRU Challenge Trophy from WRU president Sir Tasker Watkins after victory in the final against Cardiff. Jenkins is wearing a Cardiff jersey!

*Picture: Huw Evans Picture Agency, Cardiff*

# Sparkling display tames England in this first 'A' team contest

Wales A won three of their five matches during 1997-98. Gareth Wyatt and Martyn Williams each snapped up two tries in the 36-21 victory over Romania A at Sardis Road. Gareth Llewellyn also crossed and Lee Davies converted one try and kicked three penalty goals. Byron Hayward was the star with 26 points as Wales A won their first meeting with England A 41-22 at Leicester. Hayward, Garin Jenkins, scrum half Andy Moore and Dafydd James crossed and Hayward converted three tries and put over five penalty shots. Lock Andy Moore was cited for a punch on Ben Clarke and banned for one match.

Scotland rocked Wales to 18-10 defeat at Rodney Parade in atrocious conditions. "Our lineout was a major disappointment," said manager David Pickering. Matthew Lloyd scored the home try; Hayward converted and kicked a penalty goal. Ireland led 17-6, but a storming second half performance saw Wales A 42-27 winners. Replacement David Weatherley collected two tries to turn the game. Arwel Thomas scored a try, converted four and landed three penalty goals for 22 points and scrum half Andy Moore and Chris Wyatt also crossed. France A took it 27-18 at Bridgend. Chris Wyatt and Dean Thomas scored Welsh tries, Arwel Thomas converted one and fired in two penalty goals.

**WALES A 36, ROMANIA A 21. WALES A:** L Davies (Swansea); G Wyatt (Pontypridd), D James (Pontypridd), J Lewis (Pontypridd), N Walker (Cardiff); M Lewis (Bridgend), Rhodri Jones (Swansea); I Buckett (Swansea), R McBryde (Llanelli), C Anthony (Swansea), Gareth Llewellyn (Harlequins, capt), N Watkins (Neath), A Gibbs (Llanelli), C Wyatt (Llanelli), M Williams (Pontypridd). Reps: D Case (Neath) for Davies, M Lloyd (Pontypridd) for Watkins.

**ENGLAND A 22, WALES A 41. WALES A:** K Morgan (Pontypridd); G Wyatt (Pontypridd), J Lewis (Pontypridd), M Taylor (Swansea), D James (Pontypridd); B Hayward (Ebbw Vale), A Moore (Richmond); A Griffiths (Pontypridd), G Jenkins (Swansea), C Anthony (Swansea), Andy Moore (Swansea), S Roy (Pontypridd), M Lloyd (Pontypridd), C Wyatt (Llanelli), K Jones (Ebbw Vale, capt). Reps: V Cooper (Llanelli) for Roy, I Boobyer (Neath) for Lloyd.

**WALES A 10, SCOTLAND A 18. WALES A:** J Thomas (Cardiff); G Wyatt (Pontypridd), N Boobyer (Llanelli), J Lewis (Pontypridd), D. James (Pontypridd); R Hayward (Ebbw Vale), A Moore (Richmond, capt); A Griffiths (Pontypridd), B Williams (Richmond), C Anthony (Swansea), Gareth Llewellyn (Harlequins), C Stephens (Bridgend), M Lloyd (Pontypridd), C Wyatt (Llanelli), M Williams (Pontypridd). Reps: R McBryde (Llanelli) for B Williams, I Boobyer (Neath) for Lloyd.

**IRELAND A 27, WALES A 42. WALES A:** J Thomas (Cardiff); G Wyatt (Pontypridd), J Lewis (Pontypridd), D. James (Pontypridd), R Rees (Swansea); A Thomas (Swansea), A Moore (Richmond, capt); A Griffiths (Pontypridd), R McBryde (Llanelli), C Anthony (Swansea), Gareth Llewellyn (Harlequins), C Stephens (Bridgend), M Lloyd (Pontypridd), C Wyatt (Llanelli), M Williams (Pontypridd). Reps: D Weatherley (Swansea) for J Thomas, C Warlow (Llanelli) for G Wyatt, N Eynon (Pontypridd) for Griffiths, I Gough (Newport) for Stephens, I Boobyer (Neath) for C Wyatt.

**WALES A 18, FRANCE A 27. WALES A:** J Thomas (Cardiff); R Rees (Swansea), M Taylor (Swansea), J Lewis (Pontypridd), S Hill (Cardiff); A Thomas (Swansea), A Moore (Richmond, capt); A Griffiths (Pontypridd), R McBryde (Llanelli), C Anthony (Swansea), Gareth Llewellyn (Harlequins), C Stephens (Bridgend), M Lloyd (Pontypridd), C Wyatt (Llanelli), I Boobyer (Neath). Reps: D Weatherley (Swansea) for Lewis, D Llewellyn (Ebbw Vale) for Moore, I Gough (Newport) for Stephens, D Thomas (Swansea) for Boobyer.

# Hero Gareth saves his side
# from that dreaded whitewash

Wales averted a nightmare whitewash for the season with a splendid 14-3 success at Waterton Cross thanks to hero Gareth Cull. The full back provided all the points with a thrilling late try after he had kicked three penalty goals. Basic errors faulted Wales when they crashed to 46-7 defeat in their opening game against England U-21 at Worcester. There was just one try for Wales, by hooker Chris Wells, which Lee Jarvis converted. "We haven't any excuses," admitted skipper Jarvis.

A penalty goal by Jarvis presented Wales with their only score as Scotland U-21 won 10-3 despite the Welsh pack securing some 70 per cent of the possession. The game was scheduled for Virginia Park, but the Caerphilly pitch was waterlogged. The match was switched to BSC ground at Llanwern, where conditions were still daunting. Fly half Chris Paterson scored all Scotland's points with a try, conversion and penalty goal.

The third defeat came 27-25 to Ireland U-21 at Donnybrook, where centre Steve Winn was sent off by referee Ed Murray after a massed brawl. Chris Wells supplied the Welsh try which Jarvis converted; and when Jarvis put over his sixth penalty goal six minutes from the end it looked as if Wales would win. Alas, Gareth McCullough fired over a penalty shot with the last kick of the match in the fourth minute of injury time.

**ENGLAND U-21 46, WALES U-21 7. WALES U-21:** C Morgan (Cardiff); S Greenaway (Bridgend), S Winn (Bridgend), T Davies (Neath), R Shorney (UWIC); L Jarvis (Cardiff, capt), A Jenkins (Bridgend); I Poley (UWIC), C Wells (Swansea), K Jones (Cwmllynfell), W James (Pontypool), I Gough (Newport), G Newman (Treorchy), M Cook (UWIC), A Grabham (Swansea). Reps: S Jones (Llanelli) for Davies, D Case (Neath) for Shorney, G Lucas (Bridgend) for Newman, P Matthews (UWIC).

**WALES U-21 3, SCOTLAND U-21 10. WALES U-21:** G Cull (Bridgend); M Giraud (London Welsh), S Winn (Bridgend), T Davies (Neath), S Greenaway (Bridgend); L Jarvis (Cardiff, capt), G Downes (Bridgend); I Thomas (Ebbw Vale), C Wells (Swansea), I Poley (UWIC), W James (Pontypool), I Gough (Newport), A Grabham ( Bridgend), M Cook (UWIC), A Lloyd (Merthyr). Reps: G Thomas (Bridgend) for Wells, N Hennessy (Swansea) for Poley.

**IRELAND U-21 27, WALES U-21 25. WALES U-21:** G Cull (Bridgend); S Greenaway (Bridgend), S Winn (Bridgend), T Davies (Neath), M Giraud (London Welsh); L Jarvis (Cardiff, capt), G Downes (Bridgend); I Thomas (Ebbw Vale), C Wells (Swansea), I Poley (UWIC), V Cooper (Llanelli), W James (Pontypool), A Grabham (Bridgend), A Lloyd (Merthyr), M Cook (UWIC). Reps: J Griffiths (Swansea) for James, R Field (Pontypool) for Grabham, S Jones (Llanelli) for Lloyd.

**WALES U-21 14, FRANCE U-21 3. WALES U-21:** G Cull (Bridgend); S Greenaway (Bridgend), T Davies (Neath), S Jones (Llanelli), M Giraud (London Welsh); L Jarvis (Cardiff, capt), G Downes (Bridgend); I Thomas (Ebbw Vale), C Wells (Swansea), I Poley (UWIC), V Cooper (Llanelli), W James (Pontypool), A Grabham (Bridgend), R Field (Pontypool), M Cook (UWIC).

# Lively Luke's breaks baffle French for Welsh victory

A dynamic display by Wales Schools to defeat France Schools 28-25 at the Gnoll in February was the highlight of the senior group performances during 1997-98. French officials were greatly impressed and offered unstinted praise. The French boys snapped up 12 points during a late recovery, but they had been outplayed. Fly half Luke Richards proved the star with incisive running, perceptive kicking and shrewd link work. He kicked three penalty goals and converted two of the tries by Rhys Williams, Ryan Powell and Alix Popham.

Wales lost 26-13 to NSW High Schools at Glamorgan Wanderers ground in December (David Brown and Gethin Worgan scored home tries and Worgan kicked a penalty goal), but defeated Scotland 54-0 at Brynteg School ground in January (switched from waterlogged SW Police Ground). This was a record Welsh score at this age group with 10 tries. Centre Rhys Williams collected a hat-trick and other tries came from skipper Adam Jones, Adrian Chiffi, all the front row of Ian Jones, Dean Colclough and Gary Powell, and two from Richard Johnson. One each was converted by Jason Larkman and Luke Richards.

## ENGLAND STEAL IT BY A POINT

After losing to Wales Youth 33-12 and then registering that superb victory against the always powerful French, the senior Welsh boys were pipped 11-10 by England Schools at Portsmouth in April. Rhys Williams scored the Welsh try and Luke Richards converted and fired in a penalty shot. Skipper Adam Jones suffered concussion. Another defeat followed, this time 13-6 against Ireland in Galway. Luke Richards put over two penalty goals.

**WALES SCHOOLS (senior group) v France Schools:** Richard Johnson (Neath Coll); Jason Larkman (Neath Coll), Rhys Williams (Cowbridge), Lee Banfield (Swansea Coll), David Brown (St. David's Coll, Cardiff); Luke Richards (Neath Coll), Ryan Powell (Pontypool Coll); Ian Jones (Tredegar), Dean Colclough (Morriston), Gary Powell (Llandovery Coll), James Bater (Brynteg), Adam Jones (Olchfa, capt), Adrian Chiffi (Greenhill), Alix Popham (Cross Keys Coll), Mike Owen (Bryncelynnog). Reps: Andrew George (Tasker Milward), Matthew Howells (Pontypool Coll), Kevin Lewis (Ebbw Vale), Greg Woods (Cwmcarn), Phil Wheeler (Pencoed).

The two fixtures Wales Youth most want to win each season resulted in defeats. Although the Welsh forwards surprised French Juniors in Limoges during March, there were no Welsh tries, just two Richard Davies penalty goals as the home side triumphed 15-6. David Skrela, son of French national coach and former back row star Jean-Claude Skrela, scored one of the two tries for the winners.

England Colts displayed superior forward cohesion to register a 29-20 success (also in the under-19 group) in muddy conditions at Rodney Parade in April. England scored four tries to two and no-one disputed their command. Wales took the lead with a Richard Davies penalty shot before the aggressive visitors forged ahead. Richard Davies added another penalty goal and converted tries by captain Gareth Williams, who always led with inspiring example, and centre Ben Jeffries.

The season opened with 19-6 victory over Portugal Youth (under-18 group) in Oporto during January. Centre Stephen Thomas, released by Bradford Bulls as the first RL professional to play for Wales Youth, made the break for the opening try by wing Mark Jones (Builth Wells). Hooker James Jones also crossed and Mark Lovell kicked three penalty goals. Physically stronger, the Youth defeated Wales Schools 33-12 at St. Helen's. There were Youth tries by Gavin Cooper, Chris Landry, Gareth King and Jamie Evans plus a penalty try. Gareth Bowen converted four. For Schools, David Brown and Dwayne Peel were try-getters and Luke Richards converted one.

Gareth Bowen was the dominating figure in 29-13 victory over Romania at Neath and kicked a penalty goal and converted three of the tries by Gareth Cooper, Daniel Rogers, Landry and Ryan Jones. Ireland jolted Wales 15-0 at Llandovery before success returned 23-14 over Italy at Rhymney. Bowen fired in two penalty goals and converted one of the tries by Cooper, Emyr Davies and Popham. Finally, Wales won 13-11 against Scotland in Glasgow with a try by Builth wing Mark Jones two minutes from the end. Peter Williams also crossed and Peter Burridge kicked a penalty goal.

**WALES YOUTH v French Juniors:** Gareth King (Newport); James Taylor (Neath Colts), Matthew Watkins (Newport), Ben Jeffries (Pontypool), Chris Batsford (Glais); Richard Davies (Neath), Andrew Jenkins (Bridgend); Duncan Jones (Neath Colts), Gareth Williams (UWIC, capt), Gareth Mason (Ebbw Vale), John Pemberton (Neath Colts), Scott Morgan (Neath Colts), Chris Hughes (Llanelli), Mark Prosser (Pontypridd), Darren Bowles (Llanelli Wands). Reps: Chris Landry (Pontypool), Gareth Bowen (Bridgend), Gareth Cooper (Pencoed), Rhys Bowen (Abertillery), Brett Scrivens (Bridgend).

Wales Under-16 won all four matches, including two A team games. It was desperately close at Twickenham in March with Wales stealing a 13-12 verdict through a try by outside half Nicky Robinson and vital goal points from skipper Paul Fisher. He put over a conversion and two penalty shots. Prop Owain Ford enjoyed the rare satisfaction of two victories over England: he had figured in the side that won 23-11 at Bridgend the previous season. The Wales A side defeated England A 13-10 at Imber Court as Stuart Thomas kicked two penalty goals and converted the try by centre Owen Evans. No 8 Ian Hughes captained the Wales A team.

The Welsh boys were 27-7 winners against Portugal at Llanelli in April with five tries. Skipper Paul Fisher, Tom Roberts, Paul Griffiths, D David and Gavin Henson obtained the tries and Fisher converted one. Wales A defeated the Portugal A team 32-7 at Cardiff RFC ground with Stuart Thomas swooping for two tries. Daniel Evans, R Mustoe and M John also crossed. Stuart Thomas kicked a penalty goal and converted a try and M John added a conversion.

**WALES SCHOOLS (under-16) v England Schools:** Tom Roberts (Glantaf); Shabaj Ali (Dwr-y-Felin), Paul Fisher (Ysgol Strade, capt), Scott Williams (Llantarnam), Geraint Williams (Glantaf); Nicky Robinson (Glantaf), Ryan Williams (Amman Valley); Owain Ford (Llanharri), Christian Richards (Birchgrove, Swansea), Lee May (Morriston), Paul Griffiths (Birchgrove, Swansea), Craig Jones (Maes-y-Dderwen), Stephen Thomas (Lampeter CS), Gareth Williams (Maes-y-Yrfa), John Clarke (Bryngwyn CS). Reps: Aled James (Rhymney Valley), Ashley Grainger (Blaenau Gwent), Robert Snowdon-Taylor (New Coll, Cardiff).

# Just one defeat, but it puts Wales into ninth place

Disappointingly, Wales Youth finished in ninth spot in the FIRA Junior World Cup in 1998 despite losing only one game. That defeat came in the opening fixture 23-19 to Canada in Millau. It shocked the Welsh team, who led 16-10 at one stage, but lacked purpose and seemed to take success for granted. Dunvant hooker Craig Hawkins scored the Welsh try and Gareth Bowen converted and kicked four penalty goals. Canada went on to third place play-off, where they lost 68-0 to Argentina.

Wales were 20-7 winners against Scotland in Rodez in a shoot-out to decide who would finish bottom in their pool. Craig Hawkins dodged through for a cheeky try when he took a tap-penalty and Chris Landry and Gareth Cooper also crossed. Skipper Bowen converted one and landed a penalty goal. This set Wales up for a 39-10 success against Japan in Balma, near Toulouse. Centre Cerith Rees, scrum half Gareth Cooper, wing Emyr Jones, centre Jamie Evans and flanker John Stenner crossed for tries and Bowen added 14 goal points.

In their final match, Wales defeated Romania 34-19 in the play-off for ninth position. Gareth Cooper snapped up two tries and others came from full back Gareth King, wing Emyr Davies and fly half Bowen, who fired over two conversions.

Ireland were the surprise winners of the tournament, beating favourites France, who were expecting to win the cup for the eighth time in 12 years. The final in Toulouse produced a remarkable score of 18-0 for the enthusiastic Irish youngsters in this under-19 event.

---

**Varsity Match**

## WALNE WHIPS IN FOR SPARKLING TRY

Welshman Nick Walne went over for a fine solo try to help Cambridge University win the Bowring Bowl for a fourth consecutive year in front of a full Twickenham house on December 9, 1997. It was 29-17 in a thrilling tussle and critics praised the Light Blues' pack for their most impressive display during the four years of supremacy. Richard Bramley, Mark Denney and Paul Surridge were the other try scorers for Cambridge. New Zealander Surridge converted three and kicked a penalty goal for a tally of 14 points. Kevin Spicer and Nick Booth crossed for Oxford and David Kelaher converted both tries and put over a penalty shot.

# Newport's superb Scott puts the skids under Cardiff

Outside half Scott Mitchell was the star of the Welsh Youth Dragon Capital Cup final. He scored 24 points as Newport defeated Cardiff 29-17 at the Gnoll on April 27, 1998. Mitchell provided all the first half points for a 19-9 lead and controlled events coolly with methodical kicking and shrewdly taken decisions. His try was a particularly smart piece of opportunism as he jinked through from some 20 yards. He finished with a try, two conversions and five penalty goals. Centre Matthew Watkins was the other try-getter.

Although they were without their influential back row Alix Popham, injured playing for Wales Youth against Scotland, Newport were always in command of the situation. "This was the victory we really wanted to complete a notable season of success," said Newport official Dylan Parker.

Cardiff did not have anyone to produce the overall generalship of Mitchell, but skipper and second row James Roach set a tireless example. Their only try came from wing David Brown on a long-distance run three minutes from the end. Matthew Maunder kicked four penalty goals.

Llanelli and District won the MK Electric Cup 8-5 against Amman Valley at Haverfordwest and Ogwr defeated Neath and District 33-25 at Dunvant to take the DG Griffiths Cup.

---

### MARK JONES AND BATH'S YATES BANNED

Ebbw Vale's Mark Jones had to complete his 28 days' suspension after the Court of Appeal overturned a High Court order imposed on the WRU concerning their procedural process for players' appeals on sendings-off. Following criticism from the High Court the WRU amended their procedure. The No 8 was sent off for fighting in the Swansea fixture at Ebbw Vale in November 1997.

Bath's Kevin Yates was banned for six months by the RFU after he was found guilty of biting London Scottish flanker Simon Fenn in their cup-tie on January 10, 1998. Fenn needed more than 25 stitches in his left ear when a scrum collapsed. Bath suspended Yates while the RFU conducted three separate hearings and spent a total of 25 hours of deliberations.

---

# Rip-roaring Rhys makes it a happy day for try-scoring props

It was a special scoring day for props at Ashton Gate on May 23, 1998. Before Llanelli on-loan prop Martyn Madden collected the only try of the SWALEC Cup final to defeat Ebbw Vale, Bridgend and District Schools' prop Rhys Watkins pounced for two tries for his side to take the D C Thomas Cup 19-7 against Rhymney Valley Schools. This under-11 age group cup, sponsored by *The Western Mail*, was staged as usual as the curtain-raiser to the SWALEC Cup and Bridgend won for a record 13th time.

Rhymney Valley forged ahead when Michael Diggle converted a penalty try; but Nicholas Roberts equalised when he converted a penalty try before prop Watkins went over twice and Roberts added the points to one of them.

David Tame (Bishop of Llandaff) crossed for the winning try in the last few minutes for Cardiff to edge Swansea 24-23 in the first leg of the Dewar Shield at St. Helen's. It set Cardiff up to collect the shield for the 19th time as they triumphed 15-9 in the second leg. Martin Johnson (2) and Nick Harrison scored Cardiff's first leg tries; Tame, Gareth Delve and Mark Burge crossed in the second leg. James Morgan and Richie Rees were Swansea's first leg try-getters; James Horner kicked three penalty goals in the return leg.

Neath Tertiary College defeated Brynteg (Bridgend) 39-0 to win the Welsh Schools' (under-18) Cup for the fifth time with tries by Paul Bamsey (2), Kevin James (2), Gareth Noble, Carl Bowen and skipper Mark Davies. Luke Richards converted two tries.

West Wales were 15-5 winners over East Wales (under-11 group) at the Brewery Field. Darren Daniel, Stuart Allen and Scott Theye scored West tries; Sam Sullivan crossed for the East. Parc-y-Tywyn (Llanelli) and Tynewydd (Newbridge) drew in the final of the national 10-a-side tourney (junior group) at Bridgend in *The Western Mail*-sponsored event.

## REVENGE FOR NEW ZEALAND SCHOOLS

Welsh Schools' under-18 won three matches and lost three on their 1997 summer tour of New Zealand. The Test was lost 45-10 at Christchurch on August 9. Wales were disrupted by injuries, but took the lead with a Gareth Bowen drop-shot before replacement centre Ian Higgins was put over from Gareth Cooper's forceful run. Cerith Rees converted. It was revenge for NZ who had lost to Welsh Schools 17-11 in Christchurch in 1990.

**WELSH SCHOOLS v New Zealand:** Rhys Williams (Cowbridge); Daniel Rogers (Y Strade), Andrew Merrett (Cowbridge), Jamie Evans (Gowerton), Chris Landry (Pontypool College); Gareth Bowen (Neath Coll), Andrew Jenkins (Neath Coll); Duncan Jones (Neath Coll), Gareth Williams (Brynteg, capt), Gary Powell (Llandovery Coll), James Bater (Brynteg), Adam Jones (Olchfa), Adrian Chiffi (Greenhill, Tenby), Christopher Hughes (Amman Valley), Paul Williams (Olchfa). Reps: Gareth Cooper (Pencoed), Cerith Rees (Llandovery Coll), Ian Higgins (Whitchurch), Craig Hawkins (Gowerton), Marc Troake (Barry), Phillip Wheeler (Pencoed), Edward Rees (Cowbridge).

# Gwion's smart hat-trick is UWIC highlight in first Euro Cup

University of Wales Institute, Cardiff entered into the spirit of adventure that made the inaugural final of *The Times* European Students' Cup a thrilling event as Toulouse University were 52-37 winners at Cardiff RFC ground on March 17, 1998. Gwion Bowen scored a sparkling hat-trick of tries in the space of 12 minutes for UWIC to hold more experienced Toulouse to 27-all at half time.

But the power of the French pack proved decisive in the later stages after Matthew Cook and Dai Camborne had crossed for further home tries. Jonathan Williams converted three and kicked two penalty goals. David Darricarrere contributed 22 points for the winners, including one of their seven tries.

Swansea University defeated Northumbria University 17-3 at Twickenham on March 25, 1998 to take the British Universities Sports Association Rugby Cup. Coach Stan Addicott, a legend in student rugby in Wales, had seen Swansea lose seven times in the final; but at last he was rewarded and his team won worthy winners with tries by prop Wayne Meredith and Lee Davies, who crossed in the fourth minute of injury time. Lee Davies converted both tries and kicked a penalty goal. Swansea had put out UWIC in the BUSA semi-final, but UWIC second string won the BUSA second teams cup.

England Students were 24-15 winners against Wales Students at Blackheath. Skipper Rhodri Jones (Trinity Coll) and Mark O'Kelly (UWIC) scored Welsh tries. Peter Roberts (UWIC) converted one and kicked a penalty goal. Another failure followed when France Students triumphed 15-6 at Old Deer Park. Owen Jones put over two Welsh penalty kicks.

Wales Universities battled back from 15-10 down at half time to topple England Universities 24-15 at Iffley Road, Oxford. Tries came from Jonathan Williams, Gavin Evans, Gareth Cooper (all UWIC) and Peter Donovan (Swansea). Williams converted two. Then it was 7-0 success against Scotland Universities at UWIC ground, though the game was abandoned in the second half following an injury to a Scots' forward. Peter Short (UWIC) crossed and Williams converted.

Swansea retained the Firkin Brewery Trophy in the second Welsh Varsity Match at St. Helen's, defeating Cardiff 49-13. The match raised £5,000 for Oxfam. Tries for the holders came from Owen Jones, Gareth Thomas, Geraint John, Rhodri Griffiths, Neil Hennessy and Ed Lewsey, plus a penalty try. Lee Davies converted six and Dafydd Harries converted one. Cardiff's try-getter was Gareth Winkle. Adrian Twinning converted one and Richard Davies landed two penalty goals.

# LLANDOVERY'S FIRST TOVALI TITLE AND RECORD SCORE

*by* ROY WOODWARD

A record 61 clubs competed in the Tovali-sponsored West Wales Cup when the first round was played before the end of September, and culminated in Division One side Llandovery lifting the Tovali cup some eight months later. After one of the most entertaining finals in the cup's history, the Drovers beat renowned cup experts Seven Sisters 52-34 at Stradey Park – a record score for the Tovali Final. Few sides score six tries in a final only to lose, as did Seven Sisters, but Llandovery scored two more tries to lift the cup for the first time in their history.

Both sides had experienced an exhausting season, but the Division 4 outfit called on their marvellous Swalec Cup experiences to match the eventual winners all the way. Llandovery half backs Aled Williams and man of the match Jamie Roberts contributed to a fine victory with Roberts crossing for two tries and Aled Williams supplying 13 points. Two young names for the future are the respective full backs. Llandovery's Emyr Lewis, son of former Wales coach Allan Lewis, and Seven's exciting Andrew James.

Seven accounted for plucky Division 7 side Bynea in the semi-finals after brave Bynea had led at one stage 16-3. Bynea, coached by former Dunvant coach Brian Thomas, saw inspirational skipper Mark Cook cross for a try, though Seven eventually won a pulsating semi-final thanks to a late penalty try after wing Dafydd Francis had scored Seven's first touch down. Full back James kicked 11 points.

Thomas's former club Dunvant went out to Llandovery in the other semi-final, Dunvant losing 24-7 in appalling conditions in which Aled Williams was in superb form with some punishing touchline kicking and also scoring a try. Full back Emyr Lewis and centre Cerith Rees, following an interception, also touched down to put Llandovery into the final.

If Bynea were the competition's dark horses, then Swansea valley side, Ystalyfera were also cup heroes when they beat former winners Felinfoel 19-14 in round 3 and also accounted for Division 3 side Carmarthen Quins 20-13 in round 2. Holders Kidwelly were knocked out 11-8 by Pontyberem in the second round. An Emyr Lewis try and two penalty goals by Pontyberem's Matthew Rowe did the damage. Tumble's disappointing season saw the 12 times cup winners also go out in round 2, losing 24-5 at eventual winners Llandovery.

**LLANDOVERY:** Emyr Lewis; Arwel Rowlands, Huw Thomas, Cerith Rees, Stuart Doyle; Aled Williams, Jamie Roberts; Andrew Jones, John Hughes, Matthew Monahan, Hefin Morgan, Colin Lewis, Mark Lewis, Paul Jones (capt), Chris Davies. Reps: Carwyn Jones, Adrian Davies, Hywel James, Dorian Williams, John Westgarth, Gareth Thomas.

**SEVEN SISTERS:** Andrew James; Kevin Lewis, Hywel Evans (capt), Keiron Thomas, Dafydd Francis; Grant Hughes, Lloyd Paget; Nigel Hickey, Lee Griffiths, Ian Beech, James Davies, Jeff Davies, Ian Watts, Matthew Waring, Anthony Thomas. Reps: Steven Lewis, Mark Jordan, Tudor Rees, Jonathan Evans, Darren Gravell, Geraint Lewis.

Tumble's cup misery was compounded by a second successive league season that saw this once formidable team end without a single Division 4 win, while Vardre can look forward to life in Division 3 after pipping Gilfach Goch to the

Division 4 title. Tumble, however, can now start the not inconsiderable task of rebuilding their team in Division 5 (West) after winning 19 of their 22 games. Coached by former Tumble coach Clive John, who has decided to retire, the coaching duties now will be the responsibility of two other former Tumble stalwarts – brothers Gareth and Arwel Davies. Llangennech have a number of up and coming young players who could make their mark in the higher division, particularly outside half Mark Jones, No 8 Gareth Roberts, full back Geraint John and brother Hefin John, who was top try scorer on the wing for the Division 5 winners.

After just missing out on promotion to Division 1, Whitland gained some consolation by winning the Silcox-sponsored Pembrokeshire Cup after beating old rivals Tenby United 24-14 in a hard-fought final at Narberth's ground. The heatwave conditions produced some fine open rugby with no quarter asked or given. Both finalists had recorded home wins against the other; the cup final result would therefore settle the season's title as top Pembrokeshire club. Whitland scrum half Rob Phillips was the key player in the final, but man of the match was full back colleague Barrie Thomas. Hooker Steve Gerrard put Whitland ahead after 20 minutes with a barging drive to touch down. Tristan Edwards converted but the turning point came when Tenby conceded a try directly from the restart to put Whitland 14 points ahead. Dominic Setaro charged down full back Dean Bowen's clearance to score a fine opportunist try which Edwards again converted.

Tenby managed to reduce the deficit after flanker Andrew Thomas gathered a difficult ball to touch down and Gavin Scotcher converted. Whitland, however, put the game virtually beyond Tenby's reach as Rob Phillips ran a penalty and his quick thinking earned Whitland a third try as the side's changed over at 21-7.

Tenby scrum half Jonathan Dodd sparked the game into life with an early second half try which Scotcher converted as the seaside club battled bravely. Barrie Thomas was outstanding in his tackling and fielding of the high ball which Tenby rained down on him. The result was put beyond doubt as Whitland's Edwards kicked a late penalty to collect a personal tally of 11 points.

**WHITLAND:** Barry Thomas; Richard Hopkins, Dominic Setaro (capt), Carl Morgan, Spencer Rourke; Tristan Edwards, Robert Phillips; Colin Moreshead, Steve Gerrard, Nicky Carpenter, Mike Buckingham, Mike Jacobs, Anthony Griffiths, Paul Jenkins, Alan Reynolds. Reps: Jason Styles, Dai Kirk, Paul Kirk.

**TENBY UNITED:** Dean Bowen; John Dodd, Anthony Dragone, Neil Truman, Warren Leach; Gavin Scotcher, Richard Evans; Dai Balkwell, Jonathan Hudson, Dean Hadley, Rhodri Jones, Mark Boswell, Nicky Allen, Andrew Thomas, Eddie Lewis (capt). Reps: Robbie Jones, Steve Hartland, Gareth Thomas, Justin Richards, Dominic Subbiani, Richard Crockford, Richard Rossiter.

Whitland and Tenby ended up in third and fourth places respectively in Division 2, with fellow Pembrokeshire club Narberth ending in mid-table in the same division.

Cardigan enjoyed a successful campaign, gaining promotion to Division 4 after finishing runners-up in Division 5 (West). Aberystwyth, after a promising start when they led the division, ended in mid-table.

In Division 6A (West), Haverfordwest celebrated the division title and are promoted for the second successive season, while the other Pembrokeshire clubs of Pembroke Dock Quins, Pembroke and Aberaeron unfortunately occupied three of the four bottom positions.

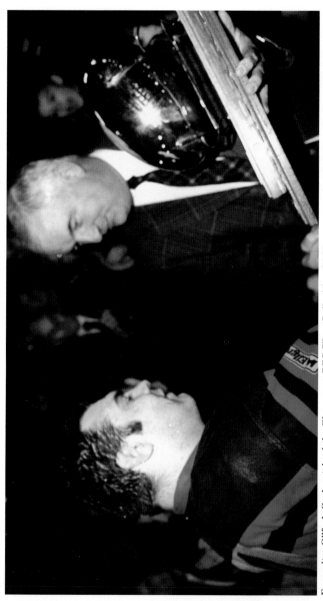

Favourites Gilfach Goch retained the Glamorgan RFC Silver Ball with a 34-22 success against first-time finalists British Steel (Port Talbot) at Sardis Road. Welsh Brewers Ltd Sales Director Brian Mills presents the trophy to Gilfach captain Jonathan James.

# Andre is top man as Gilfach
# use dynamic scrum power

Two penalty tries helped Gilfach Goch retain the Silver Ball as they defeated British Steel (Port Talbot), who were hoping to take the title for the first time, 34-22 at Sardis Road, Pontypridd on April 20, 1998. Gilfach were favourites and their powerful scrum drive was too much for the Steelmen. Referee David Davies twice ruled Gilfach had been denied tries by collapsing scrums and awarded penalty tries. Other tries were obtained by Craig Williams, Robert Stinchcombe and Paul Hughes. Craig Williams converted three and kicked a penalty goal. Gilfach's Andre Medcraft was chosen as man-of-the-match.

The Steel also had a Craig Williams as their goal-kicker and he fired over a penalty shot and converted two of the tries by Gerwyn Pugh, and David Morgan and Andrew Bucknall.

By retaining the title, Gilfach earned the right to meet Maesteg Harlequins, winners of the Hancocks Bitter Trophy as top try-scoring team in the Silver Ball, for the President's Cup. Again Gilfach triumphed, this time 24-8 at Treherbert.

| SILVER BALL WINNERS | |
|---|---|
| 1956-57 | Taibach |
| 1957-58 | Welsh Acads. |
| 1958-59 | Maesteg Celtic |
| 1959-60 | Seven Sisters |
| 1960-61 | Glynneath |
| 1961-62 | Glynneath |
| 1962-63 | Glynneath |
| 1963-64 | Llantwit Major |
| 1964-65 | Llantwit Major |
| 1965-66 | Cwmgwrach |
| 1966-67 | Cardiff Athletic |
| 1967-68 | Cardiff Athletic |
| 1968-69 | Cardiff Coll. of Ed. |
| 1969-70 | Cardiff Coll. of Ed. |
| 1970-71 | Senghenydd |
| 1971-72 | Senghenydd |
| 1972-73 | Abercynon |
| 1973-74 | Kenfig Hill |
| 1974-75 | Taffs Well |
| 1975-76 | Pyle |
| 1976-77 | Abercynon |
| 1977-78 | Pyle |
| 1978-79 | Bridgend Sports |
| 1979-80 | Bridgend Sports |
| 1980-81 | Bridgend Sports |
| 1981-82 | Aberavon Quins |
| 1982-83 | Swansea Ath. |
| 1983-84 | Cilfynydd |
| 1984-85 | Cilfynydd |
| 1985-86 | St. Peter's |
| 1986-87 | Tondu |
| 1987-88 | Neath Ath. |
| 1988-89 | Llantrisant |
| 1989-90 | Beddau |
| 1990-91 | Tondu |
| 1991-92 | Tondu |
| 1992-93 | Tondu |
| 1993-94 | Llantrisant |
| 1994-95 | Tonyrefail |
| 1995-96 | Resolven |
| 1996-97 | Gilfach Goch |
| 1997-98 | Gilfach Goch |

**GILFACH GOCH:** Craig Williams; Paul Hughes, Martin Davies, Adrian Williams, Robert Stinchcombe; Matthew Banwell, Adrian Neck; Martin Hall, Jonathan James (capt), Mark Dudding, David Purnell, Darren Jones, Andrew Williams, Kristian Jones, Andre Medcraft. Reps. Dean Howarth, Carl Donahue, Ian Davies, Paul Lucas.

**BRITISH STEEL (Port Talbot):** Richard Crayford; Phil Rosser, Jason Lowndes, Craig Williams, Richard Phillips; Mike Healey, Gerwyn Pugh; Chris O'Callaghan, Ian Nicholas, Dean Thomas, Adrian Gregory, John O'Callaghan, Barry Davies, David Morgan (capt), Andrew Bucknall. Reps: Tim Edwards, Patrick O'Callaghan.

*Referee:* David R Davies (Caerphilly).

# Mark's Merthyr men make it with six tries after 28 years' wait

**MID-DISTRICT:** Merthyr shocked Div 1 champions Caerphilly 44-36 to win the Worthington Mid-District Cup for the first time for 28 years at Sardis Road in a memorable encounter that saw Merthyr storm back after trailing 24-3. Neil Morgan, Darren Thomas, skipper Mark Dicks, Richard Williams, Dean Evans and Nick Davies were try-getters for the winners; Jeremy Lloyd dropped a goal and Stuart Hancox added the other goal points. Paul Phillips, Roger Bidgood and Steve Jones crossed for Caerphilly and Brett Davey supplied 21 goal points. En route to the final, Caerphilly had shattered Aberdare 90-0.

**GWENT:** Rhymney were winners for the first time since the Hancocks HB Ben Francis Cup was launched in 1926, when they defeated holders Newport 33-22 at Ebbw Vale with Wayne Booth scoring 23 points, including a try. Other tries came from J Hodges and D Worgan. Booth converted the three tries and kicked four penalty goals. For Newport, M Lovell, J Machecek and D Gregg crossed. S Connor and S Mitchell each converted one try and Mitchell kicked a penalty goal.

**EAST DISTRICT:** St. Peter's won a goal-kicking duel against Llanharan 12-3 at Cardiff RFC ground to earn the Brains Crown Buckley Challenge Trophy. Dean Daley put over four penalty shots for the Rocks; Wayne Jervis was on target with one for Llanharan.

**CENTRAL GLAMORGAN:** Ogmore Vale, captained by David Lake, were 17-13 winners against Cwmavon at Aberavon Green Stars ground. Wing Phil Bissmire scored Vale's only try and Kevin Baldwin put over four penalty goals. Cwmavon No 8 Phil Joseph crossed for two tries and Ian Williams fired in a penalty shot.

**NORTH WALES:** Nant Conwy defeated Ruthin 30-12 with outside half Peredur Ellis supplying 25 points. He scored two tries, kicked three penalty goals and converted the tries. Prop Glyn Roberts also crossed. Wing Julian Williams obtained both Ruthin tries. John Tudor converted one.

---

### MONMOUTHSHIRE WIN COUNTIES CUP AGAIN

Monmouthshire triumphed in the Welsh Counties Cup final for a fourth consecutive year, defeating Glamorgan 44-13 at Cross Keys on May 21, 1998. No 8 John Williams (2), Peter Ovey, Joe Powell, Ray Clark, Mike Peard and Mike Boys scored tries for the winners. Boys converted two and kicked a penalty goal. Darren Worgan added a conversion. For Glamorgan, Gafyn Stiff and Gareth Jones obtained tries. Brett Davey added a penalty shot. Monmouthshire crushed Carmarthen 67-12 in the semi-final while Glamorgan put out Breconshire 38-21.

---

# Shadow men win, but Portugal's top team spring a surprise

Portugal produced a shock victory over Welsh Districts at Pontypridd on March 27, 1998. It was 24-13 with scrum half Damien Buckland (Llanrumney) scorer of the only home try. Mike Hurn converted and kicked two penalty goals. Ironically, on the previous day the Welsh Districts Select had defeated the reserve Portugal team 19-16 at Dunvant. Llanrumney outside half Gareth Rees crossed in each half, his second coming during injury time to steal the verdict. Paul Martin scored the other try. Carwyn Jones (Llandovery) converted two.

Welsh Districts were 17-10 winners against Denmark at Aalborg in April with tries by wing Steve Jones (Llanrumney), centre Paul Martin (Cambrian Welfare) and second row Adrian Bridges (Bedlinog). Mike Hurn (Brynithel) added the conversion points to one try.

Cardiff and District won the Percy Howells Cup for the first time in 10 years with 33-13 success against North East Counties at Abercynon. Stephen Jones (2), Gareth Stockwell and Damien Buckland obtained Cardiff tries and Mark Blackwood supplied the goal points. Kelvin Davies scored the NEC try. Dewi Davies converted and put over two penalty goals. Cardiff put out Llanelli and District 31-0 in the semi-final with No 8 Peter Brito (Fairwater) scoring two of the five tries. NEC defeated Mid-Glamorgan 16-11 in the other semi-final as Dewi Davies kicked 11 decisive points.

Cambrian Welfare second row Wayne Morgan was banned for five years as a result of an incident in the match against Glyncoch involving referee Emyr Adlam.

---

**Welsh Women**

## ONLY ELEVENTH PLACE IN WORLD CUP

A 12-10 victory over Italy in their last match saw Wales finish 11th place overall in the Women's World Cup staged in Amsterdam during May 1998. Jamie Kift and Elli Green were the try scorers and Tracey Comley converted one. New Zealand won the cup for the first time, defeating USA 44-12 in the final. Wales opened with a 38-18 defeat by Spain and then were crushed 83-7 by Russia. The Welsh girls, who had finished in fourth place in the 1994 World Cup, lost 18-13 to Kazakhstan in the shield semi-final.

England, who have never lost in 12 meetings with Wales, were 29-12 winners at Waterloo after a 60-yard try by new wing Sarah Thomas had given Wales the lead. Scotland triumphed 22-12 in Swansea before a sparkling display brought Wales 27-10 success against Ireland in Limerick. Louise Rickard, Rhonwen Owens and full back Non Evans set up victory with tries and others followed from Rhian Williams and Sarah Thomas.

# LEADING SCORERS FOR WALES (to 30/6/98)

*by Howard Evans*

(* indicates all tries at 3pts; + indicates all tries at 4pts; otherwise all at 5pts each)

**Pts**

| | | |
|---|---|---|
| 594 | **Neil Jenkins** *(Pontypridd)* | 7t, 76c, 133p, 3dg. (1t at 4pts; 6t at 5pts) |
| 304 | + **Paul Thorburn** *(Neath)* | 2t, 43c, 70p |
| 173 | **Arwel Thomas** *(Bristol, Swansea)* | 10t, 24c, 25p |
| 166 | + **Phil Bennett** *(Llanelli)* | 4t, 18c, 36p, 2dg |
| 157 | **Ieuan Evans** *(Llanelli, Bath)* | 33t (8t at 4pts; 25t at 5pts) |
| 152 | + **Steve Fenwick** *(Bridgend)* | 4t, 11c, 35p, 3dg |
| 90 | * **Barry John** *(Llanelli, Cardiff)* | 5t, 6c, 13p, 8dg |
| 88 | **Gareth Edwards** *(Cardiff)* | 20t, 2c, 1p, 3dg (8t at 3pts; 12t at 4pts) |
| 88 | **Jack Bancroft** *(Swansea)* | 38c, 4p |
| 81 | + **Mark Wyatt** *(Swansea)* | 1t, 7c, 21p |
| 81 | + **Jonathan Davies** *(Neath, Llanelli, Cardiff)* | 5t, 2c, 6p, 13dg |
| 74 | **Gwyn Evans** *(Maesteg)* | 4c, 22p |
| 73 | * **Keith Jarrett** *(Newport)* | 2t, 17c, 11p |
| 72 | **Gerald Davies** *(London Welsh, Cardiff)* | 20t (8t at 3pts; 12t at 4pts) |
| 65 | **Gareth Thomas** *(Bridgend, Cardiff)* | 13t |
| 60 | **Nigel Walker** *(Cardiff)* | 12t |
| 60 | **Billy Bancroft** *(Swansea)* | 20c, 4p, 1dg, 1g from mark |
| 57 | * **Reggie Gibbs** *(Cardiff)* | 17t, 3c |
| 55 | **Wayne Proctor** *(Llanelli)* | 11t |
| 51 | * **Ken J Jones** *(Newport)* | 17t |
| 51 | * **John L Williams** *(Cardiff)* | 17t |
| 50 | **Terry Davies** *(Swansea, Llanelli)* | 7c, 12p |
| 50 | **Bert Winfield** *(Cardiff)* | 14c, 6p, 1g from mark |

# Dauntless Dean makes Brynithel
# pay for that late tackle

The Welsh Districts Cup, with Worthington as new sponsors, saw Bedlinog win the 1998 final 13-5 against Brynithel at Virginia Park, Caerphilly on April 18. It was the last time in the competition for both teams, who now step up to WRU probationary status.

Bedlinog's second success came 10 years after winning the cup. Their defiant defence blocked Brynithel's eager runners, who were spearheaded by full back Carl Mogford. After Bedlinog fly half Dean Rees had been felled by a late tackle, he recovered and added a sparkling try from half way to his penalty goal. Scrum half Ceri Powell also crossed for a smart try. Brynithel's try was scored by prop Anthony Jayne, waiting out wide for the long pass from Mike Peck following a quick penalty-tap.

## WELSH BREWERS CUP

| | | | |
|---|---|---|---|
| 1974 | Girling defeated Baglan 16-3 | 1989 | St. Alban's defeated Hartridge HSOB 13-10 |
| 1975 | Girling defeated St. Joseph's 6-3 | 1990 | Hartridge HSOB defeated Newtown 24-18 |
| 1976 | Cross Keys Utd. defeated Caldicot 9-6 | 1991 | Fairwater defeated CIAC 13-3 |
| 1977 | CIAC defeated Cross Keys Utd. 16-3 | 1992 | St. Alban's defeated Fairwater 21-20 |
| 1978 | Rumney defeated Nantyglo 25-9 | 1993 | Birchgrove defeated Wattstown 26-19 |
| 1979 | Rumney defeated Nantyglo 18-10 | | *(after extra time)* |
| 1980 | Tondu defeated Rumney 15-10 | **PRYSG/WHITBREAD CUP** | |
| 1981 | Caerleon defeated Rhydyfelin 12-9 | 1994 | Wattstown defeated Hartridge 15-6 |
| 1982 | Llantrisant defeated Glyncorrwg 18-9 | 1995 | Banwen defeated Fairwater 16-11 |
| 1983 | Baglan defeated Heol-y-Cyw 13-6 | **WD NATIONAL CUP** | |
| 1984 | Baglan defeated Cimla 12-6 | 1996 | St Alban's defeated Wattstown 15-12 |
| 1985 | Glyncorrwg defeated Llanishen 16-12 | 1997 | Cambrian W. defeated Wattstown 18-11 |
| 1986 | Tonmawr defeated CIAC 9-6 | **WORTHINGTON CUP** | |
| 1987 | CIAC defeated Hartridge 26-3 | 1998 | Bedlinog defeated Brynithel 13-5 |
| 1988 | Bedlinog defeated Forgeside 9-6 | | |

**BEDLINOG,** 1998 Worthington Cup winners: Martin Veall; Adrian Evans, Ian Thompson, P Williams, Stuart Carpenter; Dean Rees, Ceri Powell; Wayne Richards, David Rees, Andrew Hiscocks, Adrian Bridges (capt), David Coleman, Martin Morgan, Dean Thomas, Richard Smurdon. Reps: Mark Hall, Wayne Evans, Roger Heath, Raymond Fussell, Paddy McNally, David Phillips.

**SEMI-FINALS:** Llangefni failed in their attempt to become the first North Wales team to reach the final, going down after a gallant effort 16-11 to Bedlinog. Wing Adrian Evans was the try-getter for the winners; Dean Rees converted and kicked three penalty goals. Llangefni's try came from Will Bown. Dewi Jones added two penalty goals. Much fancied Fairwater fell 11-8 victims to Brynithel with Tony Jayne scoring the Gwent team's try. Carl Mogford dropped a goal and Michael Hurn fired in a penalty shot. Ricky Theaker kicked a Fairwater penalty goal and converted Richard Talbot's try.

**FIFTH ROUND:** Ricky Theaker collected 20 points in Fairwater's 35-16 victory over Abercwmboi, the team who began life in 1980 as a pub side from the King's Head in nearby Aberaman and reached the fourth round of the SWALEC Cup this season. Martin Morgan snapped up two tries for Bedlinog to beat Llangadog 34-6. Vince Kieron's two penalty goals edged Llangefni into the semis 6-5 after Steve Way crossed for Glyncoch. Brynithel won 16-14 at Bettws (Newport).

**FOURTH ROUND:** Glyncorrwg, the 1985 winners, departed 16-6 at the hands of visitors Llangefni. Brynithel, runaway winners in the previous round, scraped a 5-3 verdict at Cefn Fforest. Bedlinog had captain Adrian Bridges sent off, but his side demolished Penallta 32-0. Phil Lewis kicked four penalty goals to give Abercwmboi a 12-5 verdict at New Panteg. Fairwater defeated Deri 22-9 as Ricky Theaker planted over five penalty goals and converted a penalty try. Bettws put out Caerau (Ely) 11-8 with an Andy Taylor try and two John Whitehead penalty shots.

**THIRD ROUND:** Three times winners St. Alban's, the most successful team in the tournament's history, made their exit 13-6 at Caerau as the Ely side obtained an Ian McCoy try and Stephen Cotter added a conversion and penalty goal. A hat-trick of tries by Steve Way, who also converted one, and a try and penalty goal by brother Gwyn saw Glyncoch defeat Nant Conwy 25-0. Stuart Carpenter scored Bedlinog's only try as they won 13-9 at Dowlais. New Panteg went through because they were leading 3-0 after 37 minutes when the tie was abandoned because Machynlleth second row Huw Harding was taken to the Royal Gwent Hospital where, sadly, he died after suffering a serious spinal injury. Brynithel racked up a mammoth 79-0 victory over Morganstown while Fairwater put out Llanrumney 22-3. Abercwmboi crushed Forgeside 37-0.

## BEDLINOG KNOCK OUT HOLDERS

**SECOND ROUND:** There was a shock for cup-holders Cambrian Welfare. Despite home advantage, they went out to Bedlinog, the 1988 winners – by a whisker at 16-15. Glyncoch crushed Ferryside 59-3, but it was desperately close before Llangadog squeezed to 3-0 success over South Gower. Llanedeyrn made a rousing fight of it before losing to visitors Caerau (Ely) 36-30. It was also tight at Blackwood Stars, where Cardiff East struggled into the next round 12-10. Yet another close decision came at Glyncorrwg, where Markham made a 9-3 exit.

**FIRST ROUND:** Wattstown, the previous season's defeated finalists, were shocked out 18-14 at Penallta. Wattstown had figured in four finals during the previous five years and won the cup in 1994. Girling, winners in the first two seasons of the tourney, failed comprehensively 53-0 at St. Alban's. Another heavy defeat for old champions saw Caerleon (cup winners in 1981) dumped 43-8 by visitors Hollybush. A fourth cup winning team of the past to go out were Cardiff International Athletic Club. The CIACs, champions in 1977 and 1987, lost 53-14 at Bettws. Six Bells Saracens and Cardiff East drew 19-all, but East went through as away team.

---

### NEW PLANS FOR NATIONAL LEAGUE

**Suggestions were made during the summer of 1998 to spice the National League's premier division by introducing an end-of-season play-off system for the four top teams on a home and away basis to decide the champions. The four bottom teams could play-off to decide relegation issues.**

**Divisions 3 and 4 will be regionalised for the 1998-99 season. This passed at the emergency general meeting in May, though 12 clubs opposed the change.**

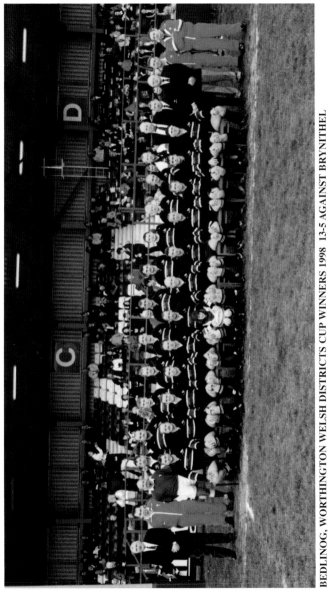

**BEDLINOG, WORTHINGTON WELSH DISTRICTS CUP WINNERS 1998 13-5 AGAINST BRYNITHEL**

*Picture: Wales News and Pictures*

# WORTHINGTON DISTRICTS CUP 1997-98

## FIRST ROUND

### Group One

St Alban's 53, Girling 0
Cwm 10, Crickhowell 18
Pontllanfraith w/o v Tylerians

Newport CS w/o v St Julian's
Beaufort 38, Ely 0

### Group Two

Deri 22, CR Caerdydd 19
Wick 7, Llanrumney 80
Brynithel 81, Aberbeeg 0

New Panteg 30, Aberbargoed 10
Bryncethin 8, Cwmtillery 13

### Group Three

Caerleon 8, Hollybush 43
Pontyfelin 17, Howardian 20
Blackwood Stars 13, Raglan 10

Caerau (Ely) 37, Abersychan 0
Six Bells Sar. 19, *Cardiff East 19
*(Through as away team)

### Group Four

Cefn Fforest 35, Hafodyrynys 12
Whitchurch 12, Trefil 22
Forgeside w/o v Cardiff CS

Glyncorrwg 18, Barry Plastics 0
Bettws 53, CIAC 14

### Group Five

Rhosllan'gog 35, Deeside 10
Castel Alun 14, Bro Ffestiniog 19
Porthmadog 6, Nant Conwy 29
Abergele 10, Holyhead 3

Benllech 11, Llangoed 6
Harlech 8, BSC Shotton 27
Flint 10, Llangefni 37
Menai Bridge 6, Bala 23

### Group Six

Penlan 7, Rhigos 3
Porth 3, Llangadog 10

Treharris 21, Ferndale 12
Penallta 18, Wattstown 14

### Group Seven

Llanwrtyd Wells 3, Glyncoch 33
Pontrhydyfen 13, Abercwmboi 43

Llanidloes 12, Cambrian W. 69
Dowlais 18, Aberfan 10

### Group Eight

Mynydd-y-Garreg 29, COBRA 12
Llanbradach 29, Cimla 5

Rhayader 14, Llandrindod W. 5

# SECOND ROUND

Abertysswg 26, Llanrumney 38
Bala 12, Llangefni 25
Beaufort 14, Llanwern 24
Bettws 33, Trefil 23
Betws 28, Llanbradach 12
Blackwood Stars 10, Cdf East 12
Brackla 7, Deri 20
Bryn Wands 8, Abercwmboi 41
BSC Shotton 24, Abergele 0
Cambrian Welfare 15, Bedlinog 16
Cefn Fforest w/o v St Joseph's
Crickhowell 3, St Alban's 19
Cwmtillery 7, Brynithel 25
Dowlais 22, Tref-y-Clawdd 3
Fairwater w/o v Howardian
Ferryside 3, Glyncoch 59

Glyncorrwg 9, Markham 3
Hollybush w/o v Newbridge Utd
Llanedeyrn 30, Caerau 36
Llangadog 3, South Gower 0
Machynlleth w/o v CMB
Morganstown 16, NASH 3
Mynydd-y-Garreg 16, Rhayader 9
Nant Conwy 50, Benllech 7
Newport CS 15, Pont'fraith 7
Penallta 31, St Clears 14
Penlan 16, Treharris 3
Penybanc 44, Aberavon NC 0
Rhos'gog 53, Bro Ffestiniog 17
Tongwynlais 0, Forgeside 29
Tregaron w/o v Mynyddbach
Whitehead 0, New Panteg 24

## THIRD ROUND

Abercwmboi 37, Forgeside 0
Bettws w/o v Cardiff East
Betws 27, Tregaron 6
Caerau (Ely) 13, St Alban's 6
Deri 19, Penlan 9
Dowlais 8, Bedlinog 13
Glyncoch 25, Nant Conwy 0
Hollybush 32, Llanwern 19

Llangefni 59, BSC Shotton 0
Llanrumney 3, Fairwater 22
Morganstown 0, Brynithel 79
Mynydd-y-Garreg 6, C. Fforest 9
New Panteg 3, Machynlleth 0
Newport CS 15, Glyncorrwg 39
Penybanc 3, Llangadog 13
Rhos'gog 10, Penallta 40

## FOURTH ROUND

Bedlinog 32, Penallta 0
Bettws 11, Caerau Ely 8
Cefn Fforest 3, Brynithel 5
Fairwater 22, Deri 9

Glyncoch 22, Betws 0
Glyncorrwg 6, Llangefni 16
Llangadog 13, Hollybush 8
New Panteg 5, Abercwmboi 12

## FIFTH ROUND

Bedlinog 32, Llangadog 6
Bettws 14, Brynithel 16

Fairwater 35, Abercwmboi 16
Llangefni 6, Glyncoch 5

## SEMI-FINALS

Bedlinog 16, Llangefni 11
*(At Maesteg)*

Brynithel 11, Fairwater 8
*(At Abercynon)*

## FINAL

Bedlinog 13, Brynithel 5
*(At Virginia Park, Caerphilly)*

# RECORD DEFEATS ON NIGHTMARE TOUR 'DOWN UNDER'

Tatterdemalion England slumped as never before when they faced Australia in Suncorp Stadium, Brisbane on June 6, 1998. It was the biggest defeat in their 127 years of international rugby at an amazing 76-0. Like Wales in South Africa, England were desperately short of key players and paid the price. Their tour of Australia, New Zealand and South Africa brought a whitewash: after the rout in Australia there were defeats by the All Blacks, first 64-22 in Dunedin (their heaviest reverse in matches against New Zealand) and then 40-10 in Auckland. On the way home, England went down 18-0 to South Africa in Cape Town.

It was not so much defeat as surrender against the Wallabies. New fly half Stephen Larkham scored three of the 11 tries. There were three also by wing Ben Tune. Other try getters were Tim Horan (2), Toutai Kefu, Matt Burke and Joe Roff. Burke converted four and put over three penalty goals. Larkham converted two.

**England's team:** T Stimpson; S Brown, M Perry, S Ravenscroft, A Healey; J Wilkinson, S Benton; G Rowntree, R Cockerill, P Vickery, D Grewcock, G Archer, B Sturnham, R Pool-Jones, A Diprose (capt). Reps: S Potter for Ravenscroft, B Clarke for Pool-Jones, D Chapman for Stimpson.

## GREWCOCK SENT OFF

The first Test in New Zealand brought dismissal for Danny Grewcock. He was banned for five weeks for stamping on Anton Oliver's head after 30 minutes at Carisbrook Park. Independent match commissioner David Gray cited NZ lock Ian Jones for stamping on Rowntree, but Jones was cleared of the charge, much to England's chagrin. Tom Beim, Richard Cockerill and Matt Dawson crossed for the tourists; Stimpson converted two and added a penalty goal. For NZ, Christian Cullen (2), Randell (2), Wilson (2), Kronfeld, Lomu and Mayerhofler were the try-getters. Andrew Mehrtens converted five and kicked three penalty goals for 19 points.

In the second Test at Eden Park, skipper Matt Dawson provided all England's points with a try, conversion and penalty goal. Jeff Wilson (2), Mayerhofler, Vidiri, Randell and Maka obtained NZ tries; Mehrtens converted two and Carlos Spencer converted three.

Conditions were appalling at Newlands on July 4, 1998. South African coach Nick Mallett asserted that his side would have piled 50 points on England on a dry day. Intstead it was only 18-0 as Joost van der Westhuizen and Stefan Terblanche scored tries and Percy Montgomery converted one and added two penalty goals.

# WELSH INTERNATIONAL PLAYERS

**Key:** E – England, S – Scotland, SA – South Africa, A – Australia, M – Maoris (1888), I – Ireland, F – France, NZ – New Zealand, NSW – New South Wales, R – Romania, FJ – Fiji, T – Tonga, WS – Western Samoa, C – Canada, N – Namibia, B – Barbarians, AR – Argentina, Z – Zimbabwe, J – Japan, P – Portugal, Sp – Spain, It – Italy.
* Denotes Replacement player.

**Ackerman, R.** *(Newport and London Welsh)* NZ. 1980; E.S.A. 1981; I.F.E.S. 1982; S.I.F.R. 1983; S.I.F.E.A. 1984; S.I.F.E.FJ 1985.

**Alexander, E.P.** *(Cambridge Univ. and Brecon)* S. 85; E.S. 86; E.I. 87.

**Alexander, W.H.** *(Llwynypia)* I.E. 98.; E.S.I. 99; S.I. 1901.

**Allen, A.** *(Newbridge)* F.E.I. 1990.

**Allen, C.P.** *(Oxford Univ. and Beaumaris)* E.S. 84.

**Andrews, F** *(Pontypool)* SA. 1912; E.S.I; 1913.

**Andrews, F.G.** *(Swansea)* E.S. 84.

**Andrews, G.** *(Newport)* E.S. 1926; E.F.I. 1927.

**Anthony, Chris** *(Swansea)* USA (1* and 2*). C*. T* 1997.

**Anthony, L.** *(Neath)* E.S.F. 1948.

**Appleyard, Rob** *(Swansea)* C. R.T.NZ. 1997; It.*E.S.I.F. 1998.

**Arnold, P.** *(Swansea)* N. 1, 2, B. 1990; E.S.I.F.A.AR.A. 1991; F.Z. (2nd) 1993; Sp. FJ. 1994; SA 1995; B* 1996.

**Arnold, W.** *(Llanelli)* S. 1903.

**Arthur, C.S.** *(Cardiff)* I.M. 88; E. 91.

**Arthur, T.** *(Neath)* S.F.I. 1927; E.S.F.I. 1929; E.S.I.F. 1930; E.S.F.I. 1931; SA. 1931; E.S. 1933.

**Ashton, C.** *(Aberavon)* E.S.I. 1959, 1960; I. 1962.

**Attewell, L.** *(Newport)* E.S.F. 1921.

**Back, M.** *(Bridgend)* F*.E*.S.I. 1995.

**Badger, O.** *(Llanelli)* E.S.I. 95; E. 96.

**Baker, A.** *(Neath)* I. 1921; E.S.F.I. 1923.

**Baker, A.M.** *(Newport)* S.F. 1909; S. 1910.

**Bancroft, J.** *(Swansea)* E.S.F.I. 1909; F.E.S.I. 1910; E.F.I. 1911; E.S.I. 1912; I. 1913; E.S.F. 1914.

**Bancroft, W.J.** *(Swansea)* S.E.I. 90; E.S.I. 91, 92, 93, 94, 95, 96; E. 97; I.E. 98; E.S.I. 99, 1900, 1901.

**Barlow, T.M.** *(Cardiff)* I. 84

**Barrell, R.** *(Cardiff)* S.F.I. 1929; I. 1933.

**Bartlett, J.D.** *(Llanelli and London Welsh)* S. 1927; E.S. 1928.

**Bassett, A.** *(Aberavon and Cardiff)* I. 1934; E.S.I. 1935; E.S. 1938.

**Bassett, J.** *(Penarth)* E.S.F.I. 1929; E.S.I. 1930; E.S.F.I.SA. 1931; E.S.I. 1932.

**Bateman, A.** *(Neath and Richmond)* S.I. N. (1, 2) 1990; SA. 1996; USA.S.F.E. R.NZ. 1997; It. E.S.I. 1998.

**Bayliss, G.** *(Pontypool)* S. 1933.

**Bebb, D.** *(Carmarthen T.C. and Swansea)* E.S.I.F. 1959; E.S.I.F.SA. 1960; E.S.I.F. 1961; E.S.F.I. 1962; E.F.NZ. 1963; E.S.F.SA. 1964; E.I.S.F. 1965; F.A. 1966; S.I.F.E. 1967.

**Beckingham, G.** *(Cardiff)* E.S. 1953; F. 1958.

**Bennett, A.** *(Aberavon)* I. 1937.

**Bennett, M.** *(Cardiff)* NZ. SA. FJ. 1995.

**Bennett, P.** *(Cardiff Harlequins)* E.S. 91; S.I. 92.

**Bennett, P.** *(Llanelli)* F.* 1969; SA.S.F. 1970; S.* 1972; NZ. 1972; E.S.I.F.A. 1973; S.I.F.E. 1974; S.*I. 1975; E.S.I.F. 1976; I.F.E.S. 1977; E.S.I.F. 1978.

**Bergiers, R.T.E.** *(Llanelli)* E.S.F.NZ. 1972; E.S.I.F.A. 1973; E. 1974; I. 1975.

**Bevan, Griff.** *(Llanelli)* E. 1947.

**Bevan, J.A.** *(Cambridge)* E. 81.

**Bevan, J.C.** *(Cardiff and Cardiff College of Education)* E.S.I.F. 1971; E.S.F. 1972; NZ. 1972; E.S. 1973.

**Bevan, J.D.** *(Aberavon)* F.E.S.A. 1975.

**Bevan, Sid.** *(Swansea)* I. 1904.

**Beynon, Ben** *(Swansea)* E.S. 1920.

**Beynon, E.** *(Swansea)* F.I. 1925.

**Bidgood, R.A.** *(Newport)* S. 1992; Z. (1st and 2nd), N.J.* 1993.

**Biggs, N.** *(Cardiff)* M. 88; I. 89, 92; E.S.I. 93; E.I. 94.

**Biggs, S.** *(Cardiff)* E.S. 95; S. 96; E. 97; I.E. 98; S.I. 99; I. 1900.

**Birch, J.** *(Neath)* S.F. 1911.

**Birt, F.W.** *(Newport)* E.S. 1911; E.S.I.SA. 1912; E. 1913.

**Bishop, D.J.** *(Pontypool)* A. 1984.

**Bishop, E.H.** *(Swansea)* S. 89.

**Blackmore, J.** *(Abertillery)* E. 1909.

**Blackmore, S.** *(Cardiff)* I.T.*C.A. 1987.

**Blake, J.** *(Cardiff)* E.S.I. 99, 1900, 1901.

**Blakemore, R.E.** *(Newport)* E. 1947.

**Bland, A.F.** *(Cardiff)* E.S.I. 87; S.I.M. 88; S.E.I. 90.

**Blyth, L.** *(Swansea)* SA. 1951; E.S. 1952.

**Blyth, W.R.** *(Swansea)* E. 1974; S.*1975; F.E.S.I. 1980.

**Boobyer, N.** *(Llanelli)* Z. (1st* and 2nd), N. 1993; F.T. 1994; F. 1998.

**Boon, R.** *(Cardiff)* S.F. 1930; E.S.I.F.SA. 1931; E.S.I.1932; E.I. 1933.

**Booth, J.** *(Pontymister)* I. 98.

**Boots, G.** *(Newport)* I.E. 98; I. 99; E.S.I 1900, 1901, 1902, 1903; E. 1904.

**Boucher, A.W.** *(Newport)* E.S.I. 92, 93; E. 94, E.S.I. 95; E.I. 96; E. 97.

**Bowcott, H.M.** *(Cardiff, Cambridge Univ. and London Welsh)* S.F.I. 1929; E. 1930; E.S. 1931; E.I. 1933.

**Bowdler, F.A.** *(Cross Keys)* NSW 1927; E.S.I.F. 1928; E.S.F.I. 1929; E. 1930; SA. 1931; E.S.I. 1932; I. 1933.

**Bowen, B.** *(S. Wales Police and Swansea)* R. 1983; S.I.F.E. 1984; FJ. 1985; E.S.I.F.FJ.T.WS. 1986; C.E.NZ.USA. 1987; E.S.I.F. 1988; S.I. 1989.

**Bowen, C.** *(Llanelli)* S.I. 1896.

**Bowen, D.H.** *(Llanelli)* E. 82; E.S.86; E. 87.

**Bowen, G.E.** *(Swansea)* S.I. 87, 88.

**Bowen, W.** *(Swansea)* S.F. 1921; E.S.I.F. 1922.

**Bowen, Wm.** *(Swansea)* E.S. 86; E.S.I. 87; M. 88; S.I. 89; S.E.I. 90; E.S. 91.

**Brace, D.O.** *(Newport, Oxford Univ. and Llanelli)* E.S.I.F. 1956; E. 1957; S.I.F. 1960; I. 1961.

**Braddock, K.J.** *(Newbridge)* A. 1966; S.I. 1967.

**Bradshaw, K.** *(Bridgend)* E.S.I.F.SA. 1964; E.S.I.F. 1966.

**Brewer, T.J.** *(Newport, Oxford Univ. and London Welsh)* E. 1950; E.S. 1955.

**Brice, A.** *(Aberavon and Cardiff)* E.S.I. 99, 1900, 1901, 1902, 1903, 1904.

**Bridges, C.** *(Neath)* N. 1, 2, B. 1990; E.* I.F.A. 1991.

**Bridie, R.** *(Newport)* I. 82.

**Britton, G.** *(Newport)* S. 1961.

**Broughton, A.** *(Treorchy)* NSW. 1927; S. 1929.

**Brown, Archie** *(Newport)* I. 1921.

**Brown, J.** *(Cardiff)* E.S.I. 1907; E.S.F. 1908; E. 1909.

**Brown, J.** *(Cardiff)* I. 1925.

**Brown, M.** *(Pontypool)* R. 1983; E.S.FJ(R).T.WS. 1986.

**Bryant, D.** *(Bridgend)* NZ.(1 and 2), WS.R. 1988, S.I.F.E. 1989.

**Buchanan, A.** *(Llanelli)* T.E.*NZ.A. 1987; I. 1988.

**Buckett, I.** *(Swansea)* T. 1994; USA.C. 1997.

**Burcher, D.** *(Newport)* I.F.E.S. 1977.

**Burgess, R.C.** *(Ebbw Vale)* I.F.E.S. 1977; I.F. 1981; F.E.S. 1982.

**Burnett, R.** *(Newport)* E. 1953.

**Burns, J.** *(Cardiff)* F.I. 1927.

**Bush, P.** *(Cardiff)* NZ. 1905; E. 1906; SA. 1906; I. 1907; E.S. 1908; S.I. 1910.

**Butler, E.T.** *(Pontypool and Cambridge Univ.)* F.E.S.I.NZ.* 1980; S. 1982; E.S.I.F.R. 1983; S.I.F.E.A. 1984.

**Cale, W.R.** *(Newbridge and Pontypool)* E.S.I. 1949; E.S.I.F. 1950.

**Carter, A.J.** *(Newport)* E.S. 1991.

**Cattell, A.** *(Llanelli)* E. 1882; S. 1883.

**Challinor, C.** *(Neath)* E. 1939.

**Charvis, Colin** *(Swansea)* A*.SA. 1996; USA.S.I.F. 1997; It*.E.S.I.F. Z*.SA. 1998.

**Clapp, T.** *(Newport)* I.E. 82; S. 83; E.S.I. 84; E.S. 85; S. 86; E.S.I. 87; S.I. 88.

**Clare, J.** *(Cardiff)* E. 82.

**Clarke, S.S.** *(Neath)* I. 82; I. 87.

**Cleaver, W.B.** *(Cardiff)* E.S.I.F.A. 1947; E.S.F.I. 1948; I. 1949; E.S.I.F. 1950.

**Clegg, B.** *(Swansea)* F. 1979.

**Clement, A.** *(Swansea)* USA. 1987; E.NZ (1), WS(R), R. 1988; NZ. 1989; S(R),I.N. (1, 2) 1990; S*.A*.F.WS.AR.A. 1991; I.F.E.S. 1992; I*.F.J.C. 1993; S.I.F.Sp.C*.T.WS.It.SA. 1994; F.E.J.NZ.I. 1995.

**Clement, W.H.** *(Llanelli)* E.S.I. 1937, 1938.

**Cobner, T.J.** *(Pontypool)* S.I.F.E. 1974; F.E.S.I. 1975; A. 1975; E.S. 1976; F.E.S. 1977; E.S.I.F.A.(1) 1978.

**Coldrick, A.P.** *(Newport)* E.S.I. 1911; E.S.F. 1912.

**Coleman, E.** *(Newport)* E.S.I. 1949.

**Coles, F.C.** *(Pontypool)* S.I.F. 1960.

**Collins, J.** *(Aberavon)* A.E.S.F. 1958; E.S.I.F. 1959; E. 1960; F. 1961.

**Collins, R.G.** *(S Wales Police, Cardiff, Pontypridd)* E*.I.I.E.NZ.USA 1987; E.S.I.F.R. 1988; E.S.I. 1990; A.F.WS. 1991; C.FJ.T.WS.R.It.SA. 1994; F.E.S.I. 1995.

**Collins, T.** *(Mountain Ash)* I. 1923.

**Cook, T.** *(Cardiff)* S.I. 1949.

**Cope, W.** *(Cardiff, Cambridge Univ. and Blackheath)* S. 96.

**Copsey, A.H.** *(Llanelli)* I.F.E.S.A. 1992; E.S.I.J.C. 1993; E*.P.Sp*.FJ.T.WS*. 1994.

**Cornish, F.H.** *(Cardiff)* E. 97; I.E. 98; I. 99.

**Cornish, R.A.** *(Cardiff)* E.S. 1923; E. 1924;E.S.F. 1925; E.S.I.F. 1926;

**Coslett, K.** *(Aberavon)* E.S.F. 1962.

**Cowey, B.T.V.** *(Newport)* E.S.I. 1934; E. 1935.

**Cresswell, B.** *(Newport)* E.S.I.F. 1960.

**Cummins, W.** *(Treorchy)* S.I.F. 1922.

**Cunningham, L.J.** *(Aberavon)* E.S.I.F. 1960; E.S.F. 1962; I. 1962; NZ. 1963; E.S.I.F.SA. 1964.

**Dacey, M.** *(Swansea)* E.S.I.F.R. 1983; S.I.F.E.A. 1984; FJ.T.WS. 1986; F*.T. 1987.

**Daniel, D.J.** *(Llanelli)* S. 91; E.S.I. 94; I.E. 98; E.I. 99.

**Daniel, L.T.D.** *(Newport)* S. 1970.

**Daniels, P.C.T.** *(Cardiff)* A. 1981; I. 1982.

**Darbyshire, G.** *(Bangor)* E. 81.

**Dauncey, F.H.** *(Newport)* E.S.I. 96.

**Davey, Claude** *(Swansea and London Welsh)* F. 1930; E.S.I.F.SA. 1931; E.S.I. 1932; E.S. 1933; E.S.I. 1934, 1935; NZ. 1935; S. 1936; E.I. 1937, 1938.

**David, R.** *(Cardiff)* I. 1907.

**David, T.P.** *(Pontypridd and Llanelli)* F.A. 1973; I.F. 1976.

**Davidge, G.** *(Newport)* F. 1959; S.I.F. 1960; SA. 1960; E.S.I. 1961; F. 1962.

**Davies, Adrian** *(Neath and Cardiff)* B*. 1990, A. 1991; Z. (1st and 2nd) J.C. 1993; FJ. 1994; J.I. 1995.

**Davies, A.C.** *(London Welsh)* I. 89.

**Davies, A.E.** *(Llanelli)* A. 1984.

**Davies, Rev. Alban** *(Swansea and Llanelli)* S.F.I. 1913; E.S.F.I. 1914.

**Davies, B** *(Llanelli)* E. 95, 96.

**Davies, Bailey** *(Oxford and Llanelli)* E. 1907.

**Davies, Carwyn** *(Llanelli)* WS. 1988, S.I(R).F. 1989.

**Davies, C.H.A.** *(Llanelli and Cardiff)* I. 1957; A.E.S.I. 1958; SA. 1960; E. 1961.

**Davies, C.L.** *(Cardiff)* E.S.I. 1956.

**Davies, C.R.** *(Bedford and Cardiff High School)* E. 1934.

**Davies, Cliff** *(Cardiff)* S.F.I.A. 1947; E.S.F.I. 1948; F. 1949; E.S.I.F. 1950; E.S.I. 1951.

**Davies, Daph.** *(Bridgend)* I. 1921. 1925.

**Davies, D. Brian** *(Llanelli)* I. 1962; E.S. 1963.

**Davies, D.G.** *(Cardiff)* E.S. 1923.

**Davies, D.H.** *(Neath)* S. 1904.

**Davies, D. Hunt** *(Aberavon)* E. 1924.

**Davies, D. Idwal** *(Swansea)* E. 1939.

**Davies D.J.** *(Neath)* I. 1962

**Davies, D.M.** *(Somerset Police)* E.S.I.F. 1950, 1951; SA. 1951; E.S.I.F. 1952; I.F.N.Z. 1953; E. 1954.

**Davies, E.** *(Aberavon)* A. 1947; I. 1948.

**Davies, Evan** *(Maesteg)* NZ. 1919.

**Davies, Ewan** *(Cardiff)* E.F. 1912.

**Davies, Geo.** *(Swansea)* E.S.I. 1900, 1901, 1905.

**Davies, Glyn** *(Pontypridd and Cambridge Univ.)* S.A. 1947; E.S.F.I. 1948; E.S.F. 1949; E.S. 1951.

**Davies, Graham** *(Llanelli)* F.I. 1921; F. 1925.

**Davies, Gwyn** *(Cardiff)* F. 1928; E. 1929; S. 1930.

**Davies, H.** *(Bridgend)* S.I.F.E. 1984.

**Davies, H.** *(Swansea)* I.E. 98; S.I. 1901.

**Davies, H.J.** *(Cambridge Univ. and Aberavon)* E.S. 1959.

**Davies, Harold** *(Newport)* S. 1924.

**Davies, Howard** *(Swansea and Llanelli)* S.I. 1939; E.S.F.I. 1947.

**Davies, Howel** *(Neath)* E.S. 1912.

**Davies, J.** *(Neath,Llanelli and Cardiff)* E.F.J. 1985; E.S.I.F.FJ.T.WS. 1986; F.E.S.I.I.T*.C.E. NZ.A. 1987; F.S.I.F.NZ. (1 and 2). WS.R. 1988; A. 1996; USA*.S*.F*.E. 1997.

**Davies, J.D.** *(Neath)* I.F. 1991, F*.Z.(2nd), J.C. 1993; S.I.F.E.P.Sp.C.WS.R.It.SA. 1994; F.E.J.NZ.I.SA. 1995; It.E.S.I.F.A.B.F.It. 1996; Z.SA. 1998

**Davies, J.H.** *(Aberavon)* I. 1923.

**Davies, I.T.** *(Llanelli)* S.F.I. 1914.

**Davies, Leigh** *(Neath and Cardiff)* It.E.S.I. F.A.B.F.It*. 1996; USA (1 and 2).C.R.T.NZ*. 1997; E*.I.F. 1998.

**Davies, Len** *(Llanelli)* F.S. 1954; I. 1955.

**Davies, Leslie** *(Swansea)* S.I. 1939.

**Davies, Lyn** *(Bridgend)* E.S.I.1966.

**Davies, Mark** *(Swansea)* A. 1981; I. 1982; FJ. 1985.

**Davies, M.J.** *(Oxford)* S.I. 1939.

**Davies, N. Glyn** *(London Welsh)* E. 1955.

**Davies, Nigel** *(Llanelli)* NZ. (2nd). WS. 1988; S.I. 1989; F. 1993; S.I.E.P.Sp.C.FJ.T*.WS.R.It. 1994; E.S.I.FJ. 1995; E.S.I.F.A. (1and 2).B.F. 1996; E. 1997.

**Davies, P.T.** *(Llanelli)* E.F.J. 1985; E.S.I.F.FJ.T. WS. 1986; F.E.It.T.C.NZ. 1987; WS.R. 1988; S.I.F.E.NZ. 1989; F.E.S. 1990; I.F.A.F.WS.AR.A. 1991; F.Z. (1st) N. 1993; S.I.F.E.C.FJ*.WS.R.It. 1994; F.I. 1995.

**Davies, R.H.** *(Oxford Univ, and London Welsh)* S.I.F. 1957; A. 1958; E.S. 1962.

**Davies, Stan** *(Treherbert)* I. 1923.

**Davies, Stuart** *(Swansea)* I.F.E.S.A. 1992; E.S.I.Z. (1st* and 2nd) N.J. 1993; F.J.I. 1995; I*.F. 1998.

**Davies, Terry** *(Swansea and Llanelli)* E.S.I.F. 1953; E.S.I.F. 1957; A.E.S.F. 1958; E.S.I.F. 1959; E.SA. 1960; E.S.F. 1961.

**Davies, T.G.R.** *(Cardiff, Cambridge Univ. and London Welsh)* A. 1966; S.I.F.E. 1967; E.S. 1968; S.I.F.NZ.(1 and 2)A. 1969; E.S.I.F. 1971; E.S.F. 1972; NZ. 1972; E.S.I.F.A. 1973; S.F.E. 1974; F.E.S.I. 1975; E.S.I.F. 1976; I.F.E.S. 1977; E.I.S.A.(1 and 2) 1978.

**Davies,T.M.** *(London Welsh and Swansea)* S.I.F. E.NZ.(1 and 2)A. 1969; SA.S.E.I.F. 1970; E.S.I.F. 1971; E.S.F. 1972; NZ. 1972; E.S.I.F.A. 1973; S.I.F.E. 1974; F.E.S.I. 1975; A. 1975; E.S.I.F. 1976.

**Davies, W.** *(Cardiff)* S. 96.

**Davies, W.** *(Swansea)* SA. 1931; E.S.I. 1932.

**Davies, W.G.** *(Cardiff and Oxford Univ.)* A.(1 and 2)NZ. 1978; S.I.F.E. 1979; F.E.S.NZ. 1980; E.S.A. 1981; I.F.E.S. 1982; S.I.F. 1985.

**Davies, W.T.H.** *(Swansea)* I. 1936; E.I. 1937; E.S.I. 1939.

**Davies, Willie** *(Aberavon)* S.I. 1912.

**Davis, C.** *(Newbridge)* A.(2) 1978; E.S. 1981.

**Davis, Mark** *(Newport)* A. 1991.

**Davis, W.E.N.** *(Cardiff)* E.S.I. 1939.

**Dawes, S.J.** *(London Welsh)* I.F.SA. 1964; E.S.I.F. 1965; A. 1966; I.F. 1968; E.NZ.(2)A. 1969; SA.S.E.I.F. 1970; E.S.I.F. 1971.

**Day, H.** *(Newport)* I. 92; E.S. 93; S.I. 94.

**Day, H.C.** *(Newport)* S.I.F. 1930; E.S. 1931.

**Day, T.** *(Swansea)* E.S.I.F.SA. 1931; E.S.I. 1932; S.I. 1934; E.S.I. 1935.

**Deacon, T.** *(Swansea)* I. 91; E.S.I. 92.

**Delahay, W.** *(Bridgend and Cardiff)* E.S.I.F. 1922; E.S.I.F. 1923; NZ. 1924; E.S.F.I. 1926; E.S.I.F. 1926; S. 1927.

**Delaney, L.** *(Llanelli)* I.F.E. 1989; E. 1990; F.WS.AR.A. 1991; I.F.E. 1992.

**Devereux, D.** *(Neath)* A.E.S. 1958.

**Devereux, J.** *(S. Glam Inst.)* E.S.I.F.FJ.T.WS. 1986; F.E.S.I.I.C*.E.NZ.A. 1987; NZ.(1 and 2) R. 1988; S.I. 1989.

**Diplock, R.** *(Bridgend)* R. 1988.

**Dobson, G.** *(Cardiff)* S. 1900.

**Dobson, T.** *(Cardiff)* I.E. 98; E.S 99.

**Donovan, A.** *(Swansea)* A.(2) 1978; I*.A. 1981; E.S. 1982.

**Donovan, R.** *(S. Wales Constab.)* F*. 1983.

**Douglas, M.H.J.** *(Llanelli)* S.I.F. 1984.

**Douglas, W.M.** *(Cardiff)* E.S. 86, 87.

**Dowell, W.** *(Newport)* E.S.I. 1907; E.S.F.I. 1908.

**Dyke, J.C.M.** *(Penarth)* SA. 1906.

**Dyke, L.M.** *(Cardiff)* I. 1910; S.F.I. 1911.

**Edmunds, A.** *(Neath)* I.(R), B. 1990.

**Edwards, A.B.** *(London Welsh and Army)* E.S. 1955.

**Edwards, B.** *(Newport)* I. 1951.

**Edwards, D.** *(Glynneath)* E. 1921.

**Edwards, G.O.** *(Cardiff and Cardiff Training College)* F.E. 1967; NZ. 1967; E.S.I.F. 1968; S.I.F.E.NZ.(1 and 2)A. 1969; SA.S.E.I.F. 1970; E.S.I.F. 1971; E.S.F. 1972; NZ. 1972; E.S.I.F.A. 1973; S.I.F.E. 1974; F.E.S.I. 1975; A. 1975; E.S.I.F. 1976; I.F.E.S. 1977; E.S.I.F. 1978.

**Eidman, I.** *(Cardiff)* S.R. 1983; I.F.E.A. 1984; S.I.F.J. 1985; E.S.I.F. 1986.

**Elliott, J.E.** *(Cardiff)* I. 94; I.E. 98.

**Elsey, W.J.** *(Cardiff)* E. 95.

**Emyr, A.** *(Swansea and Cardiff)* E.NZ. 1989; F.E.S.I.N.(1, 2) 1990; F.F.WS.AR.A. 1991.

**Evans, A.C.** *(Pontypool)* E.I.F. 1924.

**Evans, Bryn** *(Llanelli)* E.S. 1933; E.S.I. 1936; E. 1937.

**Evans, Bryn** *(Swansea)* S. 1933.

**Evans, Bryn S.** *(Llanelli)* E. 1920; E.S.I.F. 1922.

**Evans, C.** *(Pontypool)* E. 1960.

**Evans, David W.** *(Cardiff and Treorchy)* F.E.NZ. 1989; F.E.S.I.B. 1990; A.F*.A*. 1991; J*. 1995.

**Evans, D.** *(Penygraig)* S.I. 96; E. 97; E. 98.

**Evans, D.B.** *(Swansea)* E. 1926.

**Evans, D.D.** *(Cheshire and Cardiff Univ.)* E. 1934.

**Evans, D.P.** *(Llanelli and Oxford Univ.)* SA. 1960.

**Evans, D.W.** *(Cardiff and Oxford Univ.)* S.I. 89; E.I. 90; E. 91.

**Evans, Emrys** *(Llanelli)* E. 1937; S.I, 1939.

**Evans, Frank** *(Llanelli)* S. 1921.

**Evans, Garan** *(Llanelli)* SA. 1998.

**Evans, G.** *(Cardiff)* E.S.F.I.A. 1947; E.S.F.I. 1948; E.S.I. 1949.

**Evans, G.** *(Newport)* F*. 1977; F.A*.(2) 1978.

**Evans, Gwyn** *(Maesteg)* S*.I.F.A 1981; I.F.E.S. 1982; F.R. 1983.

**Evans, Ieuan** *(Llanelli, Bath)* F.E.S.I.I.C.E.NZ.A. 1987; E.S.I.F.NZ.(1 and 2) 1988; I.F.E. 1989; E.S.I.F.A.F.WS.AR.A. 1991; I.F.E.S.A. 1992; E.S.I.F.J.C. 1993; S.I.E.P.Sp.C.FJ.T.WS.R. 1994; E.S.I.J.NZ.I.SA.FJ. 1995; It.E.S.I.F.A.(1 and 2).B.F.A.SA. 1996; USA.S.I.F. 1997; It. 1998.

**Evans, Iowerth** *(London Welsh)* S.I. 1934.

**Evans, Islwyn** *(Swansea)* E.S.I.F. 1922.

**Evans, J.** *(Llanelli)* S.I. 96; E. 97.

**Evans, J.** *(Blaina)* E. 1904.

**Evans, J.** *(Pontypool)* E.S.I. 1907.

**Evans, J.D.** *(Cardiff)* I.F. 1958.

**Evans, J. Elwyn** *(Llanelli)* S. 1924.

**Evans, J.R.** *(Newport)* E. 1934.

**Evans, Luc** *(Llanelli)* F*. 1991.

**Evans, O.J.** *(Cardiff)* E.S. 87; S.I. 88.

**Evans, Peter** *(Llanelli)* E.F. 1951.

**Evans, R.** *(Bridgend)* S.I.F. 1963.

**Evans, R.** *(Cardiff)* S. 89.

**Evans, Ricky** *(Llanelli)* E.S.I.F. 1993; S.I.F.E.P. Sp.C.FJ.WS.R.It.SA. 1994; F.NZ.I*. 1995.

**Evans, R.T.** *(Newport)* F.I. 1947; E.S.I.F. 1950, 1951.

**Evans, S.** *(Neath and Swansea)* F.E. 1985; FJ.T.WS. 1986; F.E.I.T. 1987.

**Evans, T.G.** *(London Welsh)* SA.S.E.I. 1970; E.S.F. 1972.

**Evans, T.P.** *(Swansea)* F.E.S.I. 1975. A. 1975; E.S.I.F. 1976; I. 1977.

**Evans, Tom** *(Llanelli)* I. 1906; E.S.I. 1907; I.A. 1908; E.S.F.I. 1909; F.E.S.I. 1910; E.S.F.I. 1911.

**Evans, Tom** *(Swansea)* I. 1924.

**Evans, V.** *(Neath)* I.F.S. 1954.

**Evans, W.F.** *(Rhymney)* I. 82; S. 83.

**Evans, W.G.** *(Brynmawr)* I. 1911.

**Evans, W.H.** *(Llwynypia)* E.S.F.I. 1914.

**Evans, W.J.** *(Pontypool)* S. 1947.

**Evans, W.R.** *(Cardiff, Bridgend and Cambridge Univ.)* A.E.S.I.F. 1958; SA. 1960; E.S.I.F. 1961; E.S. 1962; I. 1962.

**Evans, W. Rice** *(Swansea)* S. 90; E.S. 91.

**Evans, Wynne** *(Llanelli)* A. 1958.

**Everson, W.** *(Newport)* S. 1926.

**Faulkner, A.G.** *(Pontypool)* F.E.S.I. 1975; A. 1975; E.S.I.F. 1976; E.S.I.F.A.(1 and 2)NZ. 1978; S.I.F. 1979.

**Faull, J.** *(Swansea)* I.F. 1957; A.E.S.I.F. 1958; E.S.I. 1959; E.F. 1960.

**Fauvel, T.** *(Aberavon)* *NZ.(1) 1988.

**Fear, A.** *(Newport)* S.I. 1934, 1935.

**Fender, N.** *(Cardiff)* I.F. 1930; E.S.F.I. 1931.

**Fenwick, S.P.** *(Bridgend)* F.E.S. 1975; A. 1975; E.S.I.F. 1976; I.F.E.S. 1977; E.S.I.F.A.(1 and 2), NZ. 1978; S.I.F.E. 1979; F.E.S.I.NZ. 1980; E.S. 1981.

**Finch, E.** *(Llanelli)* F.NZ. 1924; F.I. 1925; F. 1926; NSW. 1927; I. 1928.

**Finlayson, A.J.** *(Cardiff)* I.F.E. 1974.

**Fitzgerald, D.** *(Cardiff)* S.I. 94.

**Ford, F.J.V.** *(Welch Regt. and Newport)* E. 1939.

**Ford, I** *(Newport)* E.S. 1959.

**Ford, S.** *(Cardiff)* I.N.(1,2), B. 1990; E.S.I.A. 1991.

**Forward, A.** *(Pontypool and Mon. Police)* S. 1951; SA. 1951; E.S.I.F. 1952.

**Fowler, I.** *(Llanelli)* NZ. 1919.

**Francis, G.** *(Llanelli and Oxford Univ)* NZ. 1919; S. 1924.

**Francis, P.W.** *(Maesteg)* S. 1987.

**Funnell, John** *(Ebbw Vale)* Z*.SA. 1998.

**Gabe, R.T.** *(Llanelli and Cardiff)* I. 1901; E.S.I. 1902, 1903, 1904, 1905; NZ. 1905; E.I. 1906; SA. 1906; E.S.I. 1907; E.S.F.I. 1908.

**Gale, N.R.** *(Swansea and Llanelli)* I. 1960; E.S.I.NZ. 1963; E.S.I.F.SA. 1964; E.S.I.F. 1965; E.S.I.F.A. 1966; E. 1967; NZ. 1967; E. 1968; NZ.(1* and 2)A. 1969.

**Gallacher, I.S.** *(Llanelli)* F. 1970.

**Garrett, R.M.** *(Penarth)* M. 88; S. 89; E.S.I. 90; S.I. 91; E. 92.

**Geen, W.P.** *(Oxford Univ. and Newport)* SA. 1912; E.I. 1913.

**George, E.** *(Pontypridd & Cardiff)* S.I. 95; E. 96.

**George, G.M.** *(Newport)* E.S. 1991.

**Gethin, Glyn** *(Neath)* F. 1913.

**Gibbs, Andrew** *(Newbridge and Llanelli)* I.SA. 1995; A. 1996; USA (1 and 2).C. 1997.

**Gibbs, I.S.** *(Neath and Swansea)* E.S.I.F.A.F.WS. AR.A. 1991; I.F.E.S.A. 1992; E.S.I.F.J.C. 1993; It.A.SA. 1996; USA.S.I.F.T.NZ. 1997; It.E.S. 1998.

**Gibbs, R.A.** *(Cardiff)* S.I. 1906; E.S. 1907; E.S.F.I. 1908; F.E.S.I. 1910; E.S.F.I. 1911.

**Giles, S.R.** *(Aberavon)* R. 1983; FJ* 1985; C. 1987.

**Girling, B.E.** *(Cardiff)* E. 81.

**Goldsworthy, S.** *(Swansea)* I. 84; E.S. 85.

**Gore, J.** *(Blaina)* I.F.NZ. 1924; E. 1925.

**Gore, W.** *(Newbridge)* S.F.I. 1947.

**Gough, Ian** *(Newport)* SA. 1998.

**Gould, A.J.** *(Newport)* E.S. 85, 86; E.S.I. 87; S. 88; I. 89; S.E.I. 90; E.S.I. 92, 93; E.S. 94; E.S.I. 95, 96; E. 97.

**Gould, B.** *(Newport)* I. 92; S.I. 93.

**Gould, R.** *(Newport)* I.E. 82; S. 83; E.S.I. 84; E.S. 85; E. 86; E.S. 87.

**Graham, T.C.** *(Newport)* I. 90; S.I. 91; E.S. 92; E.S.I. 93; E.S. 94, 95.

**Gravell, R.W.R.** *(Llanelli)* F.E.S.I.A. 1975; E.S.I.F. 1976; E.S.I.F.A.(1 and 2)NZ. 1978; S.I. 1979; I.F. 1981; F.E.S. 1982.

**Gray, A.J.** *(London Welsh)* E.S. 1968.

**Greenslade, D.** *(Newport)* S. 1962.

**Greville, H.** *(Llanelli)* A. 1947.

**Griffin, Dr.A.** *(Edinburgh Univ.)* S. 83.

**Griffiths, C.** *(Llanelli)* E*. 1979.

**Griffiths, D.** *(Llanelli)* M. 88; I. 89.

**Griffiths, G.** *(Llanelli)* I. 89.

**Griffiths, Gareth** *(Cardiff)* E.S.I.F. 1953; NZ. 1953; I.F.S. 1954; I.F. 1955; E.S. 1957.

**Griffiths, J.** *(Llanelli)* NZ.(2nd) 1988; S. 1989.

**Griffiths, M.** *(Bridgend, Cardiff and Pontypirdd)* WS.R. 1988; S.I.F.E.NZ. 1989; F.E.N.(1,2)B. 1990; I.F.F.WS.AR.A. 1991; I.F.E.S.A. 1992; Z.(1st and 2nd)N.J.C. 1993; F*.E.S.I.J.I. 1995; SA. 1998.

**Griffiths, V.M.** *(Newport)* S.I.F. 1924.

**Gronow, B.** *(Bridgend)* F.E.S.I. 1910.

**Gwilliam, J.A.** *(Cambridge Univ., Edinburgh Wanderers and Gloucester)* A. 1947; I. 1948; E.S.I.F. 1949, 1950; E.S.I.SA. 1951; E.S.I.F. 1952; E.I.F. 1953; NZ. 1953; E. 1954.

**Gwynn, D.** *(Swansea)* E. 82; S. 87; E.I. 90; E.S. 91.

**Gwynn, W.H.** *(Swansea)* E.S.I. 84; E.S. 85.

**Hadley, A.M.** *(Cardiff)* R. 1983; S.I.F.E. 1984; F.E.FJ. 1985; E.S.I.F.FJ.T. 1986; S.*I.I.T.C. E.NZ.A.USA. 1987; E.S.I.F. 1988.

**Hall, I.** *(Aberavon)* NZ. 1967; SA.S.E. 1970; S. 1971; S.I.F. 1974.

**Hall, M.** *(Bridgend and Cardiff)* *NZ.(1) NZ.(2nd) WS.R. 1988; S.I.F.E.NZ. 1989; F.E.S. 1990; A.F.WS.AR.A. 1991; I.F.E.S.A. 1992; E.S.I. 1993; S.I.F.E.P.Sp.C.T.R.It.SA. 1994; F.S.I.J.NZ.I. 1995.

**Hall, W.** *(Bridgend)* WS. 1988.

**Hancock, F.E.** *(Cardiff)* I. 84; E.S. 85; S. 86.

**Hannan, J.** *(Newport)* M. 88; S.I. 89; S.E.I. 90; E. 91; E.S.I. 92, 93, 94, 95.

**Harding, A.F.** *(Cardiff and London Welsh)* E.S.I. 1902, 1903, 1904, 1905; NZ. 1905; E.S.I. 1906; SA. 1906; I. 1907; E.S. 1908.

**Harding, G.F.** *(Newport)* E. 81; I.E. 82; S. 83.

**Harding, Rowe** *(Swansea and Cambridge)* E.S.F.I. 1923; I.F.NZ. 1924; F.I. 1925; E.I.F. 1926; E.S.F.I. 1927; E. 1928.

**Harding, Theo** *(Newport)* M. 88; S.I. 89.

**Harris, D.J.E.** *(Pontypridd and Cardiff)* I.F. 1959; S.I.F. 1960; SA. 1960; E.S. 1961.

**Harris, Tal.** *(Aberavon)* NSW. 1927.

**Hathway, G.** *(Newport)* I.F. 1924.

**Havard, Rev. W.T.** *(Llanelli)* NZ. 1919.

**Hawkins, F.** *(Pontypridd)* I.F. 1912.

**Hayward, Byron** *(Ebbw Vale)* Z*.SA. 1998.

**Hayward, D.** *(Newbridge)* E.F. 1949; E.S.I.F. 1950; E.S.I.F. 1951; SA. 1951; E.S.I.F. 1952.

**Hayward, D.J.** *(Cardiff)* E. 1963; NZ. 1963; S.I.F.SA. 1964.

**Hayward, G.** *(Swansea)* S.F.I.A. 1908; E. 1909.

**Hellings, R.** *(Llwynypia)* E. 97; I.E. 98; S.I. 99; E.I. 1900; E.S. 1901.

**Herrera, R.** *(Cross Keys)* S.F.I. 1925; E.S.I.F. 1926; E. 1927.

**Hiams, H.** *(Swansea)* I.F. 1912.

**Hickman, Arthur** *(Neath)* E. 1930; S. 1933.

**Hiddlestone, D.** *(Neath)* E.S.I.F. 1922; NZ. 1924.

**Hill, A.F.** *(Cardiff)* S. 85; E.S. 86; S.I.M. 88; S. 89; S.I. 90; E.S.I. 93, 94.

**Hill, Simon** *(Cardiff)* Z.(1st and 2nd)N. 1993; I. *F.SA. 1994; F.SA. 1995; A.F*.It. 1996; E. 1997.

**Hinam, S.** *(Cardiff)* I. 1925; E.S.I.F. 1926.

**Hinton, J.T.** *(Cardiff)* I. 84.

**Hirst, G.L.** *(Newport)* S. 1912, 1913; E.S.F.I. 1914.

**Hodder, W.** *(Pontypool)* E.S.F. 1921.

**Hodges, J.J.** *(Newport)* E.S.I. 99, 1900; E.S. 1901; E.S.I. 1902, 1903; E.S. 1904; E.S.I. 1905; NZ. 1905; E.S.I. 1906.

**Hodgson, G.T.R.** *(Neath)* I. 1962; E.S.I.F. 1963; NZ. 1963; E.S.I.F.SA. 1966; S.I.F. 1966; I. 1967.

**Hollingdale, B.** *(Swansea)* SA. 1912; E. 1913.

**Hollingdale, T.** *(Neath)* NSW. 1927; E.S.I.F. 1928; E. 1930.

**Holmes, T.D.** *(Cardiff)* A.(2)NZ. 1978; S.I.F.E. 1979; F.E.S.I.NZ. 1980; A. 1981; I.F.E. 1982; E.S.I.F. 1983; E. 1984; S.I.F.E.FJ. 1985.

**Hopkin, W.H.** *(Newport)* S. 1937.

**Hopkins, K.** *(Cardiff and Swansea)* E. 1985; F.E.S.T.C.*USA. 1987.

**Hopkins, Phil** *(Swansea)* A. 1908; E.I. 1909; E. 1910.

**Hopkins, R.** *(Maesteg)* E*. 1970.

**Hopkins, T.** *(Swansea)* E.S.I.F. 1926.

**Hopkins, W.J.** *(Aberavon)* E.S. 1925.

**Howells, Bryn** *(Llanelli)* E. 1934.

**Howells, G.** *(Llanelli)* E.S.I.F. 1957.

**Howells, W.H.** *(Swansea)* S.I. 88.

**Howley, R.** *(Bridgend and Cardiff)* E.S.I.F.A.(1 and 2).B.F.It.A.SA. 1996; USA.S.I.F.E.T.*NZ. 1997; It.E.S.I.F.Z. 1998.

**Hughes, D.** *(Newbridge)* NZ. 1967; NZ.(2) 1969; SA.S.E.I. 1970.

**Hughes, Gomer** *(Penarth)* E.S.I. 1934.

**Hughes, H.** *(Cardiff)* S. 87, 89.

**Hughes, K.** *(Cambridge Univ. and London Welsh)* I. 1970. A. 1973; S. 1974.

**Hullin, W.** *(Cardiff)* S. 1967.

**Humphreys, J.** *(Cardiff)* NZ.I.SA.FJ. 1995; It.E. S.I.F.A.(1 and 2).B.It.A.SA.1996; S.I.F.E.T*. NZ*. 1997; It*.E*.S*.I*.F*. 1998.

**Hurrell, J.** *(Newport)* F. 1959.

**Hutchinson, F.** *(Neath)* I. 94; S.I. 96.

**Huxtable, R.** *(Swansea)* F.I. 1931.

**Huzzey, V.** *(Cardiff)* E.I. 98; E.S.I. 99.

**Hybart, A.J.** *(Cardiff)* E. 87.

**Ingledew, H.M.** *(Cardiff)* I. 90; E.S. 91.

**Isaacs, I.** *(Cardiff)* E.S. 1933.

**Jackson, T.H.** *(Swansea)* E. 95.

**James, B.** *(Bridgend)* E. 1968.

**James, C.** *(Llanelli)* A.F. 1958.

**James, Dafydd** *(Bridgend and Pontypridd)* A*.It.A.SA. 1996; I.T*. 1997; F*.Z.SA. 1998.

**James, D.R.** *(Treorchy)* F.I. 1931.

**James, David** *(Swansea)* I. 91; S.I. 92; E. 99.

**James, Evan** *(Swansea)* S. 90, I. 91; S.I. 92; E. 99.

**James, Maldwyn** *(Cardiff)* A. 1947; E.S.F.I. 1948.

**James, T.O.** *(Aberavon)* I. 1935; S. 1937.

**James, W.J.** *(Aberavon)* E.S.I.F.R 1983; S. 1984; S.I.F.E.FJ. 1985; E.S.I.F.FJ.T.WS. 1986; E.S.I. 1987.

**James, W.P.** *(Aberavon)* E.S. 1925.

**Jarman, H.** *(Newport)* E.S.I. 1910; E. 1911.

**Jarrett, K.S.** *(Newport)* E. 1967; E.S. 1968; S.I.F.E.NZ.(1 and 2)A. 1969.

**Jarvis, Lee** *(Cardiff)* R*. 1997.

**Jeffrey, J.J.** *(Cardiff College of Education and Newport)* NZ. 1967.

**Jenkins, Albert** *(Llanelli)* E.S.F.I. 1920; S.F. 1921; F. 1922; E.S.F.I. 1923; NZ. 1924; S.I. 1928.

**Jenkins, A.M.** *(Swansea)* I. 95; E. 96.

**Jenkins, D.** *(Treorchy)* E.S.I.F. 1926.

**Jenkins, D.R.** *(Swansea)* NSW. 1927; E. 1929.

**Jenkins, E.** *(Newport)* S.I. 1910.

**Jenkins, E.M.** *(Aberavon)* S.F.I. 1927; NSW. 1927; E.S.I.F. 1928; F. 1929; E.S.I.F. 1930; E.S.F.I. 1931; SA. 1931; E.S.I. 1932.

**Jenkins, G.R.** *(Pontypool and Swansea)* F.WS.*AR.A. 1991; I.F.E.S.A. 1992; C. 1993; S.I.F.E.P Sp.C.T.WS.R.It.SA. 1994; F.E.S.I.J. *SA. *FJ. 1995 *E. 1996; USA.USA.C. 1997; S.I.F.Z.SA*. 1998.

**Jenkins, J.C.** *(London Welsh)* SA. 1906.

**Jenkins, L.** *(Aberavon)* S.F. 1923.

**Jenkins, Leighton** *(Mon. Training College and Newport)* I. 1954; E.S.I.F. 1956.

**Jenkins, N.R.** *(Pontypridd)* E.S.I.F. 1991; I.F.E.S. 1992; E.S.I.F.Z. (1st and 2nd) N.J.C. 1993; S.I.F.E.P.Sp.C.T.WS.R.It.SA. 1994; F.E.S.I.J. NZ.I.SA.FJ. 1995; F.A. (1 and 2).B.F.It.A*.SA. 1996; S.I.F.E.T.NZ. 1997; It.E.S.I.F. 1998.

**Jenkins, T-Pryce** *(London Welsh)* S.I. 88.

**Jenkins, V.G.** *(Oxford Univ. London Welsh and Bridgend)* E.I. 1933; S.I. 1934; E.S. 1935; NZ. 1935; E.S.I. 1936; E. 1937; E.S. 1938; E. 1939.

**Jenkins, W.** *(Cardiff)* I.F. 1912; S.I. 1913.
**John, A.** *(Llanelli)* I. 1925; E.S.I. 1928.
**John, B.** *(Llanelli and Cardiff)* A. 1966; S. 1967;
 NZ. 1967; E.S.I.F. 1968; S.I.F.E.NZ.(1 and 2)A.
 1969; SA.S.E.I. 1970; E.S.I.F. 1971; E.S.F.
 1972.
**John, D.E.** *(Llanelli)* F.I. 1923; E.S.I. 1928.
**John, G.** *(St. Luke's College, Exeter)* E.F. 1954.
**John, J.H.** *(Swansea)* E.S.I.F. 1926; E.S.F.I.
 1927.
**John, Paul.** *(Pontypridd)* T. 1994; B*. 1996;
 USA*.USA (1 and 2).C.R.T. 1997; Z*.SA. 1998.
**John, R.** *(Neath)* E.S.I.F. 1950, 1951; SA. 1951;
 E.S.I.F. 1952; E.S.I.F. 1953; NZ. 1953; E. 1954.
**John, Spencer** *(Llanelli and Cardiff)* S.I. 1995;
 E*.T.NZ*. 1997.
**Johnson, T.** *(Cardiff)* E.F.I. 1921; E.S.F. 1923;
 E.S.NZ. 1924; E.S.F. 1925.
**Johnson, W.D.** *(Swansea)* E. 1953.
**Jones, A.H.** *(Cardiff)* E.S. 1933.
**Jones, B.J.** *(Newport)* I.F. 1960.
**Jones, Bedwellty** *(Abertillery)* E.S.F.I. 1914.
**Jones, Bert** *(Llanelli)* S.I. 1934.
**Jones, Bob** *(Llwynypia)* I. 1901.
**Jones, C.W.** *(Bridgend)* E.S.F. 1920.
**Jones, Cliff** *(Llandovery College, Cambridge
 Univ. and Cardiff)* E.S.I. 1934, 1935; NZ. 1935;
 E.S.I. 1936, 1938.
**Jones, D.** *(Neath)* NSW. 1927.
**Jones, Dan** *(Aberavon)* E. 97.
**Jones, David** *(Newport)* E.S.I.F. 1926; E. 1927.
**Jones, David** *(Swansea)* E.F.I. 1947; E.S.I.F.
 1949.
**Jones, David** *(Treherbert)* E.S.I. 1902, 1903,
 1905; NZ. 1905; E.S. 1906; SA. 1906.
**Jones, Derwyn** *(Cardiff)* SA. 1994; F.E.S.J.NZ.I.
 SA.FJ. 1995; It.E.S.I.F.A. (1and 2).B.It.A. 1996.
**Jones, Desmond** *(Llanelli)* E. 1948.
**Jones, D.K.** *(Llanelli, Cardiff and Oxford Univ.)*
 E.S.F.I. 1962; E.F.NZ. 1963; E.S.SA. 1964;
 E.S.I.F. 1966.
**Jones, D.N. Rocyn** *(St. Mary's Hospital,
 Cambridge Univ. and Newport)* I. 1925.
**Jones, D.P.** *(Pontypool)* I. 1907.
**Jones, Edgar.** *(Llanelli)* F. 1930; E.S.I 1933; E.
 1935.
**Jones, Elvet** *(Llanelli)* S. 1939.
**Jones, Gareth** *(Bridgend)* SA. 1995.
**Jones, Gary** *(Llanelli)* NZ.(2nd) 1988; F.E.NZ.
 1989; F. 1990.
**Jones, Graham** *(Cardiff)* S. 1930; I. 1933.
**Jones, Graham** *(Ebbw Vale)* S.I.F. 1963.
**Jones, G.R. Rees** *(Oxford and London Welsh)*
 E.S. 1934; I. 1935; NZ. 1935; E. 1936.
**Jones, Gwyn** *(Llanelli and Cardiff)* It.E.S.I.F.A.
 1996; USA*. S*. USA (1 and 2).R.T.NZ. 1997.
**Jones, Harold** *(Neath)* E.S. 1929.
**Jones, Harry** *(Penygraig)* S.I. 1902.
**Jones, Howel** *(Neath)* I. 1904.
**Jones, Howie** *(Swansea)* I.F. 1930.
**Jones, I.C.** *(London Welsh and Oxford Univ.)* I.
 1968.
**Jones, Iowerth** *(Llanelli)* NSW. 1927; E.S.I.F.
 1928.
**Jones, Ivor** *(Llanelli)* E.S. 1924; S.F.I. 1927;
 NSW. 1927; E.S.I.F. 1928; E.S.F.I. 1929; E.S.
 1930.
**Jones, J.** *(Aberavon)* E. 1901.
**Jones, J.A** *(Cardiff)* S. 83.

**Jones, Jim** *(Aberavon)* NZ. 1919; E.S. 1920;
 S.F.I. 1921.
**Jones, Joe** *(Swansea)* F. 1924.
**Jones, J.P.** *(Newport and Pontypool)* A. 1908;
 E.S.F.I. 1909; F.E. 1910; E.F. 1912; F.I. 1913,
 1920; E. 1921.
**Jones, J. Strand** *(Llanelli and Oxford Univ.)*
 E.S.I. 1902; E.S. 1903.
**Jones, K.D.** *(Cardiff)* SA. 1960; E.S.I. 1961; E.F.
 1962; E.S.I. 1963; NZ. 1963.
**Jones, Ken** *(Monmouth and London Welsh)* E.
 1934.
**Jones, Ken** *(Newport)* E.S.F.I.A. 1947; E.S.F.I.
 1948; E.S.I.F. 1949, 1950, 1951; SA. 1951;
 E.S.I.F. 1952, 1953; NZ. 1953; E.I.F.S. 1954;
 E.S.I.F. 1955, 1956; S. 1957.
**Jones, Kingsley** *(Ebbw Vale)* B.F.It.A. 1996; I*.E.
 1997; S.I.F*.SA. 1998
**Jones, Lewis** *(Devonport Services and Llanelli)*
 E.S.I.F. 1950; E.S. 1951; SA. 1951; E.I.F. 1952.
**Jones, Lyn** *(Llanelli)* Z.(1st and 2nd)N.J.C. 1993.
**Jones, Mark** *(Neath and Ebbw Vale)* S. 1987;
 NZ.*(2nd)   1988;   S.I.E.F.NZ.   1989;
 F.E.S.I.N.(1,2)B. 1990; Z. 1998.
**Jones, Marsden** *(Cardiff and London Welsh)* E.
 1921; NZ. 1924.
**Jones, P. Baker** *(Newport)* S. 1921.
**Jones, Percy** *(Newport and Pontypool)* SA.
 1912; E.S.F. 1913; E.S.F.I. 1914.
**Jones, R.** *(London Welsh)* E. 1929.
**Jones, R.** *(Swansea)* I. 1901, E. 1902; E.S.I.
 1904; E. 1905; F.I.A. 1908; E.S.F.I. 1909; F.E.
 1910.
**Jones, R.B.** *(Cambridge)* E.S. 1933.
**Jones, R.E.** *(Coventry)* F.E. 1967; S.I.F. 1968.
**Jones, Robert** *(Northampton)* E.S.F. 1926.
**Jones, R.N.** *(Swansea)* E.S.I.F.FJ.T.WS. 1986;
 F.E.S.I.I.T.E.NZ.A.USA. 1987; E.S.I.F.NZ(1).
 WS.R. 1988; I.F.E.NZ. 1989; F.E.S.I. 1990;
 E.S.F.WS.AR.A. 1991; I.F.E.S.A. 1992; E.S.I.
 1993; I.*P. 1994; F.E.S.I.NZ.I. 1995.
**Jones, Roy** *(Swansea)* NSW. 1927; F. 1928.
**Jones, Stephen** *(Llanelli)* SA*. 1998.
**Jones, S.T.** *(Pontypool)* S.I.F.R. 1983; S. 1984;
 E.S.F.NZ.(1 and 2) 1988.
**Jones, T.B.** *(Newport)* I.E. 82; S. 83; S. 84; E.S
 85.
**Jones, Tom** *(Newport)* E.S.I.F. 1922; E.S. 1924.
**Jones, Tuan** *(Pontypool)* S. 1913.
**Jones, W.** *(Cardiff)* I.E. 98.
**Jones, W.I.** *(Llanelli and Cambridge)* E.S.F.I.
 1925.
**Jones, W.J.** *(Llanelli)* I. 1924.
**Jones, W.K.** *(Cardiff)* NZ. 1967; E.S.I.F. 1968.
**Jones, Wyndham** *(Mountain Ash)* I. 1905.
**Jones-Davies, T.E.** *(London Welsh)* E.I. 1930;
 E.S. 1933.
**Jordan, H.M.** *(Newport)* E.S. 85; S. 89.
**Joseph, W.** *(Swansea)* E.S.I. 1902, 1903; E.S.
 1904; E.S.I.NZ. 1905; E.S.I. 1906; SA. 1906.
**Jowett, F.** *(Swansea)* E. 1903.
**Judd, S.** *(Cardiff)* E.S.I.F. 1953; NZ. 1953; E.F.S.
 1954; E.S. 1955.
**Judson, J.H.** *(Llandovery Coll.)* E. 82; S. 83.
**Kedzlie, Q.D.** *(Cardiff)* SI. 88.
**Keen, L.** *(Aberavon)* F.E.S.I. 1980.
**Knight, P.** *(Pontypridd)* N.(1,2),B.* 1990; E.S.
 1991.
**Knill, F.M.D.** *(Cardiff)* F*. 1976.

**Lamerton, A.E.** (Llanelli) F.Z.(1st and 2nd)N.J. 1993.

**Lane, S.** (Cardiff) A. (1* and 2) 1978; I.* 1979; S.I. 1980.

**Lang, J.** (Llanelli and Swansea) F.I. 1931; S.I. 1934; E.S.I. 1935; NZ. 1935; E.S.I. 1936; E. 1937.

**Law, V.J.** (Newport) I. 1939.

**Lawrence, S.** (Bridgend) S.I. 1925; S.I.F. 1926; E. 1927.

**Legge, W.G.** (Newport) I. 1937, 1938.

**Leleu, J.** (London Welsh and Swansea) E.S. 1959; F. 1960; SA. 1960.

**Lemon, A.** (Neath) I. 1929; S.I.F. 1930; E.S.F.I.SA. 1931; E.S.I. 1932; I. 1933.

**Lewis, A.J.L.** (Ebbw Vale) F. 1970; E.I.F. 1971; E.S.F. 1972; E.S.F.I. 1973.

**Lewis, Andrew** (Cardiff) It.E.S.I.A*. 1996; It.E.S. I.F. 1998.

**Lewis, A.R.** (Abertillery) E.S.I.F. 1966; A. 1966; I. 1967.

**Lewis, Bryn** (Cambridge Univ. and Swansea) I. 1912, 1913.

**Lewis, Clem** (Cardiff and Cambridge Univ.) E. 1912; S.F.I. 1913; E.S.F.I. 1914; I. 1921; E.S. 1923.

**Lewis, C.P.** (Llandovery) I.E. 82; S. 83; E.S. 84.

**Lewis, D.H.** (Cardiff) E.S. 86.

**Lewis, Emyr** (Llanelli and Cardiff) I.F.A.F.WS.AR.A. 1991; I.F.S.A. 1992; E.S.I.F.Z. (1st and 2nd) N.J.C. 1993; S.I.F.E.P.Sp.F.J. WS.R.It.SA. 1994; E.S.I.J.I. 1995; It.E.S.I.F. 1996.

**Lewis, E.J.** (Llandovery) E. 81.

**Lewis, Geraint** (Pontypridd) SA*. 1998.

**Lewis, G. Windsor** (Richmond and Cambridge Univ) E.S. 1960.

**Lewis, Howell** (Swansea) S.F.I. 1913; E. 1914.

**Lewis, J.** (Llanelli) I. 87.

**Lewis, J.R.** (Cardiff and S. Glam. Inst.) E.S.I.F. 1981; F.E.S. 1982.

**Lewis, Mark** (Treorchy) F. 1913.

**Lewis, P.I.** (Llanelli) A. 1984; S.I.F.E. 1985; E.S.I. 1986.

**Lewis, Tom** (Cardiff) E. 1926; E.S. 1927.

**Lewis, W.** (Llanelli) F. 1925.

**Lewis, Windsor** (London Welsh, Maesteg and Cambridge) I. 1926; E.F.I. 1927; NSW. 1927; F. 1928.

**Llewellyn, David** (Ebbw Vale) SA.* 1998.

**Llewellyn, D.B.** (Newport and Llanelli) SA.S.E.I.F. 1970; E.S.I.F. 1971; E.S.F. 1972; NZ. 1972.

**Llewellyn, Gareth** (Neath and Harlequins) NZ. 1989; E.S.I. 1990; E.S.A.* 1991; I.F.E.S.A. 1992; E.S.I.F.Z. (1st and 2nd) N.J.C. 1993; S.I.F.E.P.Sp.C.T. WS.R.It.SA. 1994; F.E.S.I.J. NZ.I. 1995; It.E.S.I.F.A. (1 and 2).B.F.It.A.SA. 1996; USA.S.I.F.E.USA (1 and 2).NZ. 1997; It. E. 1998.

**Llewellyn, Glyn** (Neath) N. (1, 2).B. 1990; E.S.I.F.A.F. 1991.

**Llewellyn, P.D.** (Swansea) I.F.A. 1973; S.E. 1974.

**Llewellyn, W.** (Llwynypia, London Welsh, Newport and Penygraig) E.S.I. 99, 1900, 1901, 1902; I. 1903; E.S.I. 1904, 1905; NZ. 1905.

**Loader, Christian** (Swansea) SA.F.J. 1995; F.A. (1 and 2).B.F.It.A.SA. 1996; USA.S.I.F.E.USA. R.T.NZ. 1997.

**Lloyd, D.J.** (Bridgend) E.S.I.F. 1966; A. 1966; S.I.F.E. 1967; S.I.F. 1968; S.I.F.E.NZ.(1)A. 1969; F. 1970; E.S.F. 1972; E.S. 1973.

**Lloyd, E.** (Llanelli) S. 95.

**Lloyd, G.L.** (Newport) I. 96; S.I. 99; E.S. 1900; E.S. 1901; S.I. 1902; E.S.I. 1903.

**Lloyd, P.** (Llanelli) S.E. 90; E.I. 91.

**Lloyd, R.** (Pontypool) S.F.I. 1913; E.S.F.I. 1914.

**Lloyd, T.** (Maesteg) I.F. 1953.

**Lloyd, T.C.** (Neath) F. 1909; F.I. 1913; E.S.F.I. 1914.

**Lockwood, T.W.** (Newport) E.S.I. 87.

**Long, E.** (Swansea) E.S.I. 1936; E.S. 1937; S.I. 1939.

**Lyne, H.S.** (Newport) S. 83; E.S.I. 84; E. 85.

**Maddocks, H.T.** (London Welsh) E.S.I. 1906; E.S. 1907; F. 1910.

**Maddocks, K.** (Neath) E. 1957.

**Main, D.R.** (London Welsh) E.S.I.F. 1959.

**Mainwaring, H.J.** (Swansea) F. 1961.

**Mainwaring, W.T.** (Aberavon) S.I.F.E. 1967; NZ. 1967; E. 1968.

**Major, W.** (Maesteg) F. 1949; S. 1950.

**Male, B.O.** (Cross Keys, Pontypool and Cardiff) F. 1921; S. 1923; S.I. 1924; E.S.F.I. 1927; S.I.F. 1928.

**Manfield, L.** (Mountain Ash and Cardiff) S.I. 1939; A. 1947; E.S.F.I. 1948.

**Mann, B.B.** (Cardiff) E. 81.

**Mantle, J.** (Loughborough College and Newport) E.SA. 1964.

**Margrave, F.L.** (Llanelli) E.S. 84.

**Martin, A.J.** (Aberavon) A. 1973; S.I. 1974; F.E.S.I. 1975; A. 1975; E.S.I.F. 1976; I.F.E.S. 1977; E.S.I.F.A.(1 and 2)NZ. 1978; S.I.F.E. 1979; F.E.S.I.NZ. 1980; I.F. 1981.

**Martin, W.J.** (Newport) I.F. 1912; NZ. 1919.

**Mason, J.** (Pontypridd) NZ.* (2nd) 1988.

**Mathias, R.** (Llanelli) F. 1970.

**Matthews, Rev. A.A.** (Lampeter) S. 86.

**Matthews, Chris** (Bridgend) I. 1939.

**Matthews, Jack** (Cardiff) E.A. 1947; E.S.F. 1948; E.S.I.F. 1949, 1950, 1951.

**May, P.** (Llanelli) E.S.I.F.NZ.(1 and 2) 1988; WS. 1991.

**McBryde, R.** (Swansea and Llanelli) FJ. SA.* 1994; USA. 1997.

**McCall, B.E.W.** (Welch Regt. and Newport) E.S.I. 1936.

**McCarley, A.** (Neath) E.S.I. 1938.

**McCutcheon, W.** (Swansea) S. 91; E.S. 92; E.S.I. 93; E. 94.

**McIntosh, Dale** (Pontypridd) SA. 1996; E*. 1997.

**Meek, N.** (Pontypool) E.S.I. 1993.

**Meredith, A.** (Devonport Services) E.S.I. 1949.

**Meredith, B.V.** (St. Luke's College, London Welsh and Newport) I.F.S. 1954; E.S.I.F. 1955, 1956, 1957; A.E.S.I. 1958; E.S.I.F. 1959; E.S.F. 1960; SA. 1960; E.S.I. 1961; E.S.F. 1962; I. 1962.

**Meredith, C.C.** (Neath) S. 1953; NZ. 1953; E.I.F.S. 1954; E.S.I.F. 1955; E.I. 1956; E.S. 1957.

**Meredith, J.** (Swansea) S.I. 88; E.S. 90.

**Merry, G.E.** (Pill Harriers) I.F. 1912.

**Michael, G.** (Swansea) E.S.F. 1923.

**Michaelson, R.C.B.** (Aberavon and Cambridge Univ.) E. 1963.

**Miller, F.** (Mountain Ash) I. 96; E.S.I. 1900, 1901.

113

**Mills, F.** *(Swansea and Cardiff)* E.S.I. 92, 93, 94, 95; E. 96.

**Moon, Rupert** *(Llanelli)* F.Z. (1st and 2nd) N.J.C. 1993; S.I.F.E.Sp.C.FJ.WS.R.It.SA. 1994; E*. 1995.

**Moore, Andrew** *(Swansea)* *SA. FJ. 1995; S.I.F. Z.SA. 1998.

**Moore, Andy** *(Cardiff)* J.SA.FJ. 1995; It. 1996.

**Moore, Steve** *(Swansea and Moseley)* C*.R.T. 1997.

**Moore, W.J.** *(Bridgend)* I. 1933.

**Morgan, C.H.** *(Llanelli)* I.F. 1957.

**Morgan, C.I** *(Cardiff and Bective Rangers)* I.F. 1951; SA. 1951; E.S.I. 1952; S.I.F. 1953; NZ. 1953; E.I.S. 1954; E.S.I.F. 1955, 1956, 1957, 1958.

**Morgan, D.** *(Llanelli)* I. 95; E. 96.

**Morgan, D.** *(Swansea)* S. 85, E.S. 86; E.S.I. 87; I. 89.

**Morgan, D.R.** *(Llanelli)* E.S.F.I. 1962; E.S.I.F. 1963; NZ. 1963.

**Morgan, E.** *(Llanelli)* I. 1920; E.S.F. 1921.

**Morgan, E.** *(London Welsh)* E.S.I. 1902; I. 1903; E.S.I 1904, 1905; NZ. 1905; E.S.I.SA. 1906; F. 1908.

**Morgan, E.** *(Swansea)* E.S.I. 1938; E. 1939.

**Morgan, Edgar** *(Swansea)* E.S.F.I. 1914.

**Morgan, F.L** *(Llanelli)* E.S.I. 1938; E. 1939.

**Morgan, H.J.** *(Abertillery)* E.S.I.F. 1958; I.F. 1959; E. 1960; E.S.I.F. 1961; E.S.F.I. 1962; S.I.F. 1963; E.S.I.F. 1965; E.S.I.F. 1966; A. 1966.

**Morgan, H.P.** *(Newport and Cambridge Univ.)* E.S.I.F. 1956.

**Morgan, Ivor** *(Swansea)* A. 1908; E.S.F.I. 1909; F.E.S.I. 1910; E.F.I. 1911; S. 1912.

**Morgan, J.** *(Llanelli)* SA. 1912; E. 1913.

**Morgan, Kevin** *(Pontypridd)* USA (1 and 2).C.R. NZ. 1997; S.I.F. 1998.

**Morgan, N.** *(Newport)* S.I.F. 1960.

**Morgan, P.** *(Aberavon)* E.S.F. 1961.

**Morgan, P.** *(Llanelli)* S.*I.NZ.* 1980; I. 1981.

**Morgan, R.** *(Newport)* S. 1984.

**Morgan, T.** *(Llanelli)* I. 89.

**Morgan, W. Guy** *(Cambridge Univ., Swansea and Guy's Hospital)* F.I. 1927; E.S.F.I. 1929; I.F. 1930.

**Morgan, W.L.** *(Cardiff)* S. 1910.

**Moriarty, P.** *(Swansea)* I.F.FJ.T.WS. 1986; F.E.S. I.I.T.C.E.NZ.A.USA. 1987; E.S.I.F.NZ(1). 1988.

**Moriarty, R.D.** *(Swansea)* A. 1981; I.F.E.S. 1982; E. 1983; S.I.F.E. 1984; S.I.F. 1985; FJ.T.WS. 1986; I.T.C.*E.NZ.A. 1987.

**Morley, J.C.** *(Newport)* E.S.F.I. 1929; E.I. 1930; E.S.F.I.SA. 1931; E.S.I. 1932.

**Morris, Darren** *(Neath)* Z.SA*. 1998.

**Morris, G.L.** *(Swansea)* I.E. 82; S. 83; E.S. 84.

**Morris, H.** *(Cardiff)* F. 1951; I.F. 1955.

**Morris, Ivor** *(Swansea)* E.S. 1924.

**Morris, M.** *(South Wales Police and Neath)* S.I.F. 1985; I.N.(1,2)B. 1990; I.F.WS. 1991; E. 1992.

**Morris, R.R.** *(Swansea and Bristol)* S. 1933, 1937.

**Morris, S.** *(Cross Keys)* E.S.F.I. 1920; E.S.I.F. 1922; E.S.F.I. 1923; E.S.F.NZ. 1924; E.S.F. 1925.

**Morris, W.** *(Abertillery)* NZ. 1919; F. 1920; I. 1921.

**Morris, W.D.** *(Neath)* F.E. 1967; E.S.I.F. 1968; S.I.F.E.NZ.(1 and 2)A. 1969; SA.S.E.I.F. 1970; E.S.I.F. 1971; E.S.F. 1972; NZ. 1972; E.S.I.A. 1973; S.I.F.E. 1974.

**Morris, W.J.** *(Newport)* S. 1965; F. 1966.

**Morris, W.J.** *(Pontypool)* S.I. 1963.

**Morris, William** *(Llanelli)* S.I. 96; E. 97.

**Moseley, K.** *(Pontypool and Newport)* NZ.(2nd). R. 1988; S.I. 1989; F. 1990; F.WS.AR.A. 1991.

**Murphy, C.** *(Cross Keys)* E.S.I. 1935.

**Mustoe, L.** *(Cardiff)* FJ. 1995; A. (1* and 2) 1996; USA (1 and 2).C.R*. 1997; E*.I*.F*. 1998.

**Nash, D.** *(Ebbw Vale)* SA. 1960; E.S.I.F. 1961; F. 1962.

**Neil, W.** *(Cardiff)* S.I. 1904; E.S.I. 1905; E.I. 1907; E.S.F.I. 1908.

**Newman, C.H.** *(Newport)* E. 81; I.E. 82; S. 83; E.S. 84, 85; E. 86, 87.

**Nicholas, D.** *(Llanelli)* E.S.I.F. 1981.

**Nicholas, T.J.** *(Cardiff)* NZ. 1919.

**Nicholl, C.B.** *(Cambridge and Llanelli)* I. 91; E.S.I. 92, 93; E.S. 94; E.S.I. 95, 96.

**Nicholl, D.W.** *(Llanelli)* I. 94.

**Nicholls, E.G.** *(Cardiff and Newport)* S.I. 96; E. 97; E.I. 98; E.S.I. 99; S.I. 1900; E.S.I. 1901, 1902; I. 1903; E. 1904; I.NZ. 1905; E.S.I.SA. 1906.

**Nicholls, F.E.** *(Cardiff Harlequins)* I. 92.

**Nicholls, H.** *(Cardiff)* I. 1958.

**Nicholls, S.H.** *(Cardiff)* M. 88; S.I. 89; S. 91.

**Norris, H.** *(Cardiff)* F. 1963; F. 1966.

**Norster, R.L.** *(Cardiff)* S. 1982; E.S.I.F. 1983; S.I.F.E.A. 1984; S.I.F.E.FJ. 1985; FJ.T.WS. 1986; F.E.S.I.I.C.E.USA. 1987; E.S.I.F.NZ(1) WS. 1988; F.E. 1989.

**Norton, W.B.** *(Cardiff)* I.F. 82; S. 83; E.S.I. 84.

**O'Connor, A.** *(Aberavon and Oxford Univ.)* SA. 1960; E.S. 1961; F.I. 1962.

**O'Connor, R.** *(Aberavon)* E. 1957.

**O'Shea, J.P.** *(Cardiff)* S.I. 1967; S.I.F. 1968.

**Oliver, G.** *(Pontypool)* E.S.F.I. 1920.

**Osborne, W.T.** *(Mountain Ash)* E.S.I. 1902, 1903.

**Ould, W.J.** *(Cardiff)* E.S. 1924.

**Owen, Albert** *(Swansea)* E. 1924.

**Owen, G.** *(Newport)* I.F. 1955; E.S.I.F. 1956.

**Owen, R.M.** *(Swansea)* I. 1901; E.S.I. 1902, 1903, 1904, 1905; NZ. 1905; E.S.I 1906; SA. 1906; E.S. 1907; F.I.A. 1908; E.S.F.I. 1909; F.E. 1910; E.S.F.I. 1911; E.S. 1912.

**Packer, H.** *(Newport)* E. 91; S.I. 95; E.S.I. 96; E. 97.

**Palmer, Frank** *(Swansea)* E.S.I. 1922.

**Parfitt, F.C.** *(Newport)* E.S.I. 93, 94; S. 95; S.I. 96.

**Parfitt, S.** *(Swansea)* N. 1*, B. 1990.

**Parker, D.** *(Swansea)* I.F.NZ. 1924; E.S.F.I. 1925; F.I. 1929; E. 1930.

**Parker, T.** *(Swansea)* NZ. 1919; E.S.I. 1920; E.S.F.I. 1921; E.S.I.F. 1922; E.S.F. 1923.

**Parker, W.** *(Swansea)* E.S. 99.

**Parsons, G.** *(Newport)* E. 1947.

**Pascoe, D.** *(Bridgend)* F.I. 1923.

**Pask, A.** *(Abertillery)* F. 1961; E.S.F.I. 1962; E.S.I.F. 1963; NZ. 1963; E.S.I.F.SA. 1964; E.S.I.F. 1965, 1966; A. 1966; S.I. 1967.

**Payne, G.W.** *(Army and Pontypridd)* E.S.I. 1960.

**Payne, H.** *(Swansea)* NZ. 1935.

**Peacock, H.** *(Newport)* S.F.I. 1929; S.I.F. 1930.

**Peake, E.** *(Chepstow)* E. 81.

**Pearce, G.** *(Bridgend)* I.F. 1981; I*. 1982.

115

Richards, E.S. *(Swansea)* E. 85; S. 87.
Richards, Gwyn *(Cardiff)* S. 1927.
Richards, H. *(Neath)* T.* 1986; T.E.NZ. 1987.
Richards, Idris *(Cardiff)* E.S.F.I. 1925.
Richards, K. *(Bridgend)* SA. 1960; E.S.I.F. 1961.
Richards, M.C.R. *(Cardiff)* I.F. 1968; S.I.F.E.N.Z. (1 and 2)A. 1969.
Richards, Rees *(Aberavon)* S.F.I. 1913.
Richards, Rex *(Cross Keys)* F. 1956.
Richards, T.L. *(Maesteg)* I. 1923.
Richardson, S.J. *(Aberavon)* A.(2)* 1978; E. 1979.
Rickard, A. *(Cardiff)* F. 1924.
Ring, J. *(Aberavon)* E. 1907.
Ring, M.G. *(Cardiff and Pontypool)* E. 1983; A. 1984; S.I.F. 1985; I.I.T.A.USA. 1987; E.S.I.F.NZ. (1 and 2) 1988; NZ. 1989; F.E.S.I.N. (1, 2)B. 1990; E.S.I.F.F.WS.AR.A. 1991.
Ringer, P *(Ebbw Vale and Llanelli)* NZ. 1978; S.I.F.E. 1979; F.E.NZ. 1980.
Roberts, C. *(Neath)* I.F. 1958.
Roberts, D.E.A. *(London Welsh)* E. 1930.
Roberts, E. *(Llanelli)* E. 86; I. 87.
Roberts, E.J. *(Llanelli)* S.I. 88; I. 89.
Roberts, G. *(Cardiff)* F.*E. 1985; I.T.C.E.A. 1987.
Roberts, H.M. *(Cardiff)* SA. 1960; E.S.I.F. 1961; S.F. 1962; I. 1963.
Roberts, J. *(Cardiff and Cambridge Univ.)* E.S.F.I. 1927; NSW. 1927; E.S.I.F. 1928; E.S.F.I. 1929.
Roberts, M.G. *(London Welsh)* E.S.I.F. 1971; I.F. 1973; S. 1975; E. 1979.
Roberts, T. *(Risca and Newport)* S.F.I. 1921; E.S.I.F. 1922; E.S. 1923.
Roberts, Willie *(Cardiff and Oxford Univ.)* E. 1929.
Robins, J.D. *(Birkenhead Park)* E.S.I.F. 1950, 1951; E.I.F. 1953.
Robins, R. *(Pontypridd)* S. 1953; F.S. 1954; E.S.I.F. 1955; E.F. 1956; E.S.I.F. 1957.
Robinson, I.R. *(Cardiff)* F.E. 1974.
Roderick, W.B. *(Llanelli)* I. 84.
Rosser, M. *(Penarth)* S.F. 1924.
Rowland, C.F. *(Aberavon)* I. 1926.
Rowlands, D.C.T. *(Pontypool)* E.S.I.F. 1963; NZ. 1963; E.S.I.F.SA. 1964; E.S.I.F. 1965.
Rowlands, G. *(R.A.F. and Cardiff)* NZ. 1953; E.F. 1954; F. 1956.
Rowlands, J. *(Lampeter)* E. 85.
Rowlands, K.A. *(Cardiff)* F.I. 1962; I. 1963; I.F. 1965.
Rowles, G.R. *(Penarth)* E. 92.
Rowley, Mark *(Pontypridd)* SA. 1996; USA,S.I.F. R. 1997.
Roy, Stuart *(Cardiff)* J.* 1995.
Russell, S. *(London Welsh)* USA. 1987.
Samuel, D. *(Swansea)* I. 91, 93.
Samuel, F. *(Mountain Ash)* S.I.F. 1922.
Samuel, J. *(Swansea)* I. 91.
Scourfield, T. *(Torquay)* F. 1930.
Scrines, F. *(Swansea)* E.S. 99; I. 1901.
Shanklin, J.L. *(London Welsh)* F. 1970; NZ. 1972; I.F. 1973.
Shaw, G. *(Neath)* NZ. 1972; E.S.I.F.A. 1973; S.I.F.E. 1974; I.F. 1977.
Shaw, T. *(Newbridge)* R. 1983.
Shea, Jerry *(Newport)* NZ. 1919; E.S. 1920; E. 1921.
Shell, R.C. *(Aberavon)* A.* 1973.

Simpson, H.J. *(Cardiff)* E.S.I. 84.
Skrinshire, R.T. *(Newport)* E.S.I. 99.
Skym, A. *(Llanelli and Cardiff)* E.S.I.F. 1928, 1930; E.S.F.I. 1931; SA. 1931; E.S.I. 1932, 1933; E. 1935.
Smith, J.S. *(Cardiff)* E.I. 84; E. 85.
Sparks, B. *(Neath)* I. 1954; E.F. 1955; E.S.I. 1956; S. 1957.
Spiller, W. *(Cardiff)* S.I. 1910; E.S.F.I. 1911; E.F. 1912; SA. 1912; E. 1913.
Squire, J. *(Newport and Pontypool)* I.F. 1977; E.S.I.F.A.(1)NZ. 1978; S.I.F.E. 1979; F.E.S.I.NZ. 1980; E.S.I.F.A. 1981; I.F.E. 1982; E.S.I.F. 1983.
Stadden, W.H. *(Cardiff)* I. 84; E.S. 86; I. 87; S.M. 88; S.E. 90.
Stephens, C.J. *(Llanelli)* I.F.E.A. 1992.
Stephens, Chris *(Bridgend)* E*. 1998.
Stephens, G. *(Neath)* E.S.I.F. 1912; SA. 1912; E.S.F.I. 1913; NZ. 1919.
Stephens, I. *(Bridgend)* E.S.I.F.A. 1981; I.F.E.S. 1982; I.F.E. 1984; A. 1984.
Stephens, Rev. J.G. *(Llanelli)* E.S.I.F. 1922.
Stephens, Rees *(Neath)* E.S.F.I. 1947; I. 1948; S.I.F. 1949; F. 1951; SA. 1951; E.S.I.F. 1952, 1953; NZ. 1953; E.I. 1954; E.S.I.F. 1955; S.I.F. 1956; E.S.I.F. 1957.
Stock, A. *(Newport)* F.NZ. 1924; E.S. 1926.
Stone, P. *(Llanelli)* F. 1949.
Summers, R.H.B. *(Haverfordwest)* E. 81.
Sutton, S. *(Pontypool)* F.E. 1982; E.S.I.C.NZ. *A. 1987.
Sweet-Escott, R.B. *(Cardiff)* S. 91; I. 94, 95.
Tamplin, W.E. *(Cardiff)* S.F.I.A. 1947; E.S.F. 1948.
Tanner, H. *(Swansea and Cardiff)* NZ. 1935; E.S.I. 1936, 1937, 1938, 1939; E.S.F.I. 1947, 1948; E.S.I.F. 1949.
Tarr, D.J. *(Swansea and United Services)* NZ. 1935.
Taylor, A.R. *(Cross Keys)* I. 1937, 1938; E. 1939.
Taylor, C.G. *(Blackheath and Ruabon)* E.S.I. 84; E.S. 85, 86; E.I. 87.
Taylor, Hemi *(Cardiff)* P.C.F.J.T.WS.*R.It.SA. 1994; E.S.J.NZ.I.SA.FJ. 1995; It.E.S.I.F.A.(1 and 2).It.A. 1996.
Taylor, J. *(London Welsh)* S.I.F.E. 1967; NZ. 1967; I.F. 1968; S.I.F.E.NZ.(1)A. 1969; F. 1970; E.S.I.F. 1971; E.S.F. 1972; NZ. 1972; E.S.I.F. 1973.
Taylor, Mark *(Pontypool and Swansea)* SA. 1994; F.E.S.A.* 1995; Z.SA. 1998.
Thomas, A. *(Newport)* NZ. 1963; E. 1964.
Thomas, Alun *(Cardiff and Llanelli)* E.S.I.F. 1952; S.I.F. 1953; E.I.F. 1954; S.I.F. 1955.
Thomas, Arwel *(Bristol and Swansea)* It.E.S.I. F*. SA. 1996; USA.S.I.F.USA.(1 and 2).C.R. NZ*. 1997; It.E.S*.Z.SA. 1998.
Thomas, B. *(Neath and Cambridge Univ.)* E.S.I.F. 1963; NZ. 1963; E.S.I.F.SA. 1964; E. 1965; E.S.I. 1966; NZ. 1967; S.I.F.E.NZ.(1 and 2) 1969.
Thomas, Bob *(Swansea)* E.S.I. 1900; E. 1901.
Thomas, C. *(Bridgend)* E.S. 1925.
Thomas, C.J. *(Newport)* I.M. 88; S.I. 89; S.E.I. 90; E.I. 91.
Thomas, D. *(Aberavon)* I. 1961.
Thomas, D. *(Swansea)* S.I. 1930; E.S.I. 1932; E.S. 1933; E. 1934; E.S.I. 1935.
Thomas, Denzil *(Llanelli)* I. 1954.

116

**Thomas, Dick** *(Mountain Ash)* SA. 1906; F.I. 1908; S. 1909.

**Thomas, D.J.** *(Swansea)* E. 1904; A. 1908; E.S.I. 1910; E.S.I.F. 1911; E. 1912.

**Thomas, D.L.** *(Neath)* E. 1937.

**Thomas, E.** *(Newport)* S.I. 1904; S.F.I. 1909; F. 1910.

**Thomas, G.** *(Llanelli)* E.S.F.I. 1923.

**Thomas, Gareth** *(Bridgend and Cardiff)* J.NZ.I.SA.FJ. 1995; F.A.(1 and 2).B.F.It.A. 1996; USA.S.I.F.E.USA. (1 and 2).C.R.T.NZ. 1997; It.E.S.I.F. 1998.

**Thomas, Geo.** *(Newport)* M. 88; I. 90; S. 91.

**Thomas, H.W.** *(Swansea and Cambridge Univ.)* SA. 1912; E. 1913.

**Thomas, Harold** *(Llanelli)* F. 1912.

**Thomas, Harold** *(Neath)* E.S.I. 1936, 1937.

**Thomas, Ifor** *(Bryncethin)* E. 1924.

**Thomas, Justin** *(Llanelli and Cardiff)* SA.FJ. 1995; It.E.S.I.F.B*. 1996; USA. 1997.

**Thomas, L.C.** *(Cardiff)* E.S. 85.

**Thomas, L.I.** *(Newport)* S. 94; E.I. 95.

**Thomas, M.C.** *(Newport and Devonport Services)* F. 1949; E.S.I.F. 1950, 1951; SA. 1951; E.S.I.F. 1952; E. 1953; E.S.I.F. 1956; E.S. 1957; E.S.I.F. 1958; I.F. 1959.

**Thomas, Melbourne** *(Bridgend and St. Bart's Hospital)* NZ. 1919; S.F.I. 1921; F. 1923; E. 1924.

**Thomas, Nathan** *(Bath)* SA*. 1996; USA (1* and 2). C*.R.T.NZ. 1997; Z.SA. 1998.

**Thomas, R.C.C.** *(Swansea and Cambridge Univ.)* F. 1949; I.F. 1952; S.I.F. 1953; NZ. 1953; E.I.F.S. 1954; S.I. 1955; E.S.I. 1956; E. 1957; A.E.S.I.F. 1958; E.S.I.F. 1959.

**Thomas, Rees** *(Pontypool)* F.I. 1909; S.F. 1911; E.S. 1912; SA. 1912; E. 1913.

**Thomas, R.L.** *(London Welsh and Llanelli)* S.I. 89; I. 90; E.S.I. 91; E. 92.

**Thomas, S.** *(Llanelli)* S.E. 90; I. 91.

**Thomas, W.D.** *(Llanelli)* A. 1966; S.I.F. 1968; E.NZ.(2)A. 1969; SA.S.E.I.F. 1970; E.S.I.F. 1971; E.S.F 1972; NZ. 1972; E.S.I.F. 1973; E. 1974.

**Thomas, W.H.** *(Cambridge Univ., Llanelli and London Welsh)* S. 85; E.S. 86, 87; S.I. 88; E.I. 90; S.I. 91.

**Thomas, W.J.** *(Cardiff)* F. 1961;F. 1963.

**Thomas, W.T.** *(Abertillery)* E. 1930.

**Thomas, Watcyn** *(Llanelli and Swansea)* E.S.F.I. 1927; E. 1929; E.S.SA. 1931; E.S.I. 1932, 1933.

**Thomson, J.** *(Cross Keys)* E. 1923.

**Thorburn, P.** *(Neath)* F.E.F.J. 1985; E.S.I.F. 1986; F.I.T.C.E.NZ.A.USA. 1987; S.I.F.WS.R(R). 1988; S.I.F.E.NZ. 1989; F.E.S.I.N.(1,2)B. 1990; E.S.I.F.A. 1991.

**Titley, M.H.** *(Bridgend)* R. 1983; S.I.F.E.A. 1984; S.I.F.J. 1985; F.F.J.T.WS. 1986; F.E. 1990.

**Towers, W.H.** *(Swansea)* I. 87; M. 88.

**Travers, G.** *(Pill Harriers and Newport)* E.S.I. 1903, 1905; NZ. 1905; E.S.I.SA. 1906; E.S.I. 1907; E.S.I.F.A. 1908; E.S.I. 1909; S.I.F. 1911.

**Travers, W.H.** *(Newport)* S.I. 1937; E.S.I. 1938, 1939; E.S.I.F. 1949.

**Treharne, E.** *(Pontypridd)* E. 81; E. 82.

**Trew, W.** *(Swansea)* E.S.I. 1900; E.S. 1901; S. 1903, 1905, 1906; E.S. 1907; E.S.F.I.A. 1908; E.S.F.I. 1909; F.E.S. 1910; E.S.F.I. 1911; S. 1912; S.F. 1913.

**Trott, R.F.** *(Cardiff)* E.S.F.I. 1948; E.S.I.F. 1949.

**Truman, H.** *(Llanelli)* E. 1934, 1935.

**Trump, L.** *(Newport)* E.S.I.F. 1912.

**Turnbull, B.R.** *(Cardiff and Cambridge Univ.)* I. 1925; E.S. 1927; E.F. 1928; S. 1930.

**Turnbull, M.J.** *(Cardiff)* E.I. 1933.

**Turner, P.** *(Newbridge)* I(R).F.E. 1989.

**Uzzell, H.** *(Newport)* E.S.I.F. 1912; S.F.I. 1913; E.S.F.I. 1914; E.S.F.I. 1920.

**Uzzell, J.** *(Newport)* NZ. 1963; E.S.I.F. 1965.

**Vickery, W.** *(Aberavon)* E.S.I. 1938; E. 1939.

**Vile, T.H.** *(Newport)* E.S. 1908; I. 1910; I.F. 1912; SA. 1912; E. 1913; S. 1921.

**Vincent, H.C.** *(Bangor)* I. 82.

**Voyle, M.** *(Newport and Llanelli)* A*.B. 1996; E.USA (1 and 2).C.T.NZ. 1997; It.E.S.I.F. 1998.

**Wakeford, J.** *(S.W.Police)* WS.R. 1988.

**Waldron, R.** *(Neath)* E.S.I.F. 1965.

**Walker, N.** *(Cardiff)* I.F.J. 1993; S.F.E.P.Sp. 1994; F.E. 1995; USA (1 and 2).C.R*.T.NZ. 1997; E. 1998.

**Waller, P.D.** *(Newport)* A. 1908; E.S.F.I. 1909; F. 1910.

**Walters, D.** *(Llanelli)* E. 1902.

**Wanbon, R.** *(Aberavon)* E. 1968.

**Ward, W.** *(Cross Keys)* S.I. 1934.

**Warlow, J.** *(Llanelli)* I. 1962.

**Waters, D.** *(Newport)* E.S.I.F. 1986.

**Waters, K.** *(Newbridge)* WS. 1991.

**Watkins, D.** *(Newport)* E.S.I.F. 1963; NZ. 1963; E.S.I.F.SA. 1964; E.S.I.F. 1965; 1966; I.F.E. 1967.

**Watkins, E.** *(Blaina)* S.I.F. 1926.

**Watkins, E.** *(Cardiff)* NZ. 1935; S.I. 1937; E.S.I. 1938; E.S. 1939.

**Watkins, E.** *(Neath)* E.S.I.F. 1924.

**Watkins, H.** *(Llanelli)* S.I. 1904; E.S.I. 1905; E. 1906.

**Watkins, I.** *(Ebbw Vale)* *E.S.I.F.NZ.(2nd).R. 1988; S.I.F.E. 1989.

**Watkins, L.** *(Llandaff)* E. 81.

**Watkins, M.J.** *(Newport)* I.F.E. 1984; A. 1984.

**Watkins, S.J.** *(Newport and Cardiff)* S.I.F. 1964; E.S.I.F. 1965; E.S.I.F.A. 1966; S.I.F.E. 1967; NZ. 1967; E.S. 1968; S.I.F.E.NZ.(1) 1969; E.I. 1970.

**Watkins, W.** *(Newport)* F. 1959.

**Watt, W.** *(Llanelli)* E. 1914.

**Watts, D.** *(Maesteg)* E.S.F.I. 1914.

**Watts, J.** *(Llanelli)* E.S.I. 1907; E.S.F.I.A. 1908; S.F.I. 1909.

**Watts, Wallace** *(Newport)* E.S.I. 92, 93, 94; E.I. 95; E. 96.

**Weatherley, D.** *(Swansea)* Z. 1998.

**Weaver, D.** *(Swansea)* E. 1964.

**Webb, J.** *(Abertillery)* S. 1907; E.S.F.I.A. 1908; E.S.F.I. 1909; F.E.S.I. 1910; E.S.F.I. 1911; E.S. 1912.

**Webb, J.E.** *(Newport)* M. 88; S. 89.

**Webbe, G.** *(Bridgend)* T.*WS. 1986; F.E.S.T.USA. 1987; *F.NZ(1).R. 1988.

**Webster, R.** *(Swansea)* A. 1987; B. 1990; AR.A. 1991; I.F.E.S.A. 1992; E.S.I.F. 1993.

**Wells, G.** *(Cardiff)* E.S. 1955; I.F. 1957; A.E.S. 1958.

**Westacott, D.** *(Cardiff)* I. 1906.

**Wetter, H.** *(Newport)* SA. 1912; E. 1913.

**Wetter, J.** *(Newport)* S.F.I. 1914; E.S.F.I. 1920; E. 1921; I.NZ. 1924.

**Wheel, G.A.D.** *(Swansea)* I.E.* 1974; F.E.I. 1975; A. 1975; E.S.I.F. 1976; I.E.S. 1977; E.S.I.F.A.(1 and 2)NZ. 1978; S.I. 1979; F.E.S.I. 1980; E.S.I.F.A. 1981; I. 1982.

**Wheeler, P.J.** *(Aberavon)* NZ. 1967; E. 1968.

**Whitefoot, J.** *(Cardiff)* A. 1984; S.I.F.E.FJ. 1985; E.S.I.F.FJ.T.WS. 1986; F.E.S.I.I.C. 1987.

**Whitfield, J.** *(Pill Harriers and Newport)* NZ. 1919; E.S.F.I. 1920; E. 1921; E.S.I.F. 1922; S.I. 1924.

**Whitson, G.** *(Newport)* F. 1956; S.I. 1960.

**Wilkins, G.** *(Bridgend)* T. 1994.

**Williams, Aled** *(Bridgend)* N.2* 1990; FJ.* 1995.

**Williams, Barry** *(Neath and Richmond)* F. 1996; R.T.NZ. 1997; It.E.Z*.SA. 1998.

**Williams, Bleddyn** *(Cardiff)* E.S.F.I.A. 1947; E.S.F.I. 1948; E.S.I. 1949; I. 1951; SA. 1951; S. 1952; E.S.I.F. 1953; NZ. 1953; S. 1954; E. 1955.

**Williams, Brian** *(Neath)* S.I.B. 1990; E.S. 1991.

**Williams, Bryn** *(Llanelli)* S.F.I. 1920.

**Williams, C.** *(Llanelli)* NZ. 1924; E. 1925.

**Williams, C.** *(Aberavon and Swansea)* E.S. 1977; F.E.S.I.NZ. 1980; E. 1983.

**Williams, C.D.** *(Cardiff, Neath and Oxford Univ.)* F. 1955; F. 1956.

**Williams, Darril** *(Llanelli)* SA*. 1998.

**Williams, D.** *(Ebbw Vale)* E.S.I.F. 1963; E.S.I.F.SA. 1964; E.S.I.F. 1965; E.S.I. 1966; A. 1966; F.E. 1967; NZ. 1967; E. 1968; S.I.F.E.NZ. (1and 2)A. 1969; SA.S.E.I. 1970; E.S.I.F. 1971.

**Williams, D.B.** *(Newport and Swansea)* A.(1) 1978; E.S. 1981.

**Williams, Eddie** *(Neath)* NZ. 1924; F. 1925.

**Williams, Evan** *(Aberavon)* E.S. 1925.

**Williams, Frank** *(Cardiff)* S.F.I. 1929; E.S.I.F. 1930; F.I.SA. 1931; E.S.I. 1932; I. 1933.

**Williams, G.** *(London Welsh and Llanelli)* I.F. 1950; F.I.SA. 1931; E.S.I. 1932; I. 1933.

**Williams, G.P.** *(Bridgend)* NZ. 1980; E.S.A. 1981; I. 1982.

**Williams, Gerald** *(Bridgend)* I.F. 1981; E.*S. 1982.

**Williams, Griff** *(Aberavon)* E.S.I. 1936.

**Williams, J.** *(Blaina)* E.S.I.F. 1920; S.F.I. 1921.

**Williams, J.F.** *(London Welsh)* I.NZ. 1905; S. 1906; SA. 1906.

**Williams, J.J.** *(Llanelli)* F.*A. 1973; S.I.F.E. 1974; F.E.S.I. 1975; A. 1975; E.S.I.F. 1976; I.F.E.S. 1977; E.S.I.F.A.(1 and 2)NZ. 1978; S.I.F.E. 1979.

**Williams, J.L.** *(Cardiff)* SA. 1906; E.S.I. 1907, 1908; A. 1908; E.S.F.I. 1909; I. 1910; E.S.F.I. 1911.

**Williams, J.P.R.** *(London Welsh and Bridgend)* S.I.F.E.NZ.(1 and 2)A. 1969; SA.S.E.I.F. 1970; E.S.I.F. 1971; E.S.F. 1972; NZ. 1972; E.S.I.F.A. 1973; S.I.F. 1974; F.E.S.I. 1975; A. 1975; E.S.I.F. 1976; I.F.E.S. 1977; E.S.I.F.A.(1 and 2) NZ. 1978; S.I.F.E. 1979; NZ. 1980; E.S. 1981.

**Williams, L.** *(Cardiff)* S.I.F. 1957; E.S.I.F. 1958; E.S.I. 1959; F. 1961; E.S. 1962.

**Williams, Les** *(Llanelli and Cardiff)* E.S.F.I.A. 1947; I. 1948; E. 1949.

**Williams, M.** *(Newport)* F. 1923.

**Williams, Martyn** *(Pontypridd)* B.F.It*. 1996; It.E. Z. 1998.

**Williams, Ossie** *(Llanelli)* E.S.A. 1947; E.S.F.I. 1948.

**Williams, Owain** *(Bridgend)* N. 2 1990.

**Williams, Ray** *(Llanelli)* S. 1954; F. 1957; A. 1958.

**Williams, R.D.G.** *(Abercamlais)* E. 81.

**Williams, R.F.** *(Cardiff)* SA. 1912; E.S. 1913; I. 1914.

**Williams, R.H.** *(Llanelli)* I.F.S. 1954; S.I.F. 1955; E.S.I. 1956; E.S.I.F. 1957; A.E.S.I.F. 1958; E.S.I.F. 1959; E. 1960.

**Williams, S.** *(Llanelli)* E.S.F.I. 1947; S.F. 1948.

**Williams, Sid** *(Aberavon)* E.S.I. 1939.

**Williams, Steve** *(Neath and Cardiff)* T. 1994; *E.A.(1 and 2).B.F.It.A.SA.1996;USA.S.I.F.E. USA (1 and 2*).C.R*.T*.NZ*. 1997.

**Williams, T.** *(Pontypridd)* I. 82.

**Williams, T.** *(Swansea)* S.I. 88.

**Williams, Tom** *(Swansea)* I. 1912; F. 1913; E.S.F.I. 1914.

**Williams, Trevor** *(Cross Keys)* S.I. 1935; NZ. 1935; E.S.I. 1936; S.I. 1937.

**Williams, Tudor** *(Swansea)* F. 1921.

**Williams, W.** *(Crumlin)* E.S.F.I. 1927.

**Williams, W.A.** *(Newport)* I.F. 1952; E. 1953.

**Williams, W.E.O.** *(Cardiff)* S.I. 87; S. 89, S.E. 90.

**Williams, W.H.** *(Pontymister)* E.S.I. 1900; E. 1901.

**Williams, W.O.** *(Swansea)* F. 1951; SA. 1951; E.S.I.F. 1952, 1953; NZ. 1953; E.I.F.S. 1954; E.S.I.F. 1955; E.S.I. 1956.

**Williams, W.P.J.** *(Neath)* I.F. 1974.

**Williams-Jones, H.** *(S.W. Police and Llanelli)* S(R). 1989; F(R).I. 1990; A. 1991; S.A. 1992; E.S.I.F.Z.(1st)N. 1993; FJ.T.WS.*It.* 1994; E*. 1995.

**Willis, R.** *(Cardiff)* E.S.I.F. 1950, 1951; SA. 1951; E.S. 1952; S. 1953; NZ. 1953; E.I.F.S. 1954; E.S.I.F. 1955.

**Wiltshire, M.L.** *(Aberavon)* NZ. 1967; E.S.F. 1968.

**Windsor, R.W.** *(Pontypool)* A. 1973; S.I.F.E. 1974; F.E.S.I.A. 1975; E.S.I.F. 1976; I.F.E.S. 1977; E.S.I.F.A.(1 and 2)NZ. 1978; S.I.F. 1979.

**Winfield, H.B.** *(Cardiff)* I. 1903; E.S.I. 1904; NZ. 1905; E.S.I. 1906; S.I. 1907; E.S.I.F.A. 1908.

**Winmill, S.** *(Cross Keys)* E.S.F.I. 1921.

**Wintle, Matthew** *(Llanelli)* It. 1996.

**Wintle, R.** (London Welsh) WS.(R). 1988.

**Wooller, W.** *(Rydal School, Sale, Cambridge Univ. and Cardiff)* E.S.I. 1933, 1935; NZ. 1935; E.S.I. 1936, 1937; S.I. 1938; E.S.I. 1939.

**Wyatt, Chris** *(Llanelli)* Z*.SA*. 1998.

**Wyatt, Gareth** *(Pontypridd)* T. 1997.

**Wyatt, M.** *(Swansea)* E.S.I.F. 1983; A. 1984, S.I. 1985; E.S.I. 1987.

**Young, D.** *(Swansea and Cardiff)* E.NZ.USA. 1987; E.S.I.F.NZ.(1 and 2)WS.R. 1988; S. 1989;A.SA. 1996; USA.S.I.F.E.R.NZ. 1997; It.E.S.I.F. 1998.

**Young, G.A.** *(Cardiff)* E.S. 86.

**Young, J.** *(Harrogate, Bridgend and London Welsh)* S.I.F. 1968; S.I.F.E.NZ.(1) 1969; E.I.F. 1970; E.S.I.F. 1971; E.S.F. 1972; NZ. 1972; E.S.I.F. 1973.

118

# LEADING WELSH CAP-HOLDERS

| Name | Matches | Name | Matches | Name | Matches |
|---|---|---|---|---|---|
| Ieuan Evans | 72 | Rob Howley | 24 | E. T. Butler | 16 |
| Gareth Llewellyn | 62 | D. J. Lloyd | 24 | A. H. Copsey | 16 |
| Neil Jenkins | 57 | E. Gwyn Nicholls | 24 | Cliff Davies | 16 |
| J. P. R. Williams | 55 | Hemi Taylor | 24 | R. A. Gibbs | 16 |
| Robert Jones | 54 | E. C. Davey | 23 | W. W. Joseph | 16 |
| G. O. Edwards | 53 | R. W. Gravell | 23 | Ivor Jones | 16 |
| Phil Davies | 46 | J. A. Gwilliam | 23 | E. Morgan | 16 |
| T. G. R. Davies | 46 | J. J. Hodges | 23 | Nigel Walker | 16 |
| K. J. Jones | 44 | D. F. Pickering | 23 | Mark Titley | 15 |
| Mike Hall | 42 | D. L. Quinnell | 23 | J. Bassett | 15 |
| Emyr Lewis | 41 | R. H. Williams | 23 | Allan Bateman | 15 |
| G. Price | 41 | Jeff Young | 23 | F. A. Bowdler | 15 |
| Mervyn Davies | 38 | R. Ackerman | 22 | M. Dacey | 15 |
| Garin Jenkins | 38 | S. J. Dawes | 22 | Don Hayward | 15 |
| W. Proctor | 38 | R. D. Moriarty | 22 | A. F. Hill | 15 |
| Anthony Clement | 37 | R. Prosser | 22 | G. T. R. Hodgson | 15 |
| P. Thorburn | 37 | B. L. Williams | 22 | R. Jones | 15 |
| Denzil Williams | 36 | W. O. Williams | 22 | C. B. Nicholl | 15 |
| R. M. Owen | 35 | T. J. Davies | 21 | T. Parker | 15 |
| D. I. Bebb | 34 | W. Gareth Davies | 21 | H. Uzzell | 15 |
| J. D. Davies | 34 | J. Devereux | 21 | H. B. Winfield | 15 |
| A. J. Martin | 34 | W. J. James | 21 | Paul Arnold | 15 |
| B. V. Meredith | 34 | E. M. Jenkins | 21 | Kevin Phillips | 14 |
| R. L. Norster | 34 | Paul Moriarty | 21 | W. B. Cleaver | 14 |
| W. D. Morris | 34 | Scott Quinnell | 21 | L. J. Cunningham | 14 |
| W. J. Bancroft | 33 | Mike Rayer | 21 | J. P. Jones | 14 |
| Mike Griffiths | 33 | Brian Thomas | 21 | D. K. Jones | 14 |
| Jonathan Davies | 32 | D. Watkins | 21 | Albert Jenkins | 14 |
| Scott Gibbs | 32 | W. R. Willis | 21 | V. G. J. Jenkins | 14 |
| B. Price | 32 | A. F. Harding | 20 | C. C. Meredith | 14 |
| Mark Ring | 32 | W. Llewellyn | 20 | J. C. Morley | 14 |
| J. R. G. Stephens | 32 | A. Skym | 20 | C. M. Pritchard | 14 |
| G. Wheel | 32 | Arwel Thomas | 20 | J. Idwal Rees | 14 |
| S. P. Fenwick | 30 | J. Webb | 20 | D. C. T. Rowlands | 14 |
| J. J. Williams | 30 | Steve Williams | 20 | Watcyn Thomas | 14 |
| Phil Bennett | 29 | T. J. Cobner | 19 | F. L. Williams | 14 |
| Nigel Davies | 29 | Ricky Evans | 19 | A. W. Boucher | 13 |
| C. I. Morgan | 29 | A. G. Faulkner | 19 | W. Bowen | 13 |
| J. Squire | 29 | J. Hannan | 19 | Colin Charvis | 13 |
| W. J. Trew | 29 | E. R. John | 19 | T. Day | 13 |
| Richie Collins | 28 | Derwyn Jones | 19 | Ian Eidman | 13 |
| Gareth Thomas | 28 | Chris Loader | 19 | Arthur Emyr | 13 |
| R. W. Windsor | 28 | S. Morris | 19 | W. R. Evans | 13 |
| David Young | 28 | J. Whitefoot | 19 | C. W. Jones | 13 |
| A. J. Gould | 27 | T. Arthur | 18 | D. Jones | 13 |
| A. M. Hadley | 27 | J. Bancroft | 18 | Gwyn Jones | 13 |
| H. J. Morgan | 27 | A. B. Brice | 18 | A. Lemon | 13 |
| W. C. Powell | 27 | Leigh Davies | 18 | Barry Llewellyn | 13 |
| M. C. Thomas | 27 | W. J. Delahay | 18 | F. Mills | 13 |
| J. M. Humphreys | 26 | Tom Evans | 18 | Ivor Morgan | 13 |
| A. E. I. Pask | 26 | Rupert Moon | 18 | T. W. Pearson | 13 |
| J. Taylor | 26 | S. J. Perkins | 18 | A. M. Rees | 13 |
| R. C. C. Thomas | 26 | Alan Phillips | 18 | C. F. W. Rees | 13 |
| S. J. Watkins | 26 | W. Wooller | 18 | H. E. Rees | 13 |
| N. R. Gale | 25 | D. M. Davies | 17 | J. Roberts | 13 |
| T. D. Holmes | 25 | Stuart Davies | 17 | R. J. Robins | 13 |
| B. John | 25 | Rowe Harding | 17 | I. Stephens | 13 |
| H. Tanner | 25 | J. Matthews | 17 | Alun Thomas | 13 |
| G. Travers | 25 | D. S. Richards | 17 | Mike Voyle | 13 |
| Delme Thomas | 25 | J. L. Williams | 17 | Gerwyn Williams | 13 |
| Bleddyn Bowen | 24 | H. Williams-Jones | 17 | L. H. Williams | 13 |
| R. T. Gabe | 24 | J. G. Boots | 16 | | |

## TRIPLE CROWN WINNERS

**ENGLAND 21 times** – 1882-83, 1883-84, 1891-92, 1912-13, 1913-14, 1920-21, 1922-23, 1923-24, 1927-28, 1933-34, 1936-37, 1953-54, 1956-57, 1959-60, 1979-80, 1990-91, 1991-92, 1994-95, 1995-96, 1996-97, 1997-98.

**WALES 17 times** – 1892-93, 1899-1900, 1901-02, 1904-05, 1907-08, 1908-09, 1910-11, 1949-50, 1951-52, 1964-65, 1968-69, 1970-71, 1975-76, 1976-77, 1977-78, 1978-79, 1987-88.

**SCOTLAND 10 times** – 1890-91, 1894-95, 1900-01, 1902-03, 1906-07, 1924-25, 1932-33, 1937-38, 1983-84, 1989-90.

**IRELAND 6 times** – 1893-94, 1898-99, 1947-48, 1948-49, 1981-82, 1984-85.

## GRAND SLAM WINNERS

**ENGLAND 11 times** – 1912-13, 1913-14, 1920-21, 1922-23, 1923-24, 1927-28, 1956-57, 1979-80, 1990-91, 1991-92, 1994-95.

**WALES 8 times** – 1907-08, 1908-09, 1910-11, 1949-50, 1951-52, 1970-71, 1975-76, 1977-78.

**FRANCE 6 times** – 1967-68, 1976-77, 1980-81, 1986-87, 1996-97, 1997-98.

**SCOTLAND three times** – 1924-25, 1983-84, 1989-90.

**IRELAND once** – 1947-48.

# FIVE NATIONS' CHAMPIONS

| Year | Champion | Year | Champion | Year | Champion |
|---|---|---|---|---|---|
| 1883-84 | ENGLAND | 1924-25 | SCOTLAND | 1962-63 | ENGLAND |
| 1884-85 | – | 1925-26 | IRELAND | 1963-64 | SCOTLAND |
| 1885-86 | ENGLAND | | SCOTLAND | | WALES |
| | SCOTLAND | 1926-27 | SCOTLAND | 1964-65 | WALES |
| 1886-87 | SCOTLAND | | IRELAND | 1965-66 | WALES |
| 1887-88 | | 1927-28 | ENGLAND | 1966-67 | FRANCE |
| 1888-89 | – | 1928-29 | SCOTLAND | 1967-68 | FRANCE |
| 1889-90 | ENGLAND | 1929-30 | ENGLAND | 1968-69 | WALES |
| | SCOTLAND | 1930-31 | WALES | 1969-70 | FRANCE |
| 1890-91 | SCOTLAND | | ENGLAND | | WALES |
| 1891-92 | ENGLAND | 1931-32 | WALES | 1970-71 | WALES |
| 1892-93 | WALES | | IRELAND | 1971-72 | WALES |
| 1893-94 | IRELAND | 1932-33 | SCOTLAND | 1972-73 | FIVE WAY TIE |
| 1894-95 | SCOTLAND | 1933-34 | ENGLAND | 1973-74 | IRELAND |
| 1895-96 | IRELAND | 1934-35 | IRELAND | 1974-75 | WALES |
| 1896-97 | – | 1935-36 | WALES | 1975-76 | WALES |
| 1897-98 | SCOTLAND | 1936-37 | ENGLAND | 1976-77 | FRANCE |
| 1898-99 | IRELAND | 1937-38 | SCOTLAND | 1977-78 | WALES |
| 1899-1900 | WALES | | ENGLAND | 1978-79 | WALES |
| 1900-01 | SCOTLAND | 1938-39 | WALES | 1979-80 | ENGLAND |
| 1901-02 | WALES | | IRELAND | 1980-81 | FRANCE |
| 1902-03 | SCOTLAND | 1946-47 | WALES | 1981-82 | IRELAND |
| 1903-04 | SCOTLAND | | ENGLAND | 1982-83 | FRANCE |
| 1904-05 | WALES | 1947-48 | IRELAND | | IRELAND |
| 1905-06 | IRELAND | 1948-49 | IRELAND | 1983-84 | SCOTLAND |
| | WALES | 1949-50 | WALES | 1984-85 | IRELAND |
| 1906-07 | SCOTLAND | 1950-51 | IRELAND | 1985-86 | FRANCE |
| 1907-08 | WALES | 1951-52 | WALES | | SCOTLAND |
| 1908-09 | WALES | 1952-53 | ENGLAND | 1986-87 | FRANCE |
| 1909-10 | ENGLAND | 1953-54 | ENGLAND | 1987-88 | WALES |
| 1910-11 | WALES | | FRANCE | | FRANCE |
| 1911-12 | ENGLAND | | WALES | 1988-89 | FRANCE |
| | IRELAND | 1954-55 | WALES | 1989-90 | SCOTLAND |
| 1912-13 | ENGLAND | | FRANCE | 1990-91 | ENGLAND |
| 1913-14 | ENGLAND | 1955-56 | WALES | 1991-92 | ENGLAND |
| 1919-20 | ENGLAND | 1956-57 | ENGLAND | 1992-93 | FRANCE |
| | SCOTLAND | 1957-58 | ENGLAND | 1993-94 | WALES |
| | WALES | 1958-59 | FRANCE | 1994-95 | ENGLAND |
| 1920-21 | ENGLAND | 1959-60 | FRANCE | 1995-96 | ENGLAND |
| 1921-22 | WALES | | ENGLAND | 1996-97 | FRANCE |
| 1922-23 | ENGLAND | 1960-61 | FRANCE | 1997-98 | FRANCE |
| 1923-24 | ENGLAND | 1961-62 | FRANCE | | |

# WELSH INTERNATIONAL RESULTS
# AGAINST ENGLAND

## Matches played 104    Wales 48 wins,    England 44,    12 drawn

1880-81 **ENGLAND** 7G, 1DG, 6T to 0 *(Blackheath)*

1881-82 No Match

1882-83 **ENGLAND** 2G, 4T to 0 *(Swansea)*

1883-84 **ENGLAND** 1G, 2T to 1G (Leeds)

1884-85 **ENGLAND** 1G, 4T to 1G, 1T *(Swansea)*

1885-86 **ENGLAND** 1GM, 2T to 1G *(Blackheath)*

1886-87 **DRAWN** No Score *(Llanelli)*

1887-88 and 1888-89 No Matches

1889-90 **WALES** 1T(1) to 0 *(Dewsbury)*

1890-91 **ENGLAND** 2G, 1T (7) to 1G (3) *(Newport)*

1891-92 **ENGLAND** 3G, 1T (17) to 0 *(Blackheath)*

1892-93 **WALES** 1G, 1PG, 2T (12) to 1G 3T (11) *(Cardiff)*

1893-94 **ENGLAND** 4G, 1GM, (24) to 1T (3) *(Birkenhead)*

1894-95 **ENGLAND** 1G, 3T (14) to 2T (6) *(Swansea)*

1895-96 **ENGLAND** 2G, 5T (25) to 0 *(Blackheath)*

1896-97 **WALES** 1G, 2T (11) to 0 *(Newport)*

1897-98 **ENGLAND** 1G, 3T (14) to 1DG, 1T (7) *(Blackheath)*

1898-99 **WALES** 4G, 2T (26) to 1T (3) *(Swansea)*

1899-1900 **WALES** 2G, 1PG (13) to 1T (3) *(Gloucester)*

1900-01 **WALES** 2G, 1T (13) to 0 *(Cardiff)*

1901-02 **WALES** 1PG, 2T (9) to 1G, 1T (8) *(Blackheath)*

1902-03 **WALES** 3G, 2T (21) to 1G (5) *(Swansea)*

1903-04 **DRAWN ENGLAND** 1G, 1PG, 2T (14) to **WALES** 2G, 1GM, (14) *(Leicester)*

1904-05 **WALES** 2G, 5T (25) to 0 *(Cardiff)*

1905-06 **WALES** 2G, 2T (16) to 1T (3) *(Richmond)*

1906-07 **WALES** 2G, 4T (22) to 0 *(Swansea)*

1907-08 **WALES** 3G, 1DG, 1PG, 2T (28) to 3G, 1T (18) *(Bristol)*

1908-09 **WALES** 1G, 1T (8) to 0 *(Cardiff)*

1909-10 **ENGLAND** 1G, 1PG, 1T (11) to 2T (6) *(Twickenham)*

1910-11 **WALES** 1PG, 4T, (15) to 1G, 2T (11) *(Swansea)*

1911-12 **ENGLAND** 1G, 1T (8) to 0 *(Twickenham)*

1912-13 **ENGLAND** 1G, 1DG, 1T (12) to 0 *(Cardiff)*

1913-14 **ENGLAND** 2G (10) to 1G, 1DG (9) *(Twickenham)*
1919-20 **WALES** 1G, 2DG, 1T (19) to 1G (5) *(Swansea)*
1920-21 **ENGLAND** 1G, 1DG, 3T (18) to 1T (3) *(Twickenham)*
1921-22 **WALES** 2G, 6T (28) to 2T (6) *(Cardiff)*
1922-23 **ENGLAND** 1DG, 1T (7) to IT (3) *(Twickenham)*
1923-24 **ENGLAND** 1G, 4T (17) to 3T (9) *(Swansea)*
1924-25 **ENGLAND** 1PG, 3T (12) to 2T (6) *(Twickenham)*
1925-26 **DRAWN** 1T (3) each *(Cardiff)*
1926-27 **ENGLAND** 1G, 1PG, 1GM (11) to 1PG, 2T (9) *(Twickenham)*
1927-28 **ENGLAND** 2G, (10) to 1G, 1T (8) *(Swansea)*
1928-29 **ENGLAND** 1G, 1T (8) to 1T (3) *(Twickenham)*
1929-30 **ENGLAND** 1G, 1PG, 1T (11) to 1T (3) *(Cardiff)*
1930-31 **DRAWN** ENGLAND 1G, 2PG (11) to WALES 1G, 1GM, 1T (11) *(Twickenham)*
1931-32 **WALES** 1G, 1DG, 1PG (12) to 1G (5) *(Swansea)*
1932-33 **WALES** 1DG, 1T (7) to 1T (3) *(Twickenham)*
1933-34 **ENGLAND** 3T (9) to 0 *(Cardiff)*
1934-35 **DRAWN** ENGLAND 1PG (3) to WALES 1T (3) *(Twickenham)*
1935-36 **DRAWN** No Score *(Swansea)*
1936-37 **ENGLAND** 1DG (4) to 1T (3) *(Twickenham)*
1937-38 **WALES** 1G, 2PG, 1T (14) to 1G, 1T (8) *(Cardiff)*
1938-39 **ENGLAND** 1T (3) to 0 *(Twickenham)*
1946-47 **ENGLAND** 1G, 1DG (9) to 2T (6) *(Cardiff)*
1947-48 **DRAWN** ENGLAND 1PG (3) to WALES 1T (3) *(Twickenham)*
**(Dropped goal revalued to 3pts.)**
1948-49 **WALES** 3T (9) to 1DG (3) *(Cardiff)*
1949-50 **WALES** 1G, 1PG, 1T (11) to 1G (5) *(Twickenham)*
1950-51 **WALES** 4G, 1T (23) to 1G (5) *(Swansea)*
1951-52 **WALES** 1G, 1T (8) to 2T (6) *(Twickenham)*
1952-53 **ENGLAND** 1G, 1PG (8) to 1PG (3) *(Cardiff)*
1953-54 **ENGLAND** 3T (9) to 1PG, 1T (6) *(Twickenham)*
1954-55 **WALES** 1PG (3) to 0 *(Cardiff)*
1955-56 **WALES** 1G, 1T (8) to 1PG (3) *(Twickenham)*
1956-57 **ENGLAND** 1PG (3) to 0 *(Cardiff)*
1957-58 **DRAWN** ENGLAND 1T (3) to WALES 1PG (3) *(Twickenham)*
1958-59 **WALES** 1G (5) to 0 *(Cardiff)*
1959-60 **ENGLAND** 1G, 2PG, 1T (14) to 2PG (6) *(Twickenham)*
1960-61 **WALES** 2T (6) to 1T (3) *(Cardiff)*
1961-62 **DRAWN** No Score *(Twickenham)*
1962-63 **ENGLAND** 2G, 1DG (13) to 1PG, 1T (6) *(Cardiff)*
1963-64 **DRAWN** 2T Each *(Twickenham)*
1964-65 **WALES** 1G, 1DG, 2T (14) to 1PG (3) *(Cardiff)*

1965-66 **WALES** 1G, 2PG (11) to 1PG, 1T (6) *(Twickenham)*
1966-67 **WALES** 5G, 2PG, 1DG (34) to 4PG, 3T (21) *(Cardiff)*
1967-68 **DRAWN** ENGLAND 1G, 1PG, 1T (11) to 1G, 1DG, 1T (11) *(Twickenham)*
1968-69 **WALES** 3G, 2PG, 1DG, 2T (30) to 3PG (9) *(Cardiff)*
1969-70 **WALES** 1G, 1DG, 3T (17) to 2G, 1PG (13) *(Twickenham)*
1970-71 **WALES** 2G, 2DG, 1PG, 1T (22) to 1PG, 1T (6) *(Cardiff)*
**(Try upgraded to 4pts.)**
1971-72 **WALES** 1G, 2PG (12) to 1PG (3) *(Twickenham)*
1972-73 **WALES** 1G, 1PG, 4T (25) to 2PG, 1DG (9) *(Cardiff)*
1973-74 **ENGLAND** 1G, 2PG, 1T (16) to 1G, 2PG (12) *(Twickenham)*
1974-75 **WALES** 1G, 2PG, 2T (20) to 1T (4) *(Cardiff)*
1975-76 **WALES** 3G, 1PG (21) to 3PG (9) *(Twickenham)*
1976-77 **WALES** 2PG, 2T (14) to 3PG (9) *(Cardiff)*
1977-78 **WALES** 3PG (9) to 2PG (6) *(Twickenham)*
1978-79 **WALES** 2G, 1DG, 3T (27) to 1PG (3) *(Cardiff)*
1979-80 **ENGLAND** 3PG (9) to 2T (8) *(Twickenham)*
1980-81 **WALES** 1G, 1DG, 4PG (21) to 5PG, 1T (19) *(Cardiff)*
1981-82 **ENGLAND** 3PG, 2T (17) to 1DG, 1T (7) *(Twickenham)*
1982-83 **DRAWN** WALES 2PG, 1DG, 1T (13) to ENGLAND 2PG, 1DG, 1T (13) *(Cardiff)*
1983-84 **WALES** 1G, 2DG, 4PG (24) to 5PG (15) *(Twickenham)*
1984-85 **WALES** 2G, 1DG, 3PG (24) to 1G, 1DG, 2PG (15) *(Cardiff)*
1985-86 **ENGLAND** 1DG, 6PG (21) to 1G, 1DG, 3PG (18) *(Twickenham)*
1986-87 **WALES** 5PG, 1T (19) to 4PG 12 *(Cardiff)*
1987 **WORLD CUP: WALES** 2G, 1T (16) to 1PG (3) *(BRISBANE)*
1987-88 **WALES** 1DG, 2T (11) to 1PG (3) *(Twickenham)*
1988-89 **WALES** 1G, 2PG (12) to 2PG, 1DG (9) *(Cardiff)*
1989-90 **ENGLAND** 3G, 4PG, 1T (34) to 1G (6) *(Twickenham)*
1990-91 **ENGLAND** 7PG, 1T (25) to 2PG (6) *(Cardiff)*
1991-92 **ENGLAND** 3G, 2PG (24) to 0 *(Twickenham)*
**(Try upgraded to 5pts.)**
1992-93 **WALES** 1G, 1PG (10) to 2PG, 1DG (9) *(Cardiff)*
1993-94 **ENGLAND** 1G, 1PG, 1T (15) to 1PG, 1T (8) *(Twickenham)*
1994-95 **ENGLAND** 1G, 2PG, 2T (23) to 3PG (9) *(Cardiff)*
1995-96 **ENGLAND** 1G, 3PG, 1T (21) to 1G, 1PG, 1T (15) *(Twickenham)*
1996-97 **ENGLAND** 4G, 2PG (34) to 1G, 2PG (13) *(Cardiff)*
1997-98 **ENGLAND** 7G, 2PG, 1T (60) to 3G, 1T (26) *(Twickenham)*

# AGAINST SCOTLAND
## Matches played 102    Wales 56 wins,    Scotland 44,    2 drawn

1882-83 **SCOTLAND** 3G TO 1G *(Edinburgh)*
1883-84 **SCOTLAND** 1DG, 1T TO 0 *(Newport)*
1884-85 **DRAWN** No Score *(Glasgow)*
1885-86 **SCOTLAND** 2G, 1T to 0 *(Cardiff)*

| | |
|---|---|
| 1886-87 | **SCOTLAND** 4G, 8T to 0 *(Edinburgh)* |
| 1887-88 | **WALES** 1T to 0 *(Newport)* |
| 1888-89 | **SCOTLAND** 2T to 0 *(Edinburgh)* |
| 1889-90 | **SCOTLAND** 1G, 2T (5) to 1T (1) *(Cardiff)* |
| 1890-91 | **SCOTLAND** 1G, 2DG, 5T (15) to 0 *(Edinburgh)* |
| 1891-92 | **SCOTLAND** 1G, 1T (7) to 1T (2) *(Swansea)* |
| 1892-93 | **WALES** 1PG, 3T (9) to 0 *(Edinburgh)* |
| 1893-94 | **WALES** 1DG, 1T (7) to 0 *(Newport)* |
| 1894-95 | **SCOTLAND** 1G (5) to 1GM (4) *(Edinburgh)* |
| 1895-96 | **WALES** 2T (6) to 0 *(Cardiff)* |
| 1896-97 and 1897-98 No Matches. | |
| 1898-99 | **WALES** 1GM, 2DG, 3T (21) to 2G (10) *(Edinburgh)* |
| 1899-1900 | **WALES** 4T (12) to 1T (3) *(Swansea)* |
| 1900-01 | **SCOTLAND** 3G, 1T (18) to 1G, 1T (8) *(Inverleith)* |
| 1901-02 | **WALES** 1G, 3T (14) to 1G (5) *(Cardiff)* |
| 1902-03 | **SCOTLAND** 1PG, 1T (6) to 0 *(Inverleith)* |
| 1903-04 | **WALES** 3G, 1PG, 1T (21) to 1T (3) *(Swansea)* |
| 1904-05 | **WALES** 2T (6) to 1T (3) *(Inverleith)* |
| 1905-06 | **WALES** 3T (9) to 1PG (3) *(Cardiff)* |
| 1906-07 | **SCOTLAND** 2T (6) to 1PG (3) *(Inverleith)* |
| 1907-08 | **WALES** 2T (6) to 1G (5) *(Swansea)* |
| 1908-09 | **WALES** 1G (5) to 1PG (3) *(Inverleith)* |
| 1909-10 | **WALES** 1G, 3T (14) to 0 *(Cardiff)* |
| 1910-11 | **WALES** 2G,1DG, 6T (32) to 1DG, 2T (10) *(Inverleith)* |
| 1911-12 | **WALES** 2G, 2DG, 1T (21) to 2T (6) *(Swansea)* |
| 1912-13 | **WALES** 1G, 1T (8) to 0 *(Inverleith)* |
| 1913-14 | **WALES** 2G, 2DG, 1PG, 1T (24) to 1G (5) *(Cardiff)* |
| 1919-20 | **SCOTLAND** 2PG, 1T (9) to 1G (5) *(Inverleith)* |
| 1920-21 | **SCOTLAND** 1G, 1PG, 2T (14) to 2DG (8) *(Swansea)* |
| 1921-22 | DRAWN SCOTLAND 1PG, 2T (9) to WALES 1G, 1DG (9) *(Inverleith)* |
| 1922-23 | **SCOTLAND** 1G, 2T (11) to 1G, 1PG (8) *(Cardiff)* |
| 1923-24 | **SCOTLAND** 4G,1PG, 4T (35) to 2G (10) *(Inverleith)* |
| 1924-25 | **SCOTLAND** 1G, 1DG, 5T (24) to 1G, 1PG, 2T (14) *(Swansea)* |
| 1925-26 | **SCOTLAND** 1G, 1PG (8) to 1G (5) *(Murrayfield)* |
| 1926-27 | **SCOTLAND** 1G (5) to 0 *(Cardiff)* |
| 1927-28 | **WALES** 2G, 1T (13) to 0 *(Murrayfield)* |
| 1928-29 | **WALES** 1G, 3T (14) to 1DG, 1PG (7) *(Swansea)* |
| 1929-30 | **SCOTLAND** 1G, 1DG, 1T (12) to 1G, 1DG (9) *(Murrayfield)* |
| 1930-31 | **WALES** 2G, 1T (13) to 1G, 1T (8) *(Cardiff)* |
| 1931-32 | **WALES** 1PG, 1T (6) to 0 *(Murrayfield)* |
| 1932-33 | **SCOTLAND** 1G, 1PG, 1T (11) to 1T (3) *(Swansea)* |
| 1933-34 | **WALES** 2G, 1T (13) to 1PG, 1T (6) *(Murrayfield)* |
| 1934-35 | **WALES** 1DG, 2T (10) to 2T (6) *(Cardiff)* |
| 1935-36 | **WALES** 2G, 1T (13) to 1T (3) *(Murrayfield)* |
| 1936-37 | **SCOTLAND** 2G, 1T (13) to 2T (6) *(Swansea)* |
| 1937-38 | **SCOTLAND** 1G, 1PG (8) to 2T (6) *(Murrayfield)* |

| | |
|---|---|
| 1938-39 | **WALES** 1G, 1PG, 1T (11) to 1PG (3) *(Cardiff)* |
| 1946-47 | **WALES** 2G, 1PG, 3T (22) to 1G, 1PG (8) *(Murrayfield)* |
| 1947-48 | **WALES** 1G, 1PG, 2T (14) to 0 *(Cardiff)* **(Dropped goal revalued to 3pts.)** |
| 1948-49 | **SCOTLAND** 2T (6) to 1G (5) *(Murrayfield)* |
| 1949-50 | **WALES**, 1DG, 1PG, 2T (12) to 0 *(Swansea)* |
| 1950-51 | **SCOTLAND** 2G, 1DG, 1PG, 1T (19) to 0 *(Murrayfield)* |
| 1951-52 | **WALES** 1G, 2PG (11) to 0 *(Cardiff)* |
| 1952-53 | **WALES** 1PG, 3T (12) to 0 *(Murrayfield)* |
| 1953-54 | **WALES** 1PG, 4T (15) to 1T (3) *(Swansea)* |
| 1954-55 | **SCOTLAND** 1G, 1DG, 1PG, 1T (14) to 1G, 1T (8) *(Murrayfield)* |
| 1955-56 | **WALES** 3T (9) to 1PG, (3) *(Cardiff)* |
| 1956-57 | **SCOTLAND** 1DG, 1PG, 1T (9) to 1PG, 1T (6) *(Murrayfield)* |
| 1957-58 | **WALES** 1G, 1T (8) to 1PG (3) *(Cardiff)* |
| 1958-59 | **SCOTLAND** 1PG, 1T (6) to 1G (5) *(Murrayfield)* |
| 1959-60 | **WALES** 1G, 1PG (8) to 0 *(Cardiff)* |
| 1960-61 | **SCOTLAND** 1T (3) to 0 *(Murrayfield)* |
| 1961-62 | **SCOTLAND** 1G, 1T (8) to 1DG (3) *(Cardiff)* |
| 1962-63 | **WALES** 1DG, 1PG (6) to 0 *(Murrayfield)* |
| 1963-64 | **WALES** 1G, 1PG, 1T (11) to 1T (3) *(Cardiff)* |
| 1964-65 | **WALES** 1G, 2PG, 1T (14) to 2DG, 2PG (12) *(Murrayfield)* |
| 1965-66 | **WALES** 1G, 1T (8) to 1PG (3) *(Cardiff)* |
| 1966-67 | **SCOTLAND** 1G, 1DG, 1T (11) to 1G (5) *(Murrayfield)* |
| 1967-68 | **WALES** 1G (5) to 0 *(Cardiff)* |
| 1968-69 | **WALES** 1G, 2PG, 2T (17) to 1PG (3) *(Murrayfield)* |
| 1969-70 | **WALES** 2G, 1T (18) to 1DG, 1PG, 1T (9) *(Cardiff)* |
| 1970-71 | **WALES** 2G, 1PG, 2TR (19) to 2PG, 2T (18) *(Murrayfield)* **(Try upgraded to 4pts)** |
| 1971-72 | **WALES** 3G, 3PG, 2T (35) to 1G, 2PG (12) *(Cardiff)* |
| 1972-73 | **SCOTLAND** 1G, 1T (10) to 3PG (9) *(Murrayfield)* |
| 1973-74 | **WALES** 1G (6) to 0 *(Cardiff)* |
| 1974-75 | **SCOTLAND** 3PG, 1DG (12) to 2PG, 1T (10) *(Murrayfield)* |
| 1975-76 | **WALES** 2G, 3PG, 1DG, 1T (28) to 1G (6) *(Cardiff)* |
| 1976-77 | **WALES** 2G, 2PG (18) to 1G, 1DG (9) *(Murrayfield)* |
| 1977-78 | **WALES** 1DG, 1PG, 4T (22) to 2PG, 2T (14) *(Cardiff)* |
| 1978-79 | **WALES** 1G, 3PG, 1T (19) to 3PG, 1T (13) *(Cardiff)* |
| 1979-80 | **WALES** 1G, 1PG, 2T (17) to 1G (6) *(Cardiff)* |
| 1980-81 | **SCOTLAND** 2G, 1PG (15) to 2PG (6) MURRAYFIELD) |
| 1981-82 | **SCOTLAND** 4G, 2DG, 1T (34) to 1G, 4PG (18) *(Cardiff)* |
| 1982-83 | **WALES** 1G, 3PG, 1T (19) to 1G, 3PG (15) *(Murrayfield)* |
| 1983-84 | **SCOTLAND** 2G, 1PG (15) to 1G, 1PG (9) *(Cardiff)* |
| 1984-85 | **WALES** 1G, 1DG, 4PG, 1T (25) to 2G, 2DG, 1PG (21) *(Murrayfield)* |
| 1985-86 | **WALES** 5PG, 1DG, 1T (22) to 1PG, 3T (15) *(Cardiff)* |

122

| | | | |
|---|---|---|---|
| 1986-87 | **WALES** 2G, 2PG, 1DG (21) to 1G, 2PG, 1DG (15) *(Murrayfield)* | 1992-93 | **SCOTLAND** 5PG, 1T (20) to 0 *(Murrayfield)* |
| 1987-88 | **WALES** 2G, 2DG, 1PG, 1T (25) to 4PG, 2T (20) *(Cardiff)* | 1993-94 | **WALES** 1G, 4PG, 2T (29) to 2PG (6) *(Cardiff)* |
| 1988-89 | **SCOTLAND** 1G, 2P, 1DG, 2T (23) to 1PG, 1T (7) *(Murrayfield)* | 1994-95 | **SCOTLAND** 2G, 4PG (26) to 1G, 2PG (13) *(Murrayfield)* |
| 1989-90 | **SCOTLAND** 3PG, 1T (13) to 1G, 1PG (9) *(Cardiff)* | 1995-96 | **SCOTLAND** 1G, 3PG (16) to 3PG, 1T (14) *(Cardiff)* |
| 1990-91 | **SCOTLAND** 2G, 3PG, 1DG, 2T (32) to 1G, 2PG (12) *(Murrayfield)* | 1996-97 | **WALES** 4G, 2PG (34) to 1G, 1DG, 3PG (19) *(Murrayfield)* |
| 1991-92 | **WALES** 1G, 3PG (15) to 1DG, 3PG (12) *(Cardiff)* | 1997-98 | **WALES** 1G, 4PG (19) to 1PG, 2T (13) *(Wembley)* |
| | **(Try upgraded to 5pts)** | | |

# AGAINST IRELAND

## Matches played 102    Wales 59 wins,    Ireland 37,    6 drawn

| | | | |
|---|---|---|---|
| 1881-82 | **WALES** 2G, 2T to 0 *(Dublin)* | 1925-26 | **WALES** 1G, 2T (11) to 1G, 1PG (8) *(Swansea)* |
| 1882-83 | No Match | | |
| 1883-84 | **WALES** 1DG, 2T to 0 *(Cardiff)* | 1926-27 | **IRELAND** 2G, 1PG, 2T (19) to 1G, 1DG (9) *(Dublin)* |
| 1884-85 and 1885-86 No Matches | | | |
| 1886-87 | **WALES** 1DG, 1T to 3T *(Birkenhead)* | 1927-28 | **IRELAND** 2G, 1T (13) to 2G (10) *(Cardiff)* |
| 1887-88 | **IRELAND** 1G, 1DG, 1T to 0 *(Dublin)* | 1928-29 | DRAWN 1G (5) Each *(Belfast)* |
| 1888-89 | **IRELAND** 2T to 0 *(Swansea)* | 1929-30 | **WALES** 3PG, 3T (12) to 1DG, 1PG (7) *(Swansea)* |
| 1889-90 | **DRAWN** 1G (3) Each | | |
| 1890-91 | **WALES** 1G, 1DG (6) to 1DG, 1T (4) *(Llanelli)* | 1930-31 | **WALES** 1G, 1DG, 2T (15) to 1T (3) *(Belfast)* |
| 1891-92 | **IRELAND** 1G, 2T (9) to 0 *(Dublin)* | 1931-32 | **IRELAND** 4T (12) to 1DG, 2T (10) *(Cardiff)* |
| 1892-93 | **WALES** 1T (2) to 0 *(Llanelli)* | | |
| 1893-94 | **IRELAND** 1PG (3) to 0 *(Belfast)* | 1932-33 | **IRELAND** 1DG, 1PG, 1T (10) to 1G (5) *(Belfast)* |
| 1894-95 | **WALES** 1G (5) to 1T (3) *(Cardiff)* | | |
| 1895-96 | **IRELAND** 1G, 1T (8) to 1DG (4) *(Dublin)* | 1933-34 | **WALES** 2G, 1T (13) to 0 *(Swansea)* |
| | | 1934-35 | **IRELAND** 2PG, 1T (9) to 1PG (3) *(Belfast)* |
| 1896-97 | No Match | | |
| 1897-98 | **WALES** 1G, 1PG, 1T (11) to 1PG (3) *(Limerick)* | 1935-36 | **WALES** 1PG (3) to 0 *(Cardiff)* |
| | | 1936-37 | **IRELAND** 1G (5) to 1PG (3) *(Belfast)* |
| 1898-99 | **IRELAND** 1T (3) to 0 *(Cardiff)* | 1937-38 | **WALES** 1G, 1PG, 1T (11) to 1G (5) *(Swansea)* |
| 1899-1900 | **WALES** 1T (3) to 0 *(Belfast)* | | |
| 1900-01 | **WALES** 2G (10) to 3T (9) *(Swansea)* | 1938-39 | **WALES** 1DG, 1T (7) to 0 *(Belfast)* |
| 1901-02 | **WALES** 1G, 1DG, 2T (15) to 0 *(Dublin)* | 1946-47 | **WALES** 1PG, 1T (6) to 0 *(Swansea)* |
| | | 1947-48 | **IRELAND** 2T (6) to 1T (3) *(Belfast)* |
| 1902-03 | **WALES** 6T (18) to 0 *(Cardiff)* | | **(Drop goal revalued to 3pts)** |
| 1903-04 | **IRELAND** 1G, 3T (14) to 4T (12) *(Belfast)* | 1948-49 | **IRELAND** 1G (5) to 0 *(Swansea)* |
| | | 1949-50 | **WALES** 2T (6) to 1PG (3) *(Belfast)* |
| 1904-05 | **WALES** 2G (10) to 1T (3) *(Swansea)* | 1950-51 | **DRAWN** WALES 1PG (3) to IRELAND 1T (3) *(Cardiff)* |
| 1905-06 | **IRELAND** 1G, 2T (11) to 2T (6) *(Belfast)* | | |
| 1906-07 | **WALES** 2G, 1DG, 1PG, 4T (29) to 0 *(Cardiff)* | 1951-52 | **WALES** 1G, 1PG, 2T (14) to 1PG (3) *(Dublin)* |
| 1907-08 | **WALES** 1G, 2T (11) to 1G (5) *(Belfast)* | 1952-53 | **WALES** 1G (5) to 1T (3) *(Swansea)* |
| 1908-09 | **WALES** 3G, 1T (18) to 1G (5) *(Swansea)* | 1953-54 | **WALES** 1DG, 3PG (12) to 2PG, 1T (9) *(Dublin)* |
| 1909-10 | **WALES** 1DG, 5T (19) to 1T (3) *(Dublin)* | 1954-55 | **WALES** 3G, 1PG, 1T (21) to 1PG (3) *(Cardiff)* |
| 1910-11 | **WALES** 2G, 1PG, 1T (16) to 0 *(Cardiff)* | 1955-56 | **IRELAND** 1G. 1DG, 1PG (11) to 1PG (3) *(Dublin)* |
| 1911-12 | **IRELAND** 1G, 1DG, 1T (12) to 1G (5) *(Belfast)* | 1956-57 | **WALES** 2PG (6) to 1G (5) *(Cardiff)* |
| | | 1957-58 | **WALES** 3T (9) to 1PG, 1T (6) *(Dublin)* |
| 1912-13 | **WALES** 2G, 1PG, 1T (16) to 2G, 1PG (13) *(Swansea)* | 1958-59 | **WALES** 1G, 1T (8) to 1PG, 1T (6) *(Cardiff)* |
| 1913-14 | **WALES** 1G, 2T (11) to 1T (3) *(Belfast)* | 1959-60 | **WALES** 2G (10) to 2PG, 1T (9) *(Dublin)* |
| 1919-20 | **WALES** 3G, 1DG, 3T (28) to 1DG (4) *(Cardiff)* | 1960-61 | **WALES** 2PG, 1T (9) to 0 *(Cardiff)* |
| 1920-21 | **WALES** 1PG, 1T (6) to 0 *(Belfast)* | 1961-62 | DRAWN **IRELAND** 1DG, (3) to **WALES** 1PG (3) *(Dublin)* |
| 1921-22 | **WALES** 1G, 2T (11) to 1G (5) *(Swansea)* | 1962-63 | **IRELAND** 1G, 1DG, 2PG (14) to 1DG, 1T (6) *(Cardiff)* |
| 1922-23 | **IRELAND** 1G (5) to 1DG (4) *(Dublin)* | 1963-64 | **WALES** 3G (15) to 2PG (6) *(Dublin)* |
| 1923-24 | **IRELAND** 2G, 1T (13) to 1DG, 2T (10) *(Cardiff)* | 1964-65 | **WALES** 1G, 1DG, 1PG, 1T (14) to 1G, 1PG (8) *(Cardiff)* |
| 1924-25 | **IRELAND** 2G, 1PG, 2T (19) to 1T (3) *(Belfast)* | 1965-66 | **IRELAND** 1DG, 1PG, 1T (9) to 1PG, 1T (6) *(Dublin)* |
| | | 1966-67 | **IRELAND** 1T (3) to 0 *(Cardiff)* |

| | | | |
|---|---|---|---|
| 1967-68 | **IRELAND** 1PG, 1DG, 1T (9) to 1PG, 1DG (6) *(Dublin)* | 1984-85 | **IRELAND** 2G, 3PG (21) to 1G, 1DG (9) *(Cardiff)* |
| 1968-69 | **WALES** 3G, 1PG, 1DG, 1T (24) to 1G, 2PG, (11) *(Cardiff)* | 1985-86 | **WALES** 1G, 3PG, 1T (19) to 1G, 2PG (12) *(Dublin)* |
| 1969-70 | **IRELAND** 1G, 1DG, 1PG, 1T (14) to 0 *(Dublin)* | 1986-87 | **IRELAND** 2G, 1PG (15) to 1PG, 2T (11) *(Cardiff)* |
| 1970-71 | **WALES** 1G, 1DG, 2PG, 3T (23) to 3PG (9) *(Cardiff)* | 1987 | WORLD CUP: **WALES** 2DG, 1PG, 1T (13) to 2PG (6) (WELLINGTON) |
| | **(Try upgraded to 4pts.)** | 1987-88 | **WALES** 1G, 1DG, 1PG (12) to 1G, 1PG (9) *(Dublin)* |
| 1971-72 | No Match | 1988-89 | **IRELAND** 1G, 3PG, 1T (19) to 3PG, 1T (13) *(Cardiff)* |
| 1972-73 | **WALES** 1G, 2PG, 1T (16) to 1G, 2PG (12) *(Dublin)* | 1989-90 | **IRELAND** 1G, 2T (14) to 2T (8) *(Dublin)* |
| 1973-74 | DRAWN **IRELAND** 3PG (9) to **WALES** 1G, 1PG (9) *(Dublin)* | 1990-91 | DRAWN **WALES** 2G, 2PG, 1DG, (21) **IRELAND** 1G, 1DG, 3T (21) *(Cardiff)* |
| 1974-75 | **WALES** 3G, 2PG, 2T (32) to 1T (4) *(Cardiff)* | 1991-92 | **WALES** 3PG, 1DG, 1T (16) to 1G, 3PG (15) *(Dublin)* |
| 1975-76 | **WALES** 3G, 4PG, 1T (34) to 3PG (9) *(Dublin)* | | **(Try upgraded to 5pts.)** |
| 1976-77 | **WALES** 2G, 3PG, 1DG, 1T (25) to 3PG (9) *(Cardiff)* | 1992-93 | **IRELAND** 1G, 3PG, 1DG (19) to 3PG, 1T (14) *(Cardiff)* |
| 1977-78 | **WALES** 4PG, 2T (20) to 3PG, 1DG, 1T (16) *(Dublin)* | 1993-94 | **WALES** 4PG, 1T (17) to 5PG (15) *(Dublin)* |
| 1978-79 | **WALES** 2G, 4PG (24) to 2G, 3PG (21) *(Cardiff)* | 1994-95 | **IRELAND** 1G, 1DG, 2PG (16) to 4PG (12) *(Cardiff)* |
| 1979-80 | **IRELAND** 3G, 1PG (21) to 1PG, 1T (7) *(Dublin)* | 1995 | WORLD CUP: **IRELAND** 3G, 1PG (24) to 2G, 1DG, 2PG (23) (JOHANNESBURG) |
| 1980-81 | **WALES** 2PG, 1DG (9) to 2T (8) *(Cardiff)* | 1995-96 | **IRELAND** 2G, 2PG, 2T (30) to 2G, 1PG (17) *(Dublin)* |
| 1981-82 | **IRELAND** 1G, 2PG, 2T (20) to 1G, 1DG, 1PG (12) *(Dublin)* | 1996-97 | **IRELAND** 1G, 3PG, 2T (26) to 2G, 2PG, 1T (25) *(Cardiff)* |
| 1982-83 | **WALES** 1G, 3PG, 2T (23) to 3PG (9) *(Cardiff)* | 1997-98 | **WALES** 3G, 3PG (30) to 1G, 3PG (16) *(Dublin)* |
| 1983-84 | **WALES** 1G, 4PG (18) to 3PG (9) *(Dublin)* | | |

*Includes 2 friendly matches*

# AGAINST FRANCE

## Matches played 73*    Wales 38 wins,    France 32,    3 drawn

| | | | |
|---|---|---|---|
| 1907-08 | **WALES** 1PG, 6T (36) to 1DG (4) *(Cardiff)* | 1949-50 | **WALES** 3G, 1PG, 1T (21) to 0 *(Cardiff)* |
| 1908-09 | **WALES** 7G, 4T (47) to 1G (5) *(Paris)* | 1950-51 | **FRANCE** 1G, 1PG (8) to 1T (3) *(Paris)* |
| 1909-10 | **WALES** 8G, 1PG, 2T (49) to 1G, 2PG, 1T (14) *(Swansea)* | 1951-52 | **WALES** 1DG, 2PG (9) to 1G (5) *(Swansea)* |
| 1910-11 | **WALES** 3G (15) to 0 *(Paris)* | 1952-53 | **WALES** 2T (6) to 1PG (3) *(Paris)* |
| 1911-12 | **WALES** 1G, 3T (14) to 1G, 1T (8) *(Newport)* | 1953-54 | **WALES** 2G, 3PG (19) to 2G, 1PG (13) *(Cardiff)* |
| 1912-13 | **WALES** 1G, 2T (11) to 1G, 1T (8) *(Paris)* | 1954-55 | **WALES** 2G, 2PG (16) to 1G, 1DG, 1PG (11) *(Paris)* |
| 1913-14 | **WALES** 5G, 2T (31) to 0 *(Swansea)* | 1955-56 | **WALES** 1G (5) to 1T (3) *(Cardiff)* |
| 1919-20 | **WALES** 2T (6) to 1G (5) *(Paris)* | 1956-57 | **WALES** 2G, 1PG, 2T (19) to 2G, 1T (13) *(Paris)* |
| 1920-21 | **WALES** 2PG, 2T (12) to 1DG (4) *(Cardiff)* | 1957-58 | **FRANCE** 2G, 2DG (16) to 1PG, 1T (6) *(Cardiff)* |
| 1921-22 | **WALES** 1G, 2T (11) to 1T (3) *(Paris)* | 1958-59 | **FRANCE** 1G, 1PG, 1T (11) to 1PG (3) *(Paris)* |
| 1922-23 | **WALES** 2G, 1PG, 1T (16) to 1G, 1T (8) *(Swansea)* | 1959-60 | **FRANCE** 2G, 2T (16) to 1G, 1PG (8) *(Cardiff)* |
| 1923-24 | **WALES** 1DG, 2T (10) to 2T (6) *(Paris)* | 1960-61 | **FRANCE** 1G, 1T (8) to 2T (6) *(Paris)* |
| 1924-25 | **WALES** 1G, 2T (11) to 1G (5) *(Cardiff)* | 1961-62 | **WALES** 1PG (3) to 0 *(Cardiff)* |
| 1925-26 | **WALES** 1DG, 1T (7) to 1G (5) *(Paris)* | 1962-63 | **FRANCE** 1G (5) to 1PG (3) *(Paris)* |
| 1926-27 | **WALES** 2G, 5T (25) to 1DG, 1T (7) *(Swansea)* | 1963-64 | DRAWN 1G, 2PG (11) Each *(Cardiff)* |
| 1927-28 | **FRANCE** 1G, 1T (8) to 1T (3) *(Paris)* | 1964-65 | **FRANCE** 2G, 1PG, 1DG, 2T (22) to 2G, 1T (13) *(Paris)* |
| 1928-29 | **WALES** 1G, 1T (8) to 1T (3) *(Cardiff)* | 1965-66 | **WALES** 2PG, 1T (9) to 1G, 1T (8) *(Cardiff)* |
| 1929-30 | **WALES** 2DG, 1T (11) to 0 *(Paris)* | 1966-67 | **FRANCE** 1G, 2DG, 1PG, 2T (20) to 1G, 2PG, 1DG (14) *(Paris)* |
| 1930-31 | **WALES** 5G, 1DG, 2T (35) to 1T (3) *(Swansea)* | 1967-68 | **FRANCE** 1G, 1PG, 1DG, 1T (14) to 2PG, 1T (9) *(Cardiff)* |
| 1946-47 | **WALES** 1PG (3) to 0 *(Paris)* | 1968-69 | DRAWN FRANCE 1G, 1PG (8) to WALES 1G, 1T (8) *(Paris)* |
| 1947-48 | **FRANCE** 2G, 2T (11) to 1PG (3) *(Swansea)* | 1969-70 | **WALES** 1G, 2PG (11) to 2T (6) *(Cardiff)* |
| | **(Dropped goal revalued to 3pts.)** | 1970-71 | **WALES** 1PG, 2T (9) to 1G (5) *(Paris)* |
| 1948-49 | **FRANCE** 1G (5) to 1T (3) *(Paris)* | | **(Try upgraded to 4pts.)** |

| | | | | |
|---|---|---|---|---|
| 1971-72 | **WALES** 4PG, 2T (20) to 2PG (6) *(Cardiff)* | 1986-87 | **FRANCE** 1G, 2PG, 1T (16) to 3P (9) *(Paris)* |
| 1972-73 | **FRANCE** 3PG, 1DG (12) to 1DG (3) *(Paris)* | 1987-88 | **FRANCE** 2PG, 1T (10) to 1G, 1PG (9) *(Cardiff)* |
| 1973-74 | **DRAWN** WALES 3PG, 1DG, 1T (16) to FRANCE 3PG, 1DG, 1T (16) *(Cardiff)* | 1988-89 | **FRANCE** 3G, 2PG, 1DG, 1T (31) to 4PG (12) *(Paris)* |
| 1974-75 | **WALES** 1G, 1PG, 4T (25) to 2PG, 1T (10) *(Paris)* | 1989-90 | **FRANCE** 3G, 1PG, 2T (29) to 4PG, 1DG, 1T (19) *(Cardiff)* |
| 1975-76 | **WALES** 5PG, 1T (19) to 1G, 1PG, 1T (13) *(Cardiff)* | 1990-91 | **FRANCE** 3G, 2PG, 3T (36) to 1PG (3) *(Paris)* |
| 1976-77 | **FRANCE** 1G, 2PG, 1T (16) to 3PG (9) *(Paris)* | 1991 | (Friendly) **FRANCE** 2G, 2PG, 1T (22) to 1G, 1PG, (9) *(Cardiff)* |
| 1977-78 | **WALES** 1G, 2DG, 1T (16) to 1DG, 1T (7) *(Cardiff)* | 1991-92 | **FRANCE** 1G, 1DG, 1PG (12) to 3PG (9) *(Cardiff)* |
| 1978-79 | **FRANCE** 2PG, 2T (14) to 3PG, 1T (13) *(Paris)* | | **(Try upgraded to 5 pts.)** |
| 1979-80 | **WALES** 1G, 3T (18) to 1G, 1DG (9) *(Cardiff)* | 1992-93 | **FRANCE** 1G, 3PG, 2T (26) to 1G, 1PG (10) *(Paris)* |
| 1980-81 | **FRANCE** 5PG, 1T (19) to 1G, 3PG (15) *(Paris)* | 1993-94 | **WALES** 1G, 4PG, 1T (24) to 1G, 1PG, 1T (15) *(Cardiff)* |
| 1981-82 | **WALES** 6PG, 1T (22) to 1G, 2PG (12) *(Cardiff)* | 1994-95 | **FRANCE** 1G, 3PG, 1T (21) to 3PG (9) *(Paris)* |
| 1982-83 | **FRANCE** 3PG, 1DG, 1T (16) to 1G, 1PG (9) *(Paris)* | 1995-96 | **WALES** 1G, 3PG (16) to 1G, 1PG, 1T (15) *(Cardiff)* |
| 1983-84 | **FRANCE** 1G, 4PG, 1DG (21) to 1G, 1T, 2PG (16) *(Cardiff)* | 1996 | (Friendly) **FRANCE** 4G, 4PG (40) to 3G, 4PG (33) *(Cardiff)* |
| 1984-85 | **FRANCE** 2PG, 2T (14) to 1PG (3) *(Paris)* | 1996-97 | **FRANCE** 2G, 1PG, 2T (27) to 2G, 1PG, 1T (22) *(Paris)* |
| 1985-86 | **FRANCE** 2G, 1DG, 2T (23) to 5PG (15) *(Cardiff)* | 1997-98 | **FRANCE** 5G, 2PG, 2T (51) to 0 *(Wembley)* |

## AGAINST NEW ZEALAND

## Matches played 17          Wales 3 wins,                    New Zealand 14

| | | | |
|---|---|---|---|
| 1905-06 | **WALES** 1T, (3) to 0 *(Cardiff)* | 1978 | **N.Z.** 3PG, 1T (13) to 4PG (12) *(Cardiff)* |
| 1924-25 | **N.Z.** 2G, 1PG, 2T (19) to 0 *(Swansea)* | 1980 | **N.Z.** 2G, 1PG, 2T (23) to 1PG (3) *(Cardiff)* |
| 1935-36 | **WALES** 2G, 1T (13) TO 1G, 1DG, 1T (12) *(Cardiff)* | 1987 | **WORLD CUP: N.Z.** 7G, 1PG, 1T (49) to 1G (6) *(Brisbane)* |
| 1953-54 | **WALES** 2G, 1PG (13) to 1G, 1PG, (8) *(Cardiff)* | 1988 | **N.Z.** 6G, 4T (52) to 1PG (3) *(Christchurch)* |
| 1963-64 | **N.Z.** 1PG, 1DG (6) to 0 *(Cardiff)* | 1988 | **N.Z.** 8G, 2PG (54) to 1G, 1PG (9) *(Auckland)* |
| 1967 | **N.Z.** 2G, 1PG (13) to 1PG, 1DG (6) *(Cardiff)* | 1989 | **N.Z.** 3G. 4PG, 1T (34) to 3PG (9) *(Cardiff)* |
| 1969 | **N.Z.** 2G, 1PG, 2T (19) to 0 *(Christchurch)* | 1995 | **WORLD CUP: N.Z.** 2G, 1DG, 4PG, 1T (34) to 1DG, 2PG (9) *(Johannesburg)* |
| 1969 | **N.Z.** 3G, 5PG,1DG (33) to 2PG, 2T (12) *(Auckland)* | 1997 | **N.Z.** 2G, 2PG, 1DG, 1T (42) to 1G (7) *(Wembley)* |
| 1972-73 | **N.Z.** 5PG, 1T (19) to 4PG, 1T (16) *(Cardiff)* | | |
| 1974 | **\*N.Z.** 1G, 2PG, (12) to 1PG (3) *(Cardiff)* | | *\*Unofficial Match* |

## AGAINST SOUTH AFRICA

## Matches played 11     South Africa 10 wins,                    1drawn

| | | | |
|---|---|---|---|
| 1906 | **S.A.** 1G, 2T (11) to 0 *(Swansea)* | 1994 | **S.A.** 1G, 1PG, 2T (20) to 4PG (12) *(Cardiff)* |
| 1912-13 | **S.A.** 1PG (3) to 0 *(Cardiff)* | | |
| 1931-32 | **S.A.** 1G, 1T (8) to 1T (3) *(Swansea)* | 1995 | **S.A.** 3G, 3PG, 2T (40) to 2PG, 1T (11) *(Johannesburg)* |
| 1951-52 | **S.A.** 1DG, 1T (6) to 1T (3) *(Cardiff)* | | |
| 1960-61 | **S.A.** 1PG (3) to 0 *(Cardiff)* | 1996 | **SA** 3G, 2PG, 2T (37) to 5PG, 1T (20) *(Cardiff)* |
| 1964 | **S.A.** 3G, 2PG, 1DG (24) to 1PG (3) *(Durban)* | 1998 | **SA** 9G, 1PG, 6T (96) to 1G, 2PG (13) *(Pretoria)* |
| 1970 | **Drawn** 1PG, 1T (6) Each *(Cardiff)* | | |

## AGAINST AUSTRALIA

## Matches played 19          Wales 8 wins,                    Australia 11

| | | | |
|---|---|---|---|
| 1908-09 | **WALES** 1PG, 2T (9) to 2T (6) *(Cardiff)* | 1969 | **WALES** 2G, 2PG, 1T (19) to 2G, 2PG (16) *(Sydney)* |
| 1927-28 | **AUSTRALIA (NSW)** 3G, 1T (18) to 1G, 1T (8) *(Cardiff)* | 1973-74 | **WALES** 2G, 2PG, 3T (24) to 0 *(Cardiff)* |
| 1947-48 | **WALES** 2PG (6) to 0 *(Cardiff)* | 1975-76 | **WALES** 3G, 1PG, 1DG, 1T (28) to 1PG (3) *(Cardiff)* |
| 1957-58 | **WALES** 1PG, 1DG, 1T (9) to 1T (3) *(Cardiff)* | | |
| 1966-67 | **AUSTRALIA** 1G, 1PG, 1DG, 1T (14) to 1G, 1PG, 1T (11) *(Cardiff)* | 1978 | **AUSTRALIA** 1G, 4PG, (18) to 2T (8) *(Brisbane)* |

| | | | |
|---|---|---|---|
| 1978 | **AUSTRALIA** 3PG, 2DG, 1T (19) to 2PG, 1DG, 2T (17) *(Sydney)* | 1991 | **WORLD CUP: AUSTRALIA** 4G, 2PG, 2T (38) to 1PG (3) *(Cardiff)* |
| 1981 | **WALES** 1G, 1DG, 3PG (18) to 1G, 1PG, 1T (13) *(Cardiff)* | 1992 | **AUSTRALIA** 1G, 2PG, 2T (23) to 2PG, (6) *(Cardiff)* |
| 1984 | **AUSTRALIA** 3G, 2PG, 1T (28) to 1G, 1PG (9) *(Cardiff)* | 1996 | **AUSTRALIA** 6G, 3PG, 1T (56) to 2G, 2PG, 1T (25) *(Brisbane)* |
| 1987 | **WORLD CUP: WALES** 2G, 2PG, 1T (22) to 2G, 2PG, 1DG (21) *(Rotorua)* | 1996 | **AUSTRALIA** 3G, 2PG, 3T (42) to 1PG (3) *(Sydney)* |
| 1991 | **AUSTRALIA** 6G, 1PG, 6T (63) to 1DG, 1PG (6) *(Brisbane)* | 1996 | **AUSTRALIA** 2G, 3PG, 1T (28) to 1G, 4PG (19) *(Cardiff)* |

# AGAINST MAORIS

## Matches played 2     Wales 2 wins,     Maoris 0

| | | | |
|---|---|---|---|
| 1888-89 | **WALES** 1G, 2T (5) to 0 *(Swansea)* | 1982 | **WALES** 1G, 1DG, 4PG, 1T (25) to 1G, 3PG, 1T (19) *(Cardiff)* |
| *Note:* | A goal counted 3pts., a try 1pt. | | |

# AGAINST N.Z. ARMY TEAMS

| | | | |
|---|---|---|---|
| 1919 | **N.Z. ARMY** 2PG (6) to 1PG (3) *(Swansea)* | 1946 | **\*KIWIS** 1G, 2PG (11) to 1PG (6) *(Cardiff)* |
| | | | *\*No caps awarded* |

# AGAINST NAMIBIA

## Matches played 3     Wales 3 wins

| | | | |
|---|---|---|---|
| 1990 | **WALES** 2G, 2PG (18) to 1G, 1PG (9) *(Windhoek)* | 1993 | **WALES** 2G, 3PG, 3T (38) to 2G, 3PG, (23) *(Windhoek)* |
| 1990 | **WALES** 3G, 3PG, 1DG, 1T (34) to 3G, 3PG, 1DG (30) *(Windhoek)* | | |

# AGAINST TONGA

## Matches played 5     Wales 5 wins

| | | | |
|---|---|---|---|
| 1974 | **WALES** 2PG, 5T (26) to 1PG, 1T (7) *(Cardiff)* | 1994 | **WALES** 6PG (18) to 3PG (9) *(Nuku'Alofa)* |
| 1986 | **WALES** 1G, 3PG, (15) to 1PG, 1T (7) *(Nuku'Alofa)* | 1997 | **WALES** 2G, 4PG, 4T (46) to 1G, 1T (12) *(Swansea)* |
| 1987 | **WORLD CUP: WALES** 2G, 2PG, 1DG, 2T (29) to 1G, 2PG, 1T *(Palmerston North)* | | |

# AGAINST CANADA

## Matches played 9     Wales 8 wins     Canada 1

| | | | |
|---|---|---|---|
| 1962 | **WALES U-23** 1G, 1T (8) to 0 *(Cardiff)* | 1989 | **WALES** 4G, 1PG, 1T (31) to 3G, 1DG, 2T (29) *(Edmonton)* |
| 1971 | **WALES** 5G, 1DG, 1PG, 5T (56) to 1G, 1T (10) *(Cardiff)* | 1993 | **CANADA** 2G, 4PG (26) to 8PG (24) *(Cardiff)* |
| 1973 | **WALES** 8G, 2PG, 1T (58) to 1G, 2PG, 2T (20) *(Toronto)* | 1994 | **WALES** 3G, 4PG (33) to 5PG (15) *(Toronto)* |
| 1980 | **WALES** 1G, 1DG, 5PG (24) to 1PG, 1T (7) *(Vancouver)* | 1997 | **WALES** 2G, 3PG, 1T (28) to 2G, 1PG, 1DG, 1T (25) *(Toronto)* |
| 1987 | **WORLD CUP: WALES** 4G, 4T (40) to 3PG (9) *(Invercargill)* | | |

# AGAINST USA

## Matches played 4     Wales 4 wins

| | | | |
|---|---|---|---|
| 1987 | **WALES** 4G, 2PG, 4T (46) to 0 *(Cardiff)* | 1997 | **WALES** 2G, 2PG, 2T (30) to 2G, 2PG (20) *(Wilmington)* |
| 1997 | **WALES** 4G, 2PG (34) to 3PG, 1T (14) *(Cardiff)* | 1997 | **WALES** 1G, 2PG, 3T (28) to 2G, 3PG (23) *(San Francisco)* |

# AGAINST WESTERN SAMOA

## Matches played 4     Wales 2 wins,     Western Samoa 2

| | | | |
|---|---|---|---|
| 1986 | **WALES** 2G, 3PG, 1DG, 2T (32) to 2PG, 2T (14) *(Apia)* | 1991 | **WORLD CUP: W. SAMOA** 1G, 2PG, 1T (16) to 1G, 1PG, 1T (13) *(Cardiff)* |
| 1988 | **WALES** 4G, 1T (28) to 1G (6) *(Cardiff)* | 1994 | **W. SAMOA** 2G, 5PG, 1T (34) to 3PG (9) *(Apia)* |

# AGAINST ZIMBABWE

## Matches played 3      Wales 3 wins

1993    **WALES** 3G, 2PG, 1DG, 1T (35) to 3PG, 1T (14) *(Bulawayo)*

1993    **WALES** 3G, 2PG, 3T (42) to 1G, 2PG (13) *(Harare)*

1998    **WALES** 3G, 1PG, 5T (49) to 2PG, 1T (11) *(Harare)*

# AGAINST PORTUGAL

## Matches played 1      Wales 1 win

1994    **WALES** 11G, 5T (102) to 2PG, 1T (11) *(Lisbon)*

# AGAINST BARBARIANS

## Matches played 3    Wales 1 win,     Barbarians 2 wins

1915    **BARBARIANS** 4G, 2T (26) to 1DG, 2T (10) *(Cardiff)*

1990    **BARBARIANS** 3G, 3PG, 1T (31) to 1G, 5PG, 1DG (24) *(Cardiff)*

1996    **WALES** 3G, 2T (31) to 2T (10) *(Cardiff)*

# AGAINST ITALY

## Matches played 5      Wales 5 wins

1992    **WALES** 4G, 3T (43) to 1G, 1T (12) *(Cardiff)*

1994    **WALES** 5G, 7PG, 1T (29) to 1G, 4PG (19) *(Cardiff)*

1996    **WALES** 2G, 4PG, 1T (31) to 2G, 4PG (26) *(Cardiff)*

1996    **WALES** 2G, 4PG, 1T (31) to 1G, 5PG (22) *(Rome)*

1998    **WALES** 2G, 3PG (23) to 2G, 2PG (20) *(Llanelli)*

# AGAINST ROMANIA

## Matches played 5    Wales 3 wins,       Romania 2

1979    **WALES** 2DG, 1PG, 1T (13) to 1G, 2PG (12) *(Cardiff)*

1983    **ROMANIA** 1G, 2PG, 3T (24) to 2PG (6) *(Bucharest)*

1988    **ROMANIA** 1G, 3PG (15) to 1G, 1PG (9) *(Cardiff)*

1994    **WALES** 1G, 3PG (16) to 3PG (9) *(Bucharest)*

1997    **WALES** 6G, 1PG, 5T (70) to 1G, 3PG, (21) *(Wrexham)*

# AGAINST ARGENTINA

## Matches played 4    Wales 2 wins,    Argentina 1,    1 drawn

1968    **ARGENTINA** 2PG, 1T (9) to 1G (5) *(Buenos Aires)*

1968    **DRAWN: ARGENTINA** 2PG, 1T (9), **WALES** 2PG, 1T (9) *(Buenos Aires)*

1976    **WALES** 4PG, 2T (20) to 1G, 3PG, 1T (19) *(Cardiff)*

1991    **WORLD CUP: WALES** 4PG, 1T (16) to 1PG, 1T (7) *(Cardiff)*

# AGAINST FIJI

## Matches played 7      Wales 7 wins

1964    **WALES** 2G, 1PG, 5T (28) to 2G, 4T (22) *(Cardiff)*

1969    **WALES** 5G, 1DG, 1T (31) to 1G, 1PG, 1T (11) *(Suva)*

1970    **WALES U-25** 1G, 1T (8) to 1PG, 1T (6) *(Cardiff)*

1985    **WALES** 3G, 2PG, 4T (40) to 1PG (3) *(Cardiff)*

1986    **WALES** 1G, 1DG, 3PG, 1T (22) to 2G, 1PG, (15) *(Suva)*

1994    **WALES** 2G, 3PG, (23) to 1PG, 1T (8) *(Suva)*

1995    **WALES** 3PG, 2T (19) to 1G, 1PG, 1T (15) *(Cardiff)*

# AGAINST JAPAN

## Matches played 6      Wales 6 wins

1973    **WALES** 9G, 2T (62) to 2PG, 2T (14) *(Cardiff)*

1975    **WALES** 5G, 2PG, 5T (56) to 4PG (12) *(Osaka)*

1975    **WALES** 10G, 2PG, 4T (82) to 2PG (6) *(Tokyo)*

1983    **WALES** 3G, 1PG, 2T (29) to 1G, 2PG, 3T (24) *(Cardiff)*

1993    **WALES** 5G, 4T (55) to 1T (5) *(Cardiff)*

1995    **WORLD CUP: WALES** 5G, 4PG, 2T (57) to 2T (10) *(Bloemfontein)*

# AGAINST SPAIN

## Matches played 2      Wales 2 wins

1983    **WALES** 7G, 1PG, 5T (65) to 2G, 1T (16) *(Madrid)*

1994    **WALES** 5G, 3PG, 2T (54) to 0 *(Madrid)*

# Major Fixtures 1998-99

(Some dates may be subject to change)

**1998**

SEPTEMBER
26      SWALEC Cup 1st Round

OCTOBER
24      SWALEC Cup 2nd Round

NOVEMBER
14      WALES v SOUTH AFRICA ..................................... Wembley
18      Wales A v Argentina A ......................................... Pontypridd
21      WALES v ARGENTINA .......................................... tba
28      SWALEC Cup 3rd Round

DECEMBER
19      SWALEC Cup 4th Round

**1999**

JANUARY
23      SWALEC Cup 5th Round
30      European Cup Final ............................................. tba

FEBRUARY
5       Scotland A v Wales A ........................................... tba
5       Scotland U21 v Wales U21 ...................................... tba
6       SCOTLAND v WALES ........................................... Murrayfield
6/7     Ireland v France ................................................ Dublin
19      Wales A v Ireland A ............................................ Ebbw Vale
19      Wales U21 v Ireland U21 ....................................... Caerphilly
20      WALES v IRELAND ............................................. Wembley
20/21   England v Scotland ............................................ Twickenham
27      SWALEC Cup 6th Round

MARCH
5       France A v Wales A ............................................. tba
5       France U21 v Wales U21 ........................................ tba
6       FRANCE v WALES .............................................. Paris
6/7     Ireland v England ............................................. Dublin
19      Italy A v Wales A .............................................. tba
19      Italy U21 v Wales U21 .......................................... tba
20      ITALY v WALES ............................................... tba
20/21   England v France .............................................. Twickenham
20/21   Scotland v Ireland ............................................ Murrayfield
27      SWALEC Cup 7th Round

APRIL
9       Wales Students v England Students ............................. Bridgend
9       Wales A v England A ........................................... Swansea
9       Wales U21 v England U21 ....................................... Neath
11      WALES v ENGLAND ........................................... Wembley
10/11   France v Scotland ............................................. Paris
17      SWALEC Cup semi-finals

MAY
15      SWALEC Cup Final ............................................. Millennium Stadium

Published by Welsh Brewers Ltd, Maesycoed Road, Cardiff
Printed by Provincial Printing and Publishing Co Ltd, Cardiff